EUDORA WELTY AND SURREALISM

SURRE

STEPHEN M. FULLER

University Press of Mississippi
Jackson

Eudora Welty

and

ALISM

www.upress.state.ms.us

Designed by Peter D. Halverson

The University Press of Mississippi is a member of the
Association of American University Presses.

First printing 2013

∞

Library of Congress Cataloging-in-Publication Data

Fuller, Stephen M.
Eudora Welty and surrealism / Stephen M. Fuller.
p. cm.
Includes bibliographical references and index.
ISBN 978-1-61703-673-6 (cloth : alk. paper) —
ISBN 978-1-61703-674-3 (ebook) 1. Welty, Eudora, 1909–2001—
Criticism and interpretation. 2. Surrealism (Literature)—
United States. 3. Art and literature—United States. I. Title.
PS3545.E6Z684 2013
813'.52—dc23   2012020182

British Library Cataloging-in-Publication Data available

For Melissa and Stevie

CONTENTS

ACKNOWLEDGMENTS

Many people have contributed to the making of this book, first among them Eudora Welty's heirs, Elizabeth Welty Thompson and Mary Alice Welty White, to whom I am most thankful. At the Mississippi Department of Archives and History in Jackson, Forrest Galey and her staff supplied all the assistance one could ask for, reasonably and unreasonably. Likewise, Katie Hamm at the Eudora Welty House generously gave of her time, especially in leading me on a fascinating tour of Welty's home library at Pinehurst Street. Keely Latcham at Russell and Volkening of New York gave kindly of her time, too. And, at the University Press of Mississippi, I thank Walter Biggins and copyeditor Lisa Paddock.

At the Fundació Gala-Salvador Dalí in Figueres, Spain, Mercedes Aznar helped greatly in the provision of Dalí-related materials, as did Carol Butler at the Salvador Dalí Museum Archives in St. Petersburg, Florida. In New York, Andrea Fisher at Artists Rights Society and Andrea Mihalovic-Lee at the Visual Artists and Galleries Association dispensed much necessary advice. I would also like to thank the Joseph and Robert Cornell Memorial Foundation, Joanna Ling and Katherine Marshall at Sotheby's of London, Aimee L. Marshall at the Art Institute of Chicago, Rena Schergen at the Special Collections Research Center at the University of Chicago, Photofest Digital of New York, and the unfailingly helpful Marie Difilippantonio, archivist at the Jean and Julien Levy Foundation.

At the libraries that opened their doors to me, I would like to thank Jennifer Ford of the J. D. Williams Library at the University of Mississippi, Oxford; Sybil McNeil of Willet Memorial Library, Wesleyan College, Macon; and Meredith Murray and Linda Smith of Roberts Memorial Library, Middle Georgia College, Cochran. Furthermore, President Michael Stoy of

Middle Georgia College, Crystal O'Leary Davidson, Chair of Humanities, Mary Ellen Wilson and Mary Lou Frank, Vice Presidents for Academic Affairs, and Louneil Tripp deserve special mention for their encouragement and support of this book.

Some portions of chapter six appeared in a different form in the *Southern Quarterly*, and I thank the editors Douglas Chambers and Kenneth Watson for their permission to reprint. Finally, Noel Polk and Suzanne Marrs have either read and commented on drafts of this study, or provided help when I had niggling research questions. In addition, Pearl McHaney deserves special thanks for her guidance. I thank them all wholeheartedly, as I do Rosemary, Arthur, and James Fuller, Bill and Melinda Graves, and the inimitable David Jenkins. Finally, to my wife, Melissa, who gave unstintingly, I offer my most loving gratitude.

EUDORA WELTY AND SURREALISM

1

SURREALISM AND WELTY'S EARLY YEARS IN NEW YORK[1]

1. Toward the Mysterious Threshold

> When [surrealism] broke over its founders as an inspiring dream wave, it seemed the most integral, conclusive, absolute of movements. Everything with which it came into contact was integrated. Life seemed worth living only where the threshold between waking and sleeping was worn away in everyone as by the steps of multitudinous images flooding back and forth. . . .
>
> –Walter Benjamin, "Surrealism: The Last Snapshot of the European Intelligentsia"

Benjamin's lavish recollection of surrealism's founding moment foregrounds the energy, innocence, and plenitude of the epoch. As the driving force behind the movement's dynamism and innovation, surrealism's dream wave repeatedly steepened, broke, and withdrew, exposing through its coruscating imagery the seepage of the unconscious. This international movement produced legions of followers, whose artistic provocations forever cracked the edifice of the arts establishment, redefining the contours of twentieth-century culture and leaving an indelible mark on Eudora Welty, a sharp-eyed observer of the newest cultural trends. The following extract from her 1937 story, "A Memory," plainly illuminates the flood of images that typically swell to form Benjamin's dream wave in her fiction, breaking over her unsuspecting reader:

> She was unnaturally white and fatly aware, in a bathing suit which had no relation to the shape of her body. Fat hung upon her upper arms like an arrested earthslide on a hill. With the first motion she might make, I

was afraid that she would slide down upon herself into a terrifying heap. Her breasts hung heavy and widening like pears into her bathing suit. Her legs lay prone one on the other like shadowed bulwarks, uneven and deserted, upon which, from the man's hand, the sand piled higher like the teasing threat of oblivion. A slow, repetitive sound I had been hearing for a long time unconsciously, I identified as a continuous laugh which came through the motionless open pouched mouth of the woman. (*Stories* 95)

This densely figurative passage shows some fundamental characteristics that typify Welty's fictional perspective. Part observation, part recollection, and part dream, the spectacle emerges in fine and lucid detail. The whiteness, the fat body, the bathing suit, the arms, the breasts, the legs, the head, and the mouth anchor these concrete figments in the mind's eye, which holds and stabilizes the elements—readily visualized, fully formed, and boldly evoked. However, the expressions that contribute to the graphic presentation of these details tend toward abstraction, creating a reverie of actuality by tincturing the vision's naturalism with the plasticity of a dream to establish a set of material impossibilities. Before the reader's eyes, the fat liquefies into earthslides that risk heaping, the breasts form swollen pears, the legs metamorphose into bulwarks threatening annihilation, and the laugh issues from a transfigured mouth, turned into a pouch slung open and ugly.[2]

The strength of this kind of narrative resonated particularly with Katherine Anne Porter, whose introduction to *A Curtain of Green* alludes to her preference for "A Memory" because it reveals the "mysterious threshold between dream and waking" life, and the "waking faculty of daylight reason recollecting and recording the crazy logic of the dream" (969–70). Consideration of Porter's famous recommendation for Welty's stories leads naturally to contemplating the relationship between Welty and surrealism, the European avant-garde's foremost organization for the theoretical and practical investigation of the unconscious. Welty's signature certainly never endorsed a surrealist manifesto, and she never championed the surrealist revolution, announced herself a surrealist, promoted her work as surrealist inspired, contributed to surrealist periodicals, or consorted with surrealist artists. While this series of seemingly weighty objections may appear to defeat at the outset an enterprise that insists on emphasizing the surreal in Welty's oeuvre, an analysis of her literary production reveals a fundamental, pervasive, and enduring quality in her art that establishes more than a fragile affinity. Surrealism profoundly influenced Welty's artistic corpus, which shows the imprint of one of the twentieth century's most subversive and influential cultural formations.

For decades, Welty commentators have located her work broadly in the modernist tradition. Names frequently identified as influences on her work include Virginia Woolf, Katherine Mansfield, Elizabeth Bowen, James Joyce, W. B. Yeats, T. S. Eliot, Katherine Anne Porter, Willa Cather, and William Faulkner.[3] More narrowly, critics have categorized her as a southern regionalist or grouped her with Southern Renaissance writers such as Allen Tate, Robert Penn Warren, and John Crowe Ransom.[4] However, the emphasis on these figures and their literary achievements has obscured what an interdisciplinary approach to her work can reveal.[5] Surrealism's visual productions influenced Welty's career during its formative phases and imparted a style and substance that has gone largely unnoticed and unacknowledged.[6] The movement, which made Paris its home in the 1920s, reached the United States via New York in the 1930s, and thereafter supplied a new aesthetic, an artistic strategy, a way of life, and an ideology to the world.

2. European Surrealism: Paris in the Twenties

The voluminous literature charting surrealism's history, its founders, its techniques, and its principal exponents establishes its inception in Paris following the calamity of the Great War and the disintegration of its sometimes disavowed cousin, Dada.[7] From its inception as an avant-garde literary movement, surrealism proposed a radical artistic philosophy directed against positivist definitions of reality inherited from the nineteenth century, whose predominant empirical epistemology had rendered all European social, scientific, philosophical, and artistic systems bankrupt in the face of catastrophic war (Nadeau 44–45). The poet, novelist, and theoretician André Breton led the revolutionary movement from its inaugural moment, when he published his "Surrealist Manifesto" in 1924 as a "reaction against the anarchy and aimlessness of dada" (Tashjian xvi). Allied with figures such as Louis Aragon, Robert Desnos, Benjamin Péret, and Paul Eluard, Breton spearheaded this avant-garde's rejection of purely Cartesian constructions of the subject, instead advancing a theory of subjectivity incorporating the revolutionary discoveries of psychoanalysis and premised on the Hegelian dialectic. Underwritten by the radical energies of the Freudian unconscious, surrealism abandoned the pursuit of knowledge that precluded accommodating the irrational life of dreams.

Under the leadership of Breton, the surrealists wrote poetry and prose, convened meetings, carried out experiments, founded journals, and conducted research designed to probe the permeability of the conscious mind to unconscious phenomena. In his 1924 "Manifesto of Surrealism," Breton famously declares his aim for the movement: "I believe in the future resolution of these two states, dream and reality, which are seemingly so contradictory, into a kind of absolute reality, a *surreality*, if one may so speak" (14). Later in the manifesto, he supplies further elucidation in the form of two bold pronouncements: Surrealists practice a pure "psychic automatism" that reproduces by the "written word, or in any other manner" the "actual functioning of thought" in the "absence of any control exercised by reason"; and the philosophy of surrealism assumes a "belief in the superior reality of certain forms of previously neglected associations" and studies the "omnipotence of the dream" and the "disinterested play of thought" (26). These elaborate definitions reveal two key points about the intentions of the founders. First, they warrant Maurice Nadeau's observation that surrealism was not envisaged as a "new artistic school, but as a means of knowledge" that incorporated and advanced through a "discovery of continents which had not yet been systematically explored: the unconscious, the marvelous, the dream, madness, hallucinatory states—in short, if we add the fantastic and the marvelous as they occurred throughout the world, the other side of the logical décor" (80).[8] Second, despite the prominent positions visual artists would come to adopt in the movement—particularly in the United States—the definitions indicate Breton's defining of the cause as primarily a literary one with precise philosophical objectives. Although modified and revised by subsequent interpreters—not least Breton himself—surrealism's core philosophical prejudice against a logic excluding the desire permeating the Freudian unconscious remained unchanged, and the movement's transplantation to the United States did nothing to alter this hostility.

Discontent, fractiousness, and divisiveness always marked surrealism's evolution, but 1930 represented a watershed moment. Published by Breton that year, the acerbic "Second Manifesto of Surrealism" purged the ranks of the movement by banishing some of surrealism's earliest adherents. The manifesto very publicly banished those whom he considered traitors to the movement's purity. Breton accused some of economic and artistic concessions, but he mostly reserved his animus for those he viewed as having "confused the principles of surrealism with the political tenets of the current communism in which he, Breton, could find only a feeble and limited application of the concepts of Hegel, Marx, and Engels" (Balakian *Magus* 94). Despite his long and tempestuous association with the French Communist Party, which he ultimately abandoned in 1935,[9] Breton refused to subordinate surrealism's revolutionary agenda to communist ideology. Although the second manifesto draws on Hegel's *Phenomenonology of the Mind* and "locates surrealism under the banner of dialectical materialism" (97), it stops short of designating surrealism as communism's handmaiden. While Anna Balakian[10] argues that the first manifesto "was written under the aegis of Freud" (90) and that the second "is in the orbit of Hegel" (97), she also contends that, taken together—and allowing for the six-year interval separating their publication dates—the manifestoes reveal "not so much of diffusion as of continuity and development or enlargement of surrealism when one juxtaposes them" (86). The publication of the second manifesto in the final issue of surrealism's primary journal, *La Révolution Surréaliste*, ended the "first cycle of Surrealism's history," but the dismissals "had been at least partly counterbalanced by some new memberships" (Polizzotti *Revolution* 334). By far the most influential new addition, Salvador Dalí almost singlehandedly revived Breton's flagging movement. The flamboyant Catalan's incipient theory of paranoia-criticism subtly renovated Breton's now aging surrealist apparatus and pointed the way to the future, when it would find new and receptive audiences in the United States.

3. American Surrealism: New York and Jackson in the Thirties

Disaster marked the beginning of the new decade for America generally and for Welty personally. New York's 1929 stock market crash and its corollary, the Great Depression, destroyed the dream of the twenties and, in its shadow, Welty returned to Jackson because her father had fallen gravely ill (he would die in 1931) (Marrs *Eudora* 35). On his advice, she had completed a one-year course in advertising at the Columbia Business School (Walker 133), but her hopes for extending her stay in the city that she loved met disappointment when a promised job fell through, leaving Welty stranded with an "apartment taken" and "theater tickets bought" (Wheatley 124).

In contrast, New York in the 1930s presented many surrealist artists with great opportunities—not least because of young devotees of modern art

such as Julien Levy, the individual probably most responsible for popular-
izing surrealism in the United States. The glamour of the new world excited
the creativity of the surrealists, providing new and potentially lucrative mar-
kets for their talents, and, as war again erupted in Europe, affording a haven
from Nazi aggression. One of the "Harvard modernists,"[11] Levy traveled to
Europe in the 1920s, then returned to New York to open the Julien Levy
Gallery at 602 Madison Avenue in 1931 (Watson *Portrait* 80), beginning a
seminal chapter in the history of modern art that historians have just begun
to recognize. Any careful observer of contemporary cultural life could have
acquired considerable knowledge of current trends in modern art by visiting
Levy's Madison Avenue gallery, and other commercial galleries such as the
Pierre Matisse Gallery, the John Becker Gallery, the Brummer Galleries, the
Valentine Gallery, the Wildenstein Gallery, or the newly founded Museum
of Modern Art.[12] To varying degrees, these venues, all within easy reach of
one another, constituted a beachhead for the invasion of modern art that
would rock the conservatives of the New York art world. Among galleries
known for dealing in surrealist art, Levy's and, secondly, Matisse's, took center stage. By 1936, the former had staged one-man shows for Man Ray, Max
Ernst, Salvador Dalí, Alberto Giacometti, René Magritte, and Yves Tanguy,
while the latter had sponsored solo shows for Joan Miró, André Masson, and
Giorgio de Chirico (Price "Chronology" 172–75). Of all the surrealists, Dalí
perhaps capitalized on the moment earliest. Although still based in Europe,
he turned his gaze increasingly on the United States, where he recognized
the potential of American art audiences, moving rapidly to show his work
in New York and elsewhere in the 1930s[13] and obtaining Levy as his first
American agent. In addition to the Spaniard, Levy promoted and exhibited a wide array of other artists, poets, sculptors, and photographers, both
European and American, and he tirelessly invested his time and money in
preparing American audiences for surrealism's entrance upon the American
cultural stage. In 1936, for example, he published *Surrealism*, an anthology
of surrealist work intended to educate the American public about an art
movement that Mark Polizzotti's introduction states had "already weathered
a dozen years of continuous existence in France" (v). Operating between
1931 and 1949, Levy's gallery showed a diverse mix of art "during precisely
those years of transition when the center of the cultural avant-garde moved
from Paris to New York." As a "champion of Surrealism, experimental film,
and photography, Levy was a conduit for some of the most vital aesthetic
charges originating in Europe" (Schaffner & Jacobs 10).

An economically ruined country and a devastating personal tragedy deprived Welty of full participation in the euphoria generated by those culturally exhilarating times. During her year in New York, she had continued to feed the appetite for the visual arts that she had developed during her youth in Jackson. "You couldn't take anything I did in painting seriously," she recalls, "I loved it, and I studied it, but I had no serious ambition about it. I wouldn't dream that I had any ability for that; I just loved painting. I studied art when I was growing up here" (Gretlund "Seeing Real Things" 248). Returning to Jackson, Welty found like minds in three of Mississippi's premier young artists: Karl Wolfe, Helen Jay Lotterhos, and William Hollingsworth (39). All recent graduates of the Art Institute of Chicago, these painters mostly worked in the tradition of realism, "with only slight echoes of their training in European modernism" (43) and its most innovative styles, such as cubism, surrealism, expressionism, and abstraction. Nonetheless, Mississippi artists "could not ignore the vital visual culture of the times," and the ideology of the radical schools "filtered down to them through the big city and local art schools they attended, national art magazines and exhibitions" (O'Connor 61). Lotterhos and Welty in particular developed a strong friendship, "sharing a lively interest in art and writing" and frequently going on "sketching trips around Jackson." Hollingsworth and Welty, on the other hand, knew each other as children, having grown up in the same neighborhood, and they shared a similar interest in drawing cartoons. Welty had drawn "cartoons for publications at Mississippi University for Women," while Hollingsworth "contributed cartoons to his college annual of The University of Mississippi" (Black "Back Home" 43). New York clearly eclipsed Jackson and even Chicago in the range of cultural amenities, offering a plethora of artistic attractions, and Welty indulged herself: "It was my chance, the first I ever had, to go to the theater, to the museums, to concerts, and I made use of every moment, let me tell you" (Gretlund "An Interview" 217). Columbia's business school placed few demands on this able advertising student, so Welty's New York days "were filled with theater, art, music, and the excitement of being in a vibrant city" (Black "Back Home" 35).

Although returning to Jackson precluded frequent excursions, Welty routinely visited the city throughout the 1930s and beyond, spending weeks at a time. Suzanne Marrs observes, "Welty visited New York once or twice a year after leaving Columbia, attending concerts and the theater, taking advantage of art museums and the New York Public Library" (*One Writer's*

10). During these trips, Welty attempted to establish herself as a photographer as well as a writer. She reports that on her New York journeys she would take along her pictures, and "always leave them with the publisher, along with my stories. I don't know why I thought it would be a good idea to have the pictures illustrate my stories. Oh well, none of the publishers ever thought so either" (Keith 146). One such mixed media ensemble, *Black Saturday*, assembled some early stories to correspond loosely with a selection of pictures Welty had taken as a junior publicity agent for the Works Progress Administration (Cole & Srinivasan 195). Harrison Smith and Robert Haas, the publishers to whom she sent the project in 1935, praised the work but ultimately rejected the collection as unprofitable. Similar rejections came later. In 1937 Covici-Friede declined to publish another of Welty's word and image collections, and in 1938 Story Press rejected a collection of her photographs (Marrs *Welty Collection* 78).[14] Into the late thirties, the young artist demonstrated her enthusiasm for the visual arts in both painting and the newly emerging art of photography, although she never thought she possessed a talent for the former. Despite Welty's modesty, photography formed an abiding passion that she cultivated from her "graduate student days until 1950" (78), and it complemented what she thought of as her highly visual mind, which saw "things in pictures. I'm not anything at all of a painter. I love painting. I have no talent for it. The only talent I have—for writing, I was blessed with it—is quite visual. And anything I imagine in what I read or write, I see it" (Bunting 53–54).[15] The photographic products of this visual cast of mind found exhibitors twice in Welty's career. The first[16] of her one-woman New York shows was sponsored by Lugene, Inc. Opticians, and it opened at the Photographic Galleries on March 31, 1936 (Marrs *Welty Collection* 78). Located at 600 Madison Avenue, the Photographic Galleries directly abutted the brownstone housing the Julien Levy Gallery at 602 Madison Avenue, the fulcrum on which surrealism in America turned.

It seems impossible to imagine Welty blithely declining the opportunity to visit the Levy Gallery early in 1936 when Samuel Robbins offered her a show, or when the exhibition opened in March (Marrs *Eudora* 50). The acceptance of such an invitation also seems highly likely because Welty had probably known of the Levy Gallery for at least two years prior to her show next door. A letter from Frank Lyell, a Jackson High and Columbia University comrade, to Welty in December of 1933 closely reports on his various movements around New York City, where "Goody good art shows

[are] on." After recommending the Constantin Brancusi show, probably at the Brummer Gallery (Bach, Rowell, & Temkin 390), and before extolling the "Renoir room at the Knoedler gallery," he assures Welty:

> The Salvador Dali show is no less amazing—he's a surrealist & loves intestines, fried eggs, excrement, brain fissures exposed, blood, and general depravity and degeneration. Paints very well—in rather a miniature style—but the assimilation of objects into artistic wholes defies all reason—Some was amusing, much was revolting.

Here, Lyell reports visiting the Levy Gallery and seeing Dali's first one-man show in the United States. Studying at Princeton, Lyell may have also visited Levy's prior to this occasion. Welty may have gone, too, although the gallery did not open until November 1931, after both Welty and Lyell had finished at Columbia (Schaffner & Jacobs "Introduction" 10). However, her three-week New York stay during the spring of 1932 would have provided ample opportunity to take in Levy's exhibition (Black *Early* 37), "Modern European Photography," which included such luminaries as Brassaï, André Kertész, Man Ray, and Lee Miller, Eugene Berman's first solo show in the United States, and Man Ray's first one-man photography exhibition (Jacobs "Chronology" 174). Moreover, her four-month sojourn between January and April 1933 (Marrs *Eudora* 39–41) would have yielded the chance to view "The Carnival of Venice: Photographs by Max Ewing," with an accompanying essay by Gilbert Seldes, as well as works by Mina Loy, Kurt Baasch, Pavel Tchelitchew, Berman, and Georges Roualt (Jacobs "Chronology" 175). Such opportunities to broaden her cultural education in New York may have received amplification when she visited Chicago in July of the same year. A letter Frank Lyell sent Welty in July of 1933 reveals her lodging at the La Salle Hotel, but why she had a room there remains a mystery. However, combining Welty's interest in fairs and carnivals along with her preoccupation with the visual arts may lead to identifying Chicago's 1933 world's fair as the draw and probably the Art Institute of Chicago's "A Century of Progress Exhibition of Paintings and Sculpture" as the main attraction. The institute ran this very large exhibition from June 1 to November 1, 1933, showing over twelve hundred works from the thirteenth century to the present (*Catalogue of a Century of Progress Exhibition*). Here, in a museum Welty had loved since her days at the University of Wisconsin, she could have seen many of the contemporary artists she probably also saw in New York.

Back in New York during October and November of 1934 (Marrs *Eudora* 43), she tried unsuccessfully to sell her photographs, a high but not unreasonable objective during the thirties when, Sandra S. Phillips notes, "photography would have a special florescence." Moreover, Phillips rightly points out that "we cannot know all the photographs [Welty] knew" or "all the books she saw" (72) But during October and November, Welty may well have seen Levy's "Fifty Photographs by George Platt Lynes," and his "Eight Modes of Painting: Survey of Twentieth-Century Art Movements," including work by Berman, Dalí, Marcel Duchamp, Max Ernst, Wassily Kandinsky, Paul Klee, Joan Miró, Pablo Picasso, and Tchelitchew. In addition (and particularly given Lyell's enthusiasm for Dalí's first exhibition) Welty could well have seen Dalí's second show, which ran at the Levy Gallery between November and December (Jacobs "Chronology" 176)— especially if she sought contacts like Samuel Robbins at the ritzy Lugene Opticians on Madison. In town to promote her pictures, Welty no doubt witnessed Dalí's first appearance in the United States, if only in the pages of the *New York Times*, which, on November 15 loudly announced, "Salvador Dali Arrives: Surrealist Painter Brings 25 of His Pictures for Show Here." Few possessed of a serious interest in the visual arts could have missed the media splash that he, his wife Gala, his patron Caresse Crosby, and Levy manufactured in order to drum up interest in the forthcoming exhibition.

If the embarrassment of modern art riches gracing the curving walls of the Levy Gallery did not satisfy her appetite, Welty could have consumed further delights at the Museum of Modern Art's "Modern Works of Art: Fifth Anniversary Exhibition," running from November to January 1935 (Barr *Modern Works*). The director, Alfred H. Barr, celebrated this milestone by assembling a wide-ranging show that not only drew together twentieth-century painting, sculpture, and architecture, but educated museum audiences by giving them a sense of modern art's continuity with what he called its "Pioneers of the late 19th Century" (11). Within the category of twentieth-century art, Barr represented surrealism well with a variety of works by Miró, André Masson, and Hans Arp, as well as with paintings by the artists whom he considered the current leaders of the movement, Max Ernst and Dalí (17). However, this event now seems something of a dress rehearsal for the legendary exhibitions that the Museum of Modern Art would stage the next year. Barr's 1936 shows, "Cubism and Abstract Art" and "Fantastic Art, Dada, and Surrealism," brought together literally hundreds of paintings, sculptures, films, photographs, and objects that collectively demonstrated a decisive break with the artistic traditions of the past, seeking to educate visitors (particularly through the detailed essays by Barr and others in the exhibition catalogs) about modern art's multifarious and overlapping strands. Barr's now iconic dust jacket for the "Cubism and Abstract Art" catalog charts the tangled set of interrelationships among the most prominent art movements of the preceding forty-five years. This show ran from March 2 to April 19 ("Exhibition History List"), and Welty could have attended either on her visit to New York early in 1936, or when her pictures went up at the gallery of Lugene Opticians between March 31 and April 15 (Marrs *Eudora* 50). (Marrs does not record whether Welty attended her own show.) An original copy of the exhibition catalog for the Museum of Modern Art's first exhibition largely devoted to surrealism, found in her library at Pinehurst Street, offers a tantalizing clue. Of the three thousand catalogs printed for the museum's trustees, one found its way into Welty's possession, indicating that she either obtained a copy when she saw the show between December 7, 1936, and January 17, 1937 ("Exhibition History List"), or that she acquired it at another time. Marrs gives no report of a visit coinciding with the show's run, but Welty's attendance remains a possibility. In a house that does not overflow with exhibition catalogs—especially ones dating from this early period—the existence of this one seems instructive. In her published interviews, Welty never mentioned surrealism as an influence on her work, but nobody asked her on record to contemplate the notion. She certainly never alluded to the galleries that she frequented or the surrealist art that she must have seen. But it seems obvious that before she won plaudits as a writer, Welty "was seriously considering a career in photography" (Black "Back Home" 35).

In New York in the early thirties, the Julien Levy Gallery specialized in exhibiting photographs, a "very rare inclusion" (Schaffner, "Alchemy" 20) for this time and place. In fact, the Levy gallery began life as a venue for showing avant-garde photography, closely modeled on Alfred Stieglitz's aesthetic (32–34), before bowing to economic pressure and supplanting photography with the more established media of painting and sculpture that continued as the "Levy Gallery's focus" (29). Some of Welty's earliest photographic experiments, enclosed with or literally part of letters sent to Frank Lyell in 1933, suggest the influence of photographers Welty may have seen at Levy's, figures such as Man Ray, Lee Miller, George Platt Lynes, Berenice Abbott, or André Kertész.[17] On the reverse of two pictures made as if to mimic the style of a Man Ray photograph or solarization, she gives

Welty's photograph titled "This is the souls of the mimosa going to Paradise" (1933). Reprinted by the permission of Russell & Volkening as agents for the author's estate.

the surreal images equally surreal descriptions: "This is the souls [*sic*] of the mimosa going to Paradise" and "Snow falling on a tropical tree". Produced at least as early as 1922, Man Ray's solarizations or rayographs reveal images in which "photograms of gears, darkroom equipment, crystals, and outlines of hands and faces blend irreverent machine-age art with stylish composition" (Hartshorn & Foresta 14). In another picture made in the same year—perhaps more in keeping with Man Ray's interest in machines and technology—Welty superimposes a typewriter, magnolia blooms, and what are apparently parts of a wicker basket. An avant-garde as well as a commercial artist and photographer, Man Ray produced work that spanned

Welty's photograph titled "Snow falling on a tropical tree" (1933). Reprinted by the permission of Russell & Volkening as agents for the author's estate.

these apparently antithetical categories, introducing the idiom of surrealism into the mainstream. According to Willis Hartshorn, "Man Ray was the first and, for a time, the only Surrealist photographer, an association that is apparent in his work for *Bazaar*." Following his work in this venue, the "Surrealist style was soon adopted by other fashion photographers and dominated the pages not only of *Bazaar* but most other fashion magazines of the 1930s and '40s as well" (Hartshorn 15). Welty's photographic gifts to Lyell no doubt reflect a style known to her and common in magazines of the day that were greatly influenced by Man Ray's aesthetic. But her experiments also testify to the influence of the art Welty had become familiar

Welty's photograph imitating the surrealist style of Man Ray (1933). Reprinted by the permission of Russell & Volkening as agents for the author's estate.

with in New York, where "there were probably fewer than fifteen galleries . . . at any one time in the 1930s, and only three or so concentrating on contemporary art" (Schaffner "Alchemy" 41). Therefore, it seems not only plausible but also probable that Welty knew about Levy's gallery, that like Lyell she visited it and others—such as the Pierre Matisse Gallery—and that she drew inspiration from the diversity of surrealist European imports and American work on display.

Welty's knowledge of Levy's business also seems affirmed in a 1934 letter that she sent to his one-time business partner, Berenice Abbott, applying for a place in Abbott's class on "photography at the New School for Social Research in Manhattan" (Black "Back Home" 35). In the letter Welty volunteers that she has had some "lessons in painting" and that she knows "something of certain principles in photography" (qtd. in Black 35). Lecturer, photographer, dealer, archivist, and pioneer, Abbott supplied Levy with the impetus to create his gallery after her return to New York after living in Paris.[18] As assistant to Man Ray, Abbott acquired Jean-Eugène-Auguste Atget's colossal collection of prints and negatives recording Paris at the turn of the century. Levy documents buying a "partial interest" (qtd. in Schaffner "Alchemy" 26) in the archive, thus beginning his career as a "New York art dealer representing the work of Atget." Abbott, too, promoted Atget's corpus by lecturing "extensively on his work" and by "undertaking in 1929 a project to document Manhattan, as [Atget] had in Paris, in photographs" (27). Levy wrote that Atget's photographs revealed every side of Paris, "doorways, stairways, brothels, courts, trees, street vendors, fairs, shop windows, corsets and umbrellas. All taken with beautiful quality, selection, and composition" (qtd. in Schaffner 26). Should Welty have visited, the wide-ranging diversity of subjects displayed in exhibitions of the Parisian's and Berenice Abbott's photographs staged at the Levy Gallery in the early thirties no doubt would have appealed to the aspiring photographer from Jackson.

That Welty wrote to Abbott for admittance to the New School evinces more than a modicum of admiration for the woman from Ohio who had boldly struck out for Paris in the twenties and returned to New York to have a solo exhibition of her photographs at the Julien Levy Gallery in 1932 (Jacobs "Chronology" 174). While Welty probably did not see this show, she probably did see examples of Abbott's work on other occasions and probably admired the talents of this modern woman who moved with apparent ease and success in a male-dominated art world. For a young artist of slender means, Welty would have to wait for foreign travel. As much as she may have wished, she could not simply pack up and set sail for Europe in the manner of wealthy women of her time such as Caresse Crosby, a figure to whom Welty assigns a cameo in "Going to Naples." Welty had neither the means nor the inclination to act rashly, but her deliberateness did not stop her from enjoying the lives and attitudes of women who showed great public daring and chutzpah. In 1933, Welty sent Frank Lyell some of her cartoons that suggest some appealing personalities. These include a wild depiction of a buxom Mae West and a more sober likeness of Dorothy Dix (Black *Escapades* 147), together with a quite ludicrous William Faulkner (142) and a sketch of Edward, Prince of Wales, issuing someone or something a sidelong glance. No doubt, the contemporary newsworthiness of these individuals recommended them as subjects for Welty's satire, but they also provide a glimpse of the culture at large, forming a backdrop to Welty and Lyell's lives during the thirties. More pointedly, though, the caricatures evoke the web of social orthodoxies and proprieties in which Welty's subjects found themselves caught.

Mae West's provocative and frequently campy sexuality needs little elaboration. In 1933, the year Welty sketched her likeness, it needed even less. West's box office hits, *She Done Him Wrong* and *I'm No Angel*, marked her "break-out year in Hollywood" and made her into the "first motion picture actress to sell sex talk" rather than sex itself (Doherty 182). That West

Welty's sketch titled "Mae West" (1933). Reprinted by the permission of Russell & Volkening as agents for the author's estate. ©1989 by Eudora Welty.

could take credit for writing several of her dramatic productions probably added to her appeal for Welty, who clearly enjoyed West's comedy, even to the point of imitating her signature wisecracking. In 1944, Welty saw West perform in *Catherine Was Great* (Marrs *Eudora* 117).[19] By then, however, the Hays Office, responsible for administering the cinematic Production Code, had "badly damaged her movie career" and had ended and/or greatly altered the making of many films like the ones starring West or *The Story of Temple Drake,* based on William Faulkner's scandalous *Sanctuary* (Leider 6). Premiering in 1933 and starring Miriam Hopkins as its eponymous protagonist, *The Story of Temple Drake,* with its portrayal of "rape, prostitution, and perversity among the lower orders of stunted hicks and seedy patricians," took its place among the many "vice films" titillating American audiences (Doherty 114). The dangerous games of power and sexuality that women play in these films would certainly have provoked the sobering kind of advice offered by dowagers such as Dorothy Dix in

Prince of Wales

Welty's sketch titled "Prince of Wales" (1933). Reprinted by the permission of Russell & Volkening as agents for the author's estate. ©1989 by Eudora Welty.

her agony aunt column, which made her "motherly narrative voice" a "vivid presence in every town and village" (Vella 195). Another flouter of convention and potential subject for Dix's advice, the Prince of Wales furtively peers to his left as if about to make a quick exit—the kind he literally made in 1936 after abdicating Britain's throne for Wallace Simpson. Famous for his sartorial trendsetting, the prince already had a playboy reputation by 1933. Welty acknowledged as much by choosing to heavily shade Edward's leering eyes blue and sketching his mouth pursed straight, yet with a louche round strawberry-red pout. Although she could not have foreseen his future, she perhaps sensed Edward's iconoclasm, an opinion confirmed when he chose to marry a double divorcée, an American who very much embraced ideas of modern femininity.[20] Perhaps Simpson's modernity accounts for why she engaged Elsa Schiaparelli,[21] the Italian couturier and rival of Coco Chanel, to design dresses for her wedding trousseau. In 1937, the year of Simpson's third marriage, Cecil Beaton[22] attempted to soften

Wallace Simpson
wearing Schiaparelli
and Dalí's lobster dress
(1937). Courtesy of
the Cecil Beaton Studio
Archive at Sotheby's.

her scandalous public image by photographing her for *Vogue*; however, the Schiaparelli Dalí-inspired lobster dress she wore did little to temper—and perhaps even enhanced—her reputation as a twentieth-century Hester Prynne (Blum 135).

In the year of the Windsors' marriage, Welty published "Retreat," a story she never collected that appeared in the short-lived *River* magazine. It focuses on Norris, a man who returns, disastrously, to his mother's Oedipal embrace in the wake of a botched armed robbery he has committed for his wife. As a foil to the mother's obese, cloying, and suffocating presence, Welty gives us Norris's wife, Elsa, a woman who "was flat, small, rigid, mocking" (38)—and who perhaps is a double of her namesake, Elsa Schiaparelli, who similarly appeared to symbolize a new and potentially threatening kind of femininity to which Welty aspired.[23] After World War One, Chanel changed fashion by creating clothes for women entering the public sphere, "More active, thinner, fitter, her hair was cut short, her skirt hems raised, she stepped out into the real world" (Baudot 6). As a new focus on "female form" developed, by 1928 Schiaparelli, Chanel's greatest fashion contemporary, had designed clothing in a new but still liberating context: "Unrestricted, tanned and fit, the body would henceforth dictate the shape of the garment rather than the garment the shape of the body" (7). And she found one expression of this new power in Charles Lindbergh, who had just flown the Atlantic, transforming his "flying suit, which she adapted to suit her own model heroine,—the women who skied and swam and played golf by day and at night swayed to the syncopated beat of jazz or the tango" (9–10). The author of "Powerhouse" no doubt saw and recognized the woman for whom Schiaparelli designed, the rather masculine Elsa to whom Norris cannot relate. The Elsa of "Retreat" likely symbolizes the challenge faced by men who, unlike Edward Windsor, suffer crises rather than adapt to women who assume roles very different from their mothers'. In the story, Norris fails to adjust and retreats to Vicksburg. Elsa nevertheless follows him in repeated nightmares and in the form of a high-wire walker in a traveling circus: "The girl on the wire, with a knowing smile at him, suddenly threw something which fell into his lap. It was a dead pink rose. All faces turned inward toward him. He felt as if he would faint. He summoned the strength to throw the rose far from him. He stumbled out of the tent and up the hill, with the rattling drums in pursuit" (39). The guilt associated with his crime—but more significantly his inability to change—has doomed his marriage and ultimately drives him to insanity.

Traces in Welty's fiction of Schiaparelli and other figures she admired or followed reflect the preoccupation the author had with such individuals in her life outside of writing. Progressive notions of femininity and fashion merged with surrealism in the culture at large, sometimes running hard up against the bulwark of tradition, and Welty reproduced this synthesis in the alchemy of her fiction. Her interest in this world of beauty shows in the mock advertisement for cosmetics she and her friends created, sending up Elizabeth Arden and Helena Rubenstein. "We were satirizing the advertising game," Welty recollects, "In the thirties you could laugh at advertising. It was all fun. A lot of it came out of our admiration of the smart world, our longing for the artistic scene we were keeping up with: the theatre, art, and music" (*Eudora Welty: Photographs* 201). As subjects for parody, Arden and Rubinstein certainly presented choice targets, but beyond the satire lay a more serious preoccupation with women—represented by such figures

as Abbott, Schiaparelli, and Chanel—who defied the odds by achieving no-
table economic and/or artistic success. As Lindy Woodhead, biographer of
Arden and Rubinstein, observes:

> Each established a flourishing international business, harnessing the
> emergent trend for skincare to the great commercial consumer growth of
> the twentieth century. That they did it at a time when women could expect
> little, if any, financial support from husband, family or banks, and even
> less from the male-dominated pharmaceutical industry from which they
> purchased supplies, makes their achievements all the more remarkable.
> They exercised autonomous control as sole owners and operators of their
> companies, which achieved multimillion-dollar turnovers, at a time when
> women rarely achieved commercial leadership, and job opportunities for
> women of their class were often limited to being a nurse, secretary or shop
> assistant, perhaps with the hope of making a suitable marriage. (1)

That Welty chose these women for a comic skit reveals a level of respect
somewhat submerged by the humor of the presentation but nonetheless apparent. Moreover, the satire on advertising continued when Welty and her
friends—Helen Lotterhos, Margaret Harmon, and Anne Long—dressed up
as women of fashion "with jars of pampas grass, and rising cigarette smoke.
Subtle lighting" (*Eudora Welty: Photographs* 201–2). These exploits show
fashion as humorous diversion, but Welty also turned her hand to some
freelance fashion photography to earn money, taking "one picture every
Sunday for a shop called Oppenheimer's. And the Emporium later. I got
my friends and my brother's girlfriends to pose" (Cole & Srinivason 201).[24]
    The surrealists, operating hundreds of miles away in New York, certainly
did not retreat from exploiting the financial opportunities presented to
them in the city, for "Surrealism became the extreme instance of an avant-
garde movement that entered the orbit of commercial interests. No other
movement up to that time was so courted by high fashion and at such
length" (Tashjian 69).[25] The thirties witnessed surrealists such as Man Ray
and Salvador Dalí—together with "allied artists" (70) such as George Platt
Lynes, Erwin Blumenfeld, and Pavel Tchelitchew—enter into collaboration
with high fashion's flagship publications: *Vanity Fair*, *Harper's Bazaar*, and
Vogue. Such magazines disseminated surrealist iconography and style nationwide, making for moments like the one reported to Frank Lyell and
shared between Welty and her friend in October, 1934: "Schiaparelli's last

models look indecisive—But I should worry, I should fret. Margaret and I lounged in Cain's all afternoon reading *Vogue*." Welty's contemporary account clearly confirms Schaffner's observation that opening a "contemporary issue of *Harper's Bazaar* or *Vogue* . . . you will find an essay by Jean-Paul Sartre, models posed in a tableau by de Chirico or photographed by Man Ray, ads for Elsa Schiaparelli designed by Dalí, and items about the Julien Levy Gallery, where there was always something amusing going on" ("Alchemy" 36). Surrealism, then, became ensconced in the national consciousness not just through the numerous exhibitions held at galleries and museums, or through various small magazines such as *The Little Review*, *transition*, and *View* (Tashjian 6),[26] but also through exposure in the mainstream press, where the "surrealists gained virtual celebrity status in high fashion and advertising" (xviii).

Above all others who colluded in the mass marketing of their art, Dalí emerged as Madison Avenue's darling and "most vocal spokesman" (Lubar xiii). From 1935, when he first partnered with *Harper's Bazaar* to create "Dream Fashions," to 1941, the year of his first one-man show at the Museum of Modern Art, Dalí exploited the "commercial possibilities of his surrealist activities" more than any of his contemporaries (Tashjian 83–90). Between 1936 and 1938, for example, he collaborated with Schiaparelli to create "suits and coats with pockets that looked like miniature drawers, complete with dangling handles," a jacket showing a pair of "Mae West lips" (Blum 123), and hats shaped like shoes and inkwells (123–24). In September of 1936, Schiaparelli promoted surrealist ideas on the front cover of *Vogue*, while in 1937 she and Dalí collaborated to produce their "most powerful effect" (Tashjian 84), a flowing gown and headscarf patterned with trompe l'oeil tears. Two years later, Bonwit Teller, a large New York department store, commissioned Dalí to dress their windows. He and his wife, Gala, "worked through the night" to complete the display, which showed a store mannequin stepping into a hirsute bathtub (86). Owing to customer complaints, upon their return in the afternoon, they found the mannequins replaced by "clothed figures." Outraged by the store's impudence, Dalí stormed into the window and attempted to "overturn the hairy bathtub filled with water" (87), but he only succeeded in sending himself and the tub through the store's front window, a moment of havoc widely reported in the *Daily Mirror*, the *World Telegraph*, the *Herald Tribune*, and the *New York Times* (87–88) that clinched his "image with the American public" (85).[27]

Between New York adventures, Welty and her coterie of Jackson friends remained current with the smart set by reading precisely those publications responsible for diffusing surrealism nationwide.[28] Regular readers of the *New Yorker, Harper's Bazaar,* and *Vanity Fair,* Welty and her friends both admired and enjoyed lampooning figures representing New York's high society. In the "hut," a structure in the woods behind Welty's house, the Jackson group organized parties, decorating the walls with "photos out of *Vanity Fair*—our favorite performers in the New York theatre—Noel Coward, the Lunts, the Astaires" (Cole & Srinivason 205). Lehman Engel, a student at Juilliard and a regular at the Welty home, posed in one of Welty's family photographs showing these torn pages in the background. Welty's friends invented their own entertainments during the Depression, playing—among other word and drawing games—"Heads and Tails" (Black *Early* 3 9–40), a version of the absurdist sketching entertainment the surrealists called "Exquisite Corpse," enjoyed by Yves Tanguy, Joan Miró, Max Ernst, and André Breton in the late twenties (Barr *Fantastic* 266). The Jackson circle also held dinner parties for which they would dress up, aping the chic gatherings photographed by Cecil Beaton (Cole & Srinivason 201) and mimicking the celebrities appearing in the pages of *Vanity Fair,* a publication that "deemed itself the magazine in the know and hence an arbiter of taste and high culture for American society at large" (Tashjian 68).[29] Beaton and the celebrity world that he captured in his photography of the thirties often were a subject of the comedy evident in several of the letters that passed between Welty and Frank Lyell during this decade, so when Lyell momentarily entered that rarified company at a cocktail party in New York in 1935, he wrote Welty about the event the very next day.[30]

The letter describes starting the evening at the apartment of Mississippi siblings Ruth and Charles Henri Ford, whom Lyell gives the moniker "Bubber." Use of Charles Ford's nickname certainly suggests familiarity, perhaps born of shared origins, but Lyell seems less acquainted the other partygoers, about whom he reports almost breathlessly. These include: Cecil Beaton, George Hoyningen-Heuné,[31] Djuna Barnes,[32] George Balanchine,[33] William Dollar,[34] Peter Neagoe,[35] James Pendleton,[36] Augustus John,[37] Nicolai Nabokoff [*sic*],[38] and Paul Bowles.[39] However, the evening had only just begun, for Lyell later went to the "maddest party you've ever heard of or conceived at <u>Cecil's</u> apartment in the Waldorf—It would take weeks to describe the place to you—he's done it all over—dozens of artificial flowers, pictures, paintings, scrapbooks (full of Tallulah,[40] Daisy,[41] Tilly,[42] Elsa, the Sitwells,[43] Royalty, etc, etc)." Then he has an experience that he later reports made him nearly fall "into the fireplace": Hoyningen-Heuné offers to photograph him the next day. Lyell records that he and Hoyningen-Heuné, one of *Vogue*'s leading photographers, reached a quick understanding: "After half-an-hour's conversation with him at the Fords' we were fast friends— He's really a swell guy—hates Dali, mad music, photography, painting, seems a sincere conservative at heart." Opening such a letter, Welty must surely have shared Lyell's obvious sense of disbelief and excitement; however, as a struggling artist who sought to make New York both her home and a base where she could establish work contacts, she must also have envied the opportunities offered.

By 1935, the year Lyell wrote this letter, scores of female modernists like Welty routinely faced the challenge of making their work relevant in a literary context dominated by men. In a 1932 cartoon Welty drew and sent to Lyell, she symbolizes her predicament in a comic image that apparently parodies Dalí and his signature motif, the great masturbator. In a chatty fourteen-page letter (which one could categorize as surreal), Welty reports on a miscellany of Jackson topics, illustrating the events she retells in order to provide Lyell with "pictures to entertain you while you are reading the letter." The second of several sketches shows a parody of a Dalínian figure, both male and female, standing above a Weltian great masturbator, an amorphously shaped head bearing at least three eyes and a full curve of long eyelashes. The letter recounts Welty's trip accompanying her mother to the fair, which probably provides the immediate source for the "Halfmanhalfwoman" who mysteriously "offers the remaining fact for ten cents but is not taken up." A remote and probably bemused patron stands watching in the background of the sketch, perhaps confused by the implication that the figure has anything further to expose—even for a dime. The spectator only stares blankly, as if paralyzed by this monstrous challenge to orthodoxy. This image, then, seems at once to illustrate the strong cultural influence that surrealism exerted on Welty's life, and to express how she felt bisected, a woman attracted to activities—writing, publishing, photography, and travel—traditionally associated with maleness. When Marrs draws attention to Welty's "camaraderie with bright young men" such as Frank Lyell, Lehman Engel, Robert Daniel, and Hubert Creekmore (*Eudora* 55), she underlines an argument that the author made visually in her cartoon.

Welty's sketch titled
"Halfmanhalfwoman"
(1932). Reprinted by the
permission of Russell &
Volkening as agents for the
author's estate.

Influenced by surrealism from her writing career's inception, Welty would enjoy the attention of two prominent American surrealists who obviously recognized in her a member of their artistic family. Early in the forties, warm letters of praise and gratitude passed back and forth between Welty and Charles Henri Ford and Joseph Cornell. Born in Brookhaven, Mississippi, in 1913, Ford, along with Parker Tyler and Kathleen Tankersley, founded *Blues: A Magazine of New Rhythms*, an avant-garde poetry journal published out of Columbus, Mississippi, and featuring an unexpectedly impressive lineup of talent, including Harry Crosby, H.D., Kay Boyle, Gertrude Stein, Eugene Jolas, Ezra Pound, Kenneth Rexroth, and William Carlos Williams (Henningfeld; Ford *Blues* vol.1). In a 1978 letter to her editor, William Maxwell, Welty recalls Ford and *Blues*, his "little magazine in Columbus," uncertain whether she ever made a contribution to the publication (Marrs *What There* 336). She also references Ford's *View, the surrealist-oriented* literary and visual arts publication of the forties, and one of the achievements on which his reputation rests. After *Blues*, he had joined the exodus of American artists of the twenties and thirties who made Paris their destination and home. There, he fell in with Gertrude Stein's circle, met Paul Bowles and Djuna Barnes, and through the latter, Pavel Tchelitchew, who became his lover (Henningfeld). On returning to the United States, he founded *View*, a magazine that Tchelitchew's biographer, Parker Tyler, remembers as "an international magazine that will exploit not only the best avant-garde talents in America but the many modern artists who have come here to escape the European war" (422). Tyler also recalls that Ford's "practical vision grasps the strategy of making a cultural popular front between fashionable transatlantic elements and neglected aspects of American talent" (422–23). In preparation for the seminal "Americana Fantastica" issue, Ford wrote to Welty asking for a contribution:

> Dear Miss Welty: I have been meaning to write you for a long time, ever since I read the story in Accent about the second-hand clothes. The next number of VIEW will be on and of Americana Fantastica and I wonder if you do not have an incredible story which you would send us? We go to press Nov 10 and the issue will be our most elaborate to date.

Welty reproduced this missive and included it in a letter that she wrote to Frank Lyell in November 1942, reporting that she had had a "letter from Chas Henri Ford," the abbreviation of his name acknowledged familiarity and probable friendship. Certainly, Lyell would have known both Charles and his sister, Ruth, because years earlier he attended their cocktail party, where he met Hoyningen-Huené. That Ford wrote with such warmth and conviction suggests his detecting in Welty's "Ida M'Toy," the story he would have read in *Accent*, a surreal—or at least a fantastic—sensibility at work. As if to underline this opinion of her work, Welty wrote back a few months later, signing the letter in a way that mimicked Ford's having written his name in "purple ink." To a reclining and leisurely curving *E* for Eudora, she affixed a large cutout picture of a grasshopper, whose legs, body, and antennae appear to create a *W*. Even by Welty's eccentric letter writing standards, this flamboyant and surreal gesture represents a memorable highpoint.

The grasshopper surely lodged in the mind of Ford's collaborator. Joseph Cornell had read Welty's "The Winds" in 1942 and somehow came to possess the letter that she had penned to Ford. As the designer of the "Fantastica" issue, Cornell could well have suggested that Ford write a letter of invitation to Welty, as both hailed from Mississippi, and both knew Lyell. Whatever the details surrounding the 1942 solicitation, Cornell wrote to her a few years later, early in 1945. Part letter and part collage, the artwork he sent reveals his high regard for Welty's photography and fiction, for he celebrates "The Winds" and also notes having lately "caught up with the issue of VOGUE that had your photographs, and an agreeable surprise it was, especially the house at twilight." He alludes to Welty's "Literature and the Lens," an article both visual and verbal that appeared in August 1944 and clearly was the trigger for Cornell's cross-media homage, which takes Welty's atmospheric picture of a ruined house near Natchez as its point of origin. "Greatly stimulated" by this scene at twilight, Cornell's collage harkens back to the building "at the moment of its demolition," reporting that at the instant of the chimney's toppling, an "old ship's figurehead—in the shape of a Moorish pirate that had once proudly scanned the waves from an East Indiaman—arose from his crypt and shot out of the chimney with all the fury of an avenging angel." Ultimately forming a constellation, the figurehead really does illustrate Levy's description of surrealism as a "point of view" (*Surrealism* 4) amenable to literary and/or visual representation.[44]

This fascinating correspondence, recording a mixture of artistic visions shared by Welty, Ford, and Cornell presents some of the strongest evidence of Welty's indebtedness to surrealism as it broadly manifested itself in the United States. However, Ford and Cornell only drew attention to this surreal quality, which had marked her verbal and visual art from at least 1936, the year of her first published story. In the years between returning to Jackson from Columbia in 1930 and her first publishing success, she not only exhibited an inclination to educate herself about all the latest trends in modern art, but also to take advantage of opportunities to see these works even as they altered art history. This exposure sharpened Welty's desire to live in New York City and perhaps further her schooling under Berenice Abbott. Such a move would also bring her closer to the milieu celebrated in magazines like *Vanity Fair, Harper's Bazaar*, and *Vogue*, one already occupied by her friend Frank Lyell. None of these desires was fulfilled, though—at least not then and not in the way she may have imagined. Instead, she substituted residency with temporary stays in New York, remaining in Jackson. There she wrote her fiction, blending largely southern settings, themes, and characters with a style, sensibility, and spirit centered

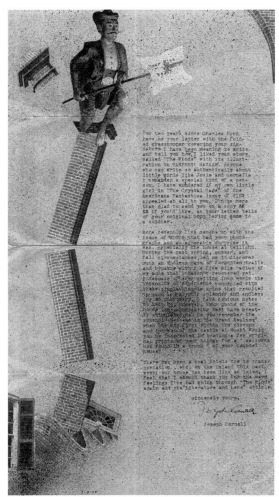

Joseph Cornell. *Letter/ collage to Eudora Welty.* 1945. Private Collection. Reprinted by the permission of Russell & Volkening as agents for the author's estate. Art © The Joseph and Robert Cornell Memorial Foundation/Licensed by VAGA, New York, NY.

in New York. A Freudian would use the term "sublimation" to describe Welty's tradeoff, sacrificing location for writing and perhaps setting a pattern for her career in fiction. Moreover, the same Freudian might also posit unconscious influence as the mechanism whereby surrealism impacted Welty's oeuvre, a theory this study does not dispute. With hindsight, Welty the surrealist almost seems to express an axiom—especially considering Katherine Anne Porter's apparent allusion to the movement in her 1941 introduction to *A Curtain of Green.* Nonetheless, Welty never guides any of her many interviewers in that direction, even when she happily advances Chekhov or Woolf as influences. More likely, she unconsciously developed this fundamental aspect of her prose style as it coalesced. As surrealism gathered strength, her writing strengthened alongside it, sometimes passing nearer and sometimes farther from the center, refracting surrealism's glow through the lens of her own writing consciousness until at least the middle fifties.

To claim the unacknowledged and unconscious influence of a large cultural movement like surrealism does not demand a major suspension of disbelief, but to identify particular personalities who the led the movement as influences may give rise to skepticism. However, evidence from Welty's life and fiction creates intriguing suggestions. For example, the strongly visual quality of her prose surely reflects her well-documented interest in modern art and probably evinces Welty as a member of what Breton biographer Mark Polizzotti describes as an English-speaking audience "deterred by the awkwardness and impenetrability of [surrealism's] poetry in English translation" and "struck instead by the much more immediate thrill of its painted imagery." Furthermore, assuming that Polizzotti's claim that "particularly in America, audiences and critics would view Surrealism almost entirely as an art movement" also applies to Welty makes only a handful of painters relevant (*Revolution* 428). These include the surrealists categorized by Alfred H. Barr as either makers of "hand-painted dream photographs" (*Fantastic* 11), or painters who show "complete spontaneity of *technique* as well as of subject matter" (12). In his introduction to the exhibition catalog for the "Fantastic Art, Dada, and Surrealism" show, Barr assigns Dalí, Tanguy, and Magritte (and secondarily de Chirico and Ernst) to the first group, while he assigns Masson and Miró to the second group, subject to the earlier influence of Kandinsky, Klee, and Arp (11–12). For decades commentators noted Welty's realistic style, an observation that tends—because of their non-representational approach, a strategy virtually impossible to simulate in fiction—to diminish the significance of Barr's second category of painters. However, the first group (with the exception of Tanguy), favored representational forms they then undermined. This surreal de-realizing of conventional representation most closely describes Welty's style as she expressed it in her fiction.

To narrow the field of surrealist influences further does not preclude the significance of other painters. Dalí, perhaps, deserves additional attention, not least because his name appears in Lyell's letters to Welty when others—such as Tanguy, Ernst, or Miró, also showing in New York—are conspicuously absent. Dalí's already high cultural profile may well have encouraged

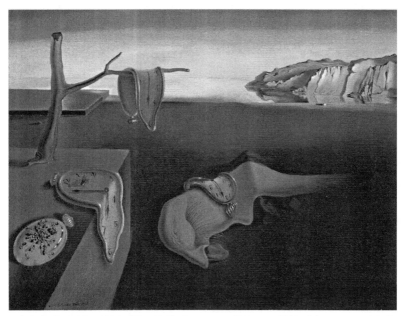

Dalí, Salvador (1904–89) © ARS, NY. *The Persistence of Memory*. 1931. Oil on canvas, 9 1/2 x 13" (24.1 x 33 cm). Given anonymously. Digital Image © The Museum of Modern Art/Licensed by SCALA/Art Resource, NY. © Salvador Dalí, Fundació Gala-Salvador Dalí/Artists Rights Society (ARS), New York 2011.

Lyell, in 1933, to visit his first one-man exhibition. Here he could have seen perhaps the most famous of all surrealist paintings, *The Persistence of Memory*, a work that had created swells of excitement in art circles ever since it "dominated" the first exhibition of surrealist art in the United States at Hartford, Connecticut's Wadsworth Atheneum (Tashjian 39). By 1934, when Welty could have seen Dalí's second solo show and witnessed his first visit to New York, he had begun to establish himself in the minds of many Americans as *the* spokesman and authority for things surreal, despite the sizable regiment of surrealist artists, and despite Breton's leadership of the movement in France. Dalí's serial grandstanding, along with sensational coverage of his antics in the American media, garnered the Spaniard such a high profile that he contributed significantly to the idea that surrealism only manifested itself through the visual arts.[45] When *Time* chose Man Ray's stylish portrait of Dalí to advertise its coverage of the Museum of Modern Art's "Fantastic Art, Dada, and Surrealism" exhibition, it acknowledged and fuelled the latter's celebrity.

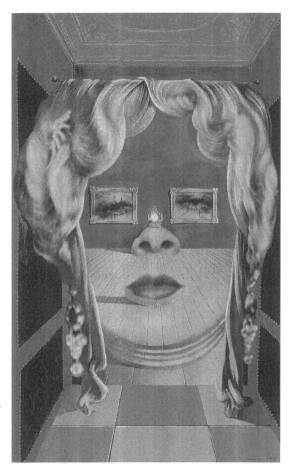

Salvador Dalí Spanish, 1904–89, *Mae West's Face which May be Used as a Surrealist Apartment*, 1934–35. Gouache, with graphite, on commercially printed magazine page, 283 x 178 mm (sight). Gift of Mrs. Charles B. Goodspeed, 1949. 517, The Art Institute of Chicago. © Salvador Dalí, Fundació Gala-Salvador Dalí/Artists Rights Society (ARS), New York 2011.

Welty no doubt saw and felt the power of many great surrealist artists, but Dalí alone moved through and enhanced the glamour of the smart set, as reflected in the pages of *Vogue, Harper's Bazaar, Vanity Fair,* or the *New York Times.* It was a world occupied by the likes of Schiaparelli and the Windsors, photographed by Beaton and Hoyningen-Heuné, and satirized by Mae West. Dalí's immortalization of this contemporary siren in his 1934–35 *Mae West's Face which May be Used as a Surrealist Apartment* reveals the extent to which both he and Welty engaged with the popular culture of their day, both cherishing and lampooning its vulgarity. Love of this milieu could well have resulted in Welty's Dalí parody, her allusion to *The Persistence of Memory* in the title of her short story, "A Memory," and to the grasshopper signature she created when writing to Charles Henri

Eric Schaal's exterior photograph of Salvador Dalí's *Dream of Venus* pavilion at the New York World's Fair (1939). Eric Schaal © Fundació Gala-Salvador Dalí, Figueres, 2011.

Ford in 1943. By then, the head of Dalí's great masturbator motif, as well as the grasshopper, had appeared in so many of his paintings they formed part of his unique mythology. One wonders, too, about the significance of New York's 1939 World's Fair, where Dalí installed his "Dream of Venus," a kitschy surrealist pavilion adorned inside and out with scantily-clad mermaids and located in the fair's amusement zone.[46] An August 1940 postcard from Welty to Lyell locates her at the fair in its final weeks and, perhaps under the influence of surrealism, apparently subject to hallucinations. Showing "The Crest," a sculpture by Brenda Putnam of a male swimmer balanced on a wave, the postcard puns, "Hasn't the crest fallen? I thought I saw Chalmers Alexander, Reba Tull, Allie Blanche Ruff, + Miss Fletcher all this afternoon on the St. Must have been an illusion. E."[47] Had Welty visited the seamier side of the fair and walked by or even paid admittance to the hallucinatory "Dream of Venus" funhouse? Had its shocking and bizarre design sent her imagination reeling, tickled her eccentric sense of humor, and lead her to affix the postcard's stamp upside down? Numerous well-known photographs of sideshows at fairs in Mississippi suggest a taste for this kind of entertainment. The postcard yields no clear answer and tantalizes with its silence.[48]

4. Surrealism in Theory: Julien Levy, Salvador Dalí, and Eudora Welty

A committed observer of New York's ascendant cultural life, Welty could not have failed to note surrealism's American debut during the early thirties. Seriously deliberating about careers in writing, photography, or both,[49] she wrote and made pictures redolent of the zeitgeist, an intellectual climate receptive to surrealism's overtures and open to change under its influence. As part of the American artistic interpretation of the movement, Welty produced much of her fiction of the thirties, forties, and fifties, and, by the final decade, had accrued enough literary success to produce two important essays expressing her artistic vision: "Writing and Analyzing a Story" and "Place in Fiction." The two pieces, which she published 1955, contain some of her most sustained theorizing about her writing philosophy. Beyond evidence of surrealism as it influenced her life and fiction, these essays offer further support for the connection—especially when read alongside some of the more famous codifications of surrealist ideas intended for consumption by American audiences. Texts that rank highly among the small number of works of this kind include Julien Levy's seminal introduction to the movement, *Surrealism* (1936), and Dalí's *Conquest of the Irrational*, published by Levy a year earlier.[50]

Welty may have read one, both, or neither of these books, but it seems reasonable to assume that she must have read at least some surrealist theory, especially considering the very close parallels linking her essays to the movement. Welty's silence regarding Breton's founding manifestoes may seem an oversight, but complete English translations of these works did not exist until 1969. Knowing little French, Welty could not have read the original statements very closely, but she would have had access to Levy's and Dalí's publications, which translate, quote, and closely paraphrase Breton. In addition, she would have had access to various exhibition catalogues (including the one that she owned, the Museum of Modern Art's "Fantastic Art, Dada, Surrealism"), as well as to surrealist ideas disseminated in the mass market.[51] In particular, Levy's *Surrealism* seems a strong candidate for a text with which Welty had familiarity, especially owing to an apparent allusion to the book in her story "The Winds." The Joseph Cornell designed cover of Levy's work shows a young boy using a cake icing tube as an instrument, blowing through it to produce the letters in "surrealism." The letters ascend from the flower-shaped opening in a curving pattern that

Joseph Cornell's dust jacket for Julien Levy's *Surrealism* (1936). Art © The Joseph and Robert Cornell Memorial Foundation/Licensed by VAGA, New York, NY. Image provided by the Jean and Julien Levy Foundation.

playfully advertises the book's subject. Several years later, Welty seems to reprise this image in "The Winds," a story Cornell clearly admired which pays homage to him via Welty's protagonist, Josie, and Josie's revered elder, Cornella. At the story's close, Josie and her family visit a Chautauqua tent where a beautiful cornet player (another echo of Cornell) gives a virtuoso performance: "If morning-glories had come out of the horn instead of those sounds, Josie would not have felt a more astonished delight. She was pierced with pleasure" (*Stories* 265). All these elements—the innocent child, the raised instrument, the punning on names, and the unexpected but exultant emissions (letters in Cornell and flowers in Welty)—together suggest Welty's knowledge of Levy's seminal work.

Surrealism's appearance in 1936 supplied American readers with a two-hundred-page handbook that gives a short history of the movement from its nineteenth-century influences to its twentieth-century practitioners. Levy prefaces his introduction with a quotation from Breton, surrealism's primary theoretician "who organized the program" (12). Levy goes on to quote liberally from Breton in outlining the philosophy's chief tenets. As an author who had primarily come to understand surrealism from a distance and through its visual productions, Levy, who spoke fluent French, penned a guide for English-speaking audiences by mediating Breton's published manifestoes. For Breton's biographer, Polizzotti, Levy accomplishes this act of interpretation and intercontinental transmission artfully. Polizzotti writes: "We can therefore celebrate Levy's achievement nearly sixty years after its first appearance, both for its laudable fidelity to the surrealist 'point of view' (including the recognition that Surrealism *was*, before anything else, a point of view) and for the intelligence of its assemblage" (Introduction viii). In addition to his interpretation of surrealist philosophy, Levy reproduces a generous assortment of surrealist works from a diverse range of media.

Levy's successful transmitting of the fundamental constituents of surrealist thought justifies Polizzotti's high praise. Levy derives these constituents directly from Breton's first and second manifestoes, summarizing these elements as follows: surrealism revolts against "positivist dissections of the eighteenth and nineteenth centuries" and the painter's or writer's mechanical and "literal recording of fact" (7); surrealism represents a "point of view, and as such applies to painting, literature, photography, cinema, politics, architecture, play and behaviour" (4); surrealism allies itself with Sigmund Freud's psychoanalysis in urging an exploration of dreams, the unconscious, and their "introactive" relationship with "reality" (5); surrealism advocates "man as psychology instead of anatomy" and embraces Marx and Engels's formulation of "modern dialectics" as a procedure reconciling "philosophic *materialism*" and "metaphysical *idealism*"; and finally, surrealism asserts the primacy of myth, fetish, parable, proverb, and metaphor in order for the artist to "explain his intuition" and subsequently to arouse a "corresponding intuition in others" (6)[52].

While Dalí broadly accepted and had long acknowledged these central tenets of the surrealist revolution, his irrepressible creativity opened fissures between Breton's orthodoxy and his own developing line of surrealist theory, paranoiac criticism. "Most of [Dalí's] theoretical texts," Haim Finkelstein observes, "indeed, reflect his continuous efforts to be accepted into the ranks of the Surrealists, but on his own terms, with full recognition of his originality and uniqueness" (*Collected* 2). The artist's writings of the early thirties display the tension resulting from his "innately anarchic and self-indulgent imagination" and the pressure to conform to Breton's dictates (3). However, by the mid thirties, these tensions diminished, and Dalí, buoyed by his New York successes, began to shift his "sights to the American public," a contention that "is well attested to by the fact that most of the texts he wrote in the late 1930s—well before fleeing in 1940 to the United States—and through the 1940s were originally published in English." These essays in "catalogues accompanying exhibitions of his work" or articles in popular magazines such as "*Vogue, Harper's Bazaar*, or *Esquire*" eliminated "all the ambiguities and mystifications needed by Dalí in order to maintain his intellectual acrobatics vis-à-vis Surrealist theory." Beyond serving as fora for the development of Dalí's theory, these magazines enabled a more "straightforward" formulation of his ideas to gain nationwide exposure, and, in addition, showcasing that theory through its general application in the world of fashion photography (4).

The Conquest of the Irrational appeared in English and French in the same year, 1935, and it represents Dalí's clearest single statement outlining the aims and methods of paranoiac criticism, a methodology that had steadily evolved in the previous five years, and a theory of knowledge which he viewed as relevant broadly to the "whole field of human experience as a general theory of Surrealist knowledge ('connaissance'), with application in every aspect of life, culture, and aesthetics" (Finkelstein *Collected* 273). In a division of the book entitled "My Fortresses," Dalí mounts a defense of his theory and his artistic practice against those who would define, identify, and therefore foreclose the play of signification in his paintings. He proposes that the operation of paranoiac criticism reveals the "concrete irrational subject" because the artist creates in response to his or her paranoia and, as a consequence, mobilizes a similar set of reactions in the audience. In painting, the procedure requires the deployment of trompe l'oeil effects that draw images of irrationality into correspondence with the "means of expression approaching those of the great realist painting—Velázquez and Vermeer of Delft." Such a synthesis supplies moments of "concrete irrationality" that simulate the "phenomenally real" through painting "realistically according to irrational thought" and "according to the unknown imagination" ("Conquest" 265). Finkelstein notes that Dalí obtained support for his theory of paranoiac and delusional interpretive acts in Jacques Lacan's doctoral thesis, *De La Psychose Paranoïaque dans ses Rapports avec la Personalité* (*Collected* 216). In 1930, Lacan read Dalí's essay, "The Rotting Donkey," that appeared in *Surréalisme au Service de la*

Révolution. According to Lacan's biographer, Elisabeth Roudinesco, Dalí's theoretical analysis of paranoiac metaphors in the visual arts led Lacan to develop his theory of the relationship between language and psychosis (31). While respecting Breton's insistence on the dialectical method, his allegiance to the psychoanalytic paradigm, his discrediting of positivist philosophy, and his allegiance to all forms of figuration, Dalí revises a tenet of classical surrealist doctrine by dispensing with the "exclusively passive and receptive role of the Surrealist subject." As if the egomaniac in Dalí could no longer brook Breton's authority or tolerate the collateral role he assigned to the artist—second to the mystery of the unconscious—in surrealist experiments, he elevates the artist to the status of one who creates by exploiting the "systematic associations that are peculiar to paranoia" ("Conquest" 266). Accordingly, as a theoretical construct, he defines paranoiac critical activity as a "*spontaneous method of irrational knowledge based in the interpretive critical association of delirious phenomena.*" Rejecting the implication that the process involves "voluntary directed thought," Dalí grants artist and audience a capacity for delirious cultural production and reception that modifies orthodox surrealist theory by substituting the "passive, disinterested, contemplative, and aesthetic attitude vis-à-vis irrational phenomena" for an "active, systematic, organizing, cognoscitive attitude" (267). Notwithstanding the obvious excesses of Dalí's ludicrously florid prose, his book essentially proposes and defends the role of the surrealist, who intentionally simulates the paranoia of consciousness in order to foreground irrationality and the power of the unconscious in shaping human behavior.

In the visual arts, the unsettling illusion of trompe l'oeil constitutes one practical manifestation of this theory. The paranoiac critical method employs these double or multiple figurations as metaphors exhibiting the complexity of the mind. Dalí contends that success in response to such trompe l'oeil relies on the "paranoic capacity of the author." Volunteering his own composition as an example that presents six perfectly complete "simultaneous images" of an "athlete, lion's head, general's head, horse, bust of a shepherdess, skull," he claims that "different viewers see in this picture different images," despite his mode of representation, which "is scrupulously realistic"[53] ("Conquest" 268). The significance of double or multiple configuration, then, resides in its insistence on mimicking the delusional condition of visual perception through destabilizing naturalistic representation. Moreover, Dalí's theory perhaps predicts Lacan's development of the mirror stage, because according to Lacanian psychoanalysis, exposure to the specular image of the subject reflected in a mirror organizes the viewer's personality at a fundamental level, creating a "drama whose internal thrust is precipitated from insufficiency to anticipation" (Lacan "The Mirror Stage" 4). This moment of reflection forms the origin of the subject's enduring sense of absence and his or her misconstruction (méconnaissance) of himself or herself as capable of perfect knowledge. Thus, Dalí's theory and practice challenge the reliability of sight, and, drawing on Lacan's dissertation, he represents in his art states of paranoia and hallucination that fully acknowledge the Freudianism that many Victorians had sought to repress.

Welty subscribed to no such nineteenth-century myopia. Born in 1909, growing up in the years preceding World War I, and maturing as artist in the decades that witnessed global depression and Germany's dissolution, militarization, and imperialism, she well understood human irrationality and fallibility. She knew civilization had meaning only in relation to the repression of its inherent barbarism. By the thirties, American fiction writers had turned to realism and naturalism as artistic responses to a decade of despair. For instance, Malcolm Bradbury notes that "there was proletarian realism and bourgeois realism, urban realism and rural realism, WASP realism and Dustbowl realism, white realism and black realism" (137). But as the example of Henry Miller demonstrates, the "novel of radical extremity took other than directly social form in the Thirties" (147). Many of the leading fiction writers of that decade, such as William Faulkner, Ernest Hemingway, and F. Scott Fitzgerald had "begun their careers in the Twenties," so the "new social emphasis did not fully displace their modernism." The avant-garde experimentalism of the twenties carried over into the next decade, shaping the work of other writers, such as John Dos Passos, whose innovative *U.S.A.* demonstrates a "radical expressionism," and Djuna Barnes or Nathanael West, both of whom employed "grotesque surrealism" (127).[54] Welty's earliest reviewers tended to align her with the sensationalism of such figures as Erskine Caldwell and the "pre-Nobel laureate reputation of William Faulkner as the headmaster of a literary 'school of cruelty'" (Kreyling *Understanding* 9), rather than grouping her with the decade's surrealists, who extended and nurtured the project initiated by the European avant-garde.

Welty's two essays from the 1950s outline explicitly her heretofore-implicit artistic philosophy that illustrates her avant-garde inheritance, particularly in relation to her literary treatment of physical locations or place

in her fiction. In "Writing and Analyzing a Story," she begins by considering her fiction retrospectively, averring that a writer's "stories have repeated
themselves in shadowy ways" and that, despite obvious variations, stories
return to "certain themes," conforming subjectively to "some pattern that's
been very early laid down" (773). For Welty, that recurring theme and patterning in her narrative often resides in what Reynolds Price describes as
her ubiquitous method, the "yoking of disparate sights into a single image
of startling freshness" (x). This surrealist juxtaposing of unlikely and often
contradictory images clearly parallels the multiple figurations central to the
art of a surrealist like Dalí, yet such formations in turn derive from Breton's
emphasis in the "Manifesto of Surrealism" on the light which pulses from
two images brought into unlikely contact. "The value of the image," Breton
theorizes, "depends upon the beauty of the spark obtained; it is, conse-
quently, a function of the difference of potential between the two conduc-
tors. When the difference exists only slightly, as in a comparison, the spark
is lacking" (37). Like Dalí's Bretonian theory of multiple images that express
the paranoiac and delusional condition of perception, Welty's use of language demonstrates a parallel conceptualizing of the dialectic between the
subject and his or her material environment or place. Commenting on her
own writing process, she argues that all the elements of her fiction hang on
"a sort of double thunderclap at the author's ears: the break of the living
world upon what is already stirring inside the mind, and the answering impulse that in a moment of high consciousness fuses impact and image and
fires them off together" ("Writing and Analyzing" 780). She seems to offer
a construction of multiple image theory when she describes the dialectical
fusion between the mind's insides and the "living world," which collide
to produce an "impact" and, most significantly, an "image." Indeed, the
lengthy series of visual metaphors that Welty deploys in this essay to analyze her story writing testifies to the central position visually charged language occupies in her canon. Writers "call up into view" (774). They work
out into space away from the "vanishing point" (775). They imagine the
"image of the story's predicament," and the writer's point of view detaches
itself, floating free from the "surrounding scene" and hanging "suspended,"
seemingly like a picture affixed to a wall (777).

The analysis of place and its representation in language in "Writing and
Analyzing a Story" repeatedly undermines the notion that in writing mere
similarities between the representational and the actual create the ideal
artwork. Taking Ian Watt's classic definition of realism in literature and

comparing it to the theory Welty propounds in this article provides a clari-
fying contrast. Watt's *The Rise of the Novel* charts the historical evolution
of realist writing from its origins in the English eighteenth-century, which
saw novelists such as Daniel Defoe and Samuel Richardson develop and
popularize "formal realism," a new or novel genre of writing that proposed
to create a "full and authentic report of human experience" by supplying
"such details of the story as the individuality of the actors concerned, the
particulars of the times and places of their actions, details which are presented through a more largely referential use of language than is common
in other literary forms" (32). This general approach guided the production
of thousands of novels throughout the eighteenth and nineteenth centuries,
until the modernist revolution challenged and badly damaged the prestige
of formal realism. Welty undoubtedly was part of this widespread revolt,
an assertion well illustrated in "Writing and Analyzing a Story," an essay
which critiques referential writing as it constructs place. "For no matter
whether the 'likeness' is there for all to see or not," Welty proclaims, "the
place, once entered into the writer's mind in a story, is, in the course of
writing the story, *functional*" (778). Here, in a close analysis of her writing practice, she clearly lays a fundamental stress on the writer's mind as
the crucible that transforms place, charging it with symbolic desires. The
dialectical exchange Welty identifies is for her the creative process itself:
The artist merges the "abstract" thesis with the "concrete" antithesis to generate the narrative's synthesis, an alloy of the abstract in the concrete and
the concrete in the abstract (779). When she alludes to her realism, she
refers not to the tradition of Defoe and Richardson, but to the reality of the
world's mystery she views as bound up in the exchange and commerce of
relationships, Welty's term for the dialectic.

    In the second essay, "Place in Fiction," Welty returns to her conceptu-
alization of fiction, exploring it in greater depth and with more examples.
Working against the condescending prejudice of critics who sought to tax-
onomize her as a regional writer, this complex and subtle essay extends the
inquiry begun in "Writing and Analyzing a Story" by again diminishing
the role of place in the novel. "Place is one of the lesser angels," she opens,
"that watch over the racing hand of fiction," while "others, like character,
plot, symbolic meaning, and so on, are doing a good deal of wingbeating
about her chair, and feeling, who in my eyes carries the crown, soars high-
est of them all and rightly relegates place into the shade" ("Place" 781). Here
are the rudiments of a central statement establishing the principles of her

artistic practice by focusing attention on the relationship or the dialectic that clearly operates when she produces fiction. Out of her observation of material reality comes language that represents the concrete, while undermining its solidity to produce a surreal prose that persists in destabilizing traditional representational techniques.

Like "Writing and Analyzing a Story," "Place in Fiction" repeatedly evinces Welty's preoccupation with fiction as a form of representation that inevitably elevates sight over the other senses, and that can accommodate the surreal point of view. Her choice of metaphor to describe fiction's aims shows this bias toward vision and seeing. A good novel should "be steadily alight." It should "be steadily visible from its outside." It should present a "pleasing and finished surface to the eye." Its plausibility risks foundering if the "visibility is only partial or intermittent" (784). It must at every second seem "within reach as the world of appearance" And its "world of appearance" must seem to be "actuality," bringing place to "life in the round before the reader's eye" (785). This artist's predilection for the specular in fiction obviously influenced the writer, whom Katherine Anne Porter, in her early introduction to Welty's *A Curtain of Green*, commended as someone who for several years "believed she was going to be a painter, and painted quite earnestly while she wrote without much effort" (966). Welty's painter's eye clearly reveals itself when she claims that the writer sees place composed in a "brimming" frame that displays spectacle as a "product of personal experience and time" that "is burnished with feelings and sensibilities, charged from moment to moment with the sun-points of imagination" ("Place" 789). For Welty, the fiction writer conveys a dream to the audience, a strategy reinforced when she dwells on the significance of the writer's skill in creating a plausible illusion of appearances—and, therefore, a successful story. She claims that the author

> must accurately choose, combine, superimpose upon, blot out, shake up, alter the outside world for one absolute purpose, the good of his story. To do this, he is always seeing double, two pictures at once in his frame, his and the world's, a fact that he constantly comprehends; and he works best in a state of constant and subtle and unfooled reference between the two. It is his clear intention—his passion, I should say—to make the reader see only one of the pictures—the author's—under the pleasing illusion that it is the world's; this enormity is the accomplishment of a good story. (789)

Using a typically visual metaphor of the artist as painter or perhaps photographer, Welty argues for fiction's need to "alter the outside world" with vehemence and totality in order for the world represented in language to take on the truthfulness of a convincing hallucination—and frequently to partake of the strangeness of an hallucination, too.

The requirement that a modernist writer possess a kind of double vision only develops a point made earlier in the essay, when Welty introduces the discussion of a nightlight by which she slept as a child. This symbol epitomizes her surrealist sensibility, but for many it also encapsulates misguided ideas about the aim of good writing:

> Some of us grew up with the china night-light, the little lamp whose lighting showed its secret and with that spread enchantment. The outside is painted with a scene, which is one thing; then, when the lamp is lighted, through the porcelain sides a new picture comes out through the old, and they are seen as one. A lamp I knew of was a view of London till it was lit; but then it was the Great Fire of London, and you could go beautifully to sleep by it. The lamp alight is the combination of internal and external, glowing in the imagination as one; and so is the good novel. Seeing that these inner and outer surfaces do lie so close together and so implicit in each other, the wonder is that human life so often separates them, or appears to, and it takes a good novel to put them back together. ("Place" 784)

In this passage, the china vessel stands as an emblem for the synthesis that good fiction achieves. Repudiating empiricist pressures that force a wedge between the internal and external surfaces of the lamp, Welty deems the novel eminently equipped to meld the material with the immaterial, synthesizing the seen with the emotionally or imaginatively experienced. One cannot help but recognize the debt Welty reveals to the teachings of European romanticism, a large cultural movement that (at least in England) enacted a parallel project—albeit through poetry and not fiction. The nightlight glows, revealing a dual surreal image: a view of London, and then, that view ravaged by flames. And some would recommend flames for the style of writing that Welty produced using this approach. For example, Diana Trilling's unyielding review of *The Wide Net* in 1943 lambasts the collection for its ostentatious "subjectivism" (4), an accusation that leads her instructively on to pair Welty and Dalí, who both are mythologists and creators of legend, both take their metaphors from dreams, and yet both are devoted naturalists; and each has a mother-country—Dalí, Spain; Miss Welty, the Natchez country—whose atmosphere and superstition permeate his work and whose confines are determining beyond the power of travel or mature experience to enlarge them. Rather more suggestive, however, than these similarities is their common service to what amounts to a myth of modern femininity. (42)

Not altogether disparaging, this assessment creates some intriguing parallels worth contemplating, but Trilling's emphasis on Welty and Dalí's shared naturalistic style forms the most significant likeness here—one on which to close.

The nightlight sheds the kind of glow that fosters sleep, and it does so through its naturalistic recreation of London's great fire. Without exaggeration, one could claim the same kind of soporific naturalism is at work in a painting like Dalí's iconic *The Persistence of Memory*, a comparison revealing how these contemporaries used the distortion of representational forms in order to generate surreal effects. In *The Persistence of Memory*, clocks famously droop and curve, seeming to melt over the surfaces or structures that support them. In the background, a body of blue water naturalistically reflects a bluff of craggy cliffs that draw the eye toward the scene's horizon. However, these photographically reproduced elements, "the bare, hard outline of the cliffs and the crystal clear light of the sky," work harmoniously with the "empty, desert-like expanses" that "are much closer to the topography of the mind, to a dreamscape" (Radford 146). This painting, in particular, demonstrates an artistic strategy observable in the majority of Dalí's compositions, which routinely present images with a startling degree of naturalistic detail while maintaining a reverie-like atmosphere, especially through the deformation of space and depth. For this reason, Werner Haftmann, probably following Alfred H. Barr's taxonomy in *Fantastic Art, Dada, Surrealism*, classifies Dalí as the most prominent and extreme practitioner of "Veristic Surrealism" (272),[55] a variety of surrealist visual art that decomposes the world of "real things completely" (273), and

seeks to represent the irrational world of dream and imagination with such extreme realism that its truth and reality can no longer be doubted. A destructive force gnaws at the images of the visible, corrodes the curtains of appearance, and calls into play another kind of illusion, which proves to be as stubborn and vital as the first. The two realms of appearance interpenetrate, one conjures up the other. The desired result is a chaotic tangle of images in which the outer and the inner are inseparably mixed but parade before our terrified minds in the guise of a fully existing reality. Again the jungle of nature opens before us. (273)

Haftmann's "extreme realism" of "inseparably mixed" subjective and objective images coincides quite neatly with the kind of representation Welty illustrates with her porcelain lamp, a symbol that reveals a mixture of inner and outer states, expressing neither the reproduction of material circumstance nor the abstraction of immaterial thought, but a synthetic and dialectically derived surreality. In "Place in Fiction," she clearly commits to this precise and harmonious doubling in her writing when she concentrates on the verity of things: "No blur of inexactness, no cloud of vagueness, is allowable in good writing; from the first seeing to the last putting down, there must be steady lucidity and uncompromise of purpose. I speak, of course, of the ideal" (789). Here, Welty shuns excessive abstraction and opacity in displaying realistic detail because of qualities minimizing the work's capacity to validate the material environment. Instead, she and Dalí—as Trilling scornfully observed in the forties—share Breton's abiding insistence on dialectically rendering the surreality formed at the conjunction of mind and matter.

The chapters that follow chronologically survey the surreal literary effects and often the surreal substance of Welty's writing in *A Curtain of Green and Other Stories, The Wide Net, and Other Stories, Delta Wedding, The Golden Apples,* and *The Bride of the Innisfallen and Other Stories.* They exclude her other fictions written during this period, *The Robber Bridegroom* and *The Ponder Heart,* and beyond. For reasons not pertinent to this study but later contemplated in the final chapter, these works swerve away stylistically from the main path cut by the majority of her books published between 1941 and 1955. These collections of short stories and novels invariably make a literary habit of presenting apparently realistic worlds that Welty quickly and often subtly vexes, conclusively showing the determining force of dreams and the unconscious in the lives of her characters.

2

THE PERSISTENCE OF A MEMORY IN
A CURTAIN OF GREEN AND OTHER STORIES

Whether surveying André Breton's multiple codifications, Salvador Dalí's renovation of Breton, or Julien Levy's synthesis of both, surrealism—in any of its forms, European or American—never abandoned its commitment to the invention and promotion of new knowledge. The innovation of psychoanalysis acted as guarantor and as collateral securing surrealism's project, which found expression in a diverse array of media. The movement's attempt to rupture the purely rational and conscious hold that positivism exercised over philosophy produced new varieties of art that widened the epistemological gaze. While the surrealist project in France frequently risked fragmentation[1] under the pressure of competing claims for the future of the movement, all parties broadly agreed that surrealism could spawn such a diversity of cultural expression because it advanced a common "point of view," with as many applications as the number of available media (Levy *Surealism* 3). Surrealism's point of view admits *only* of a dual reality with artistic productions displaying an almost alchemical aura, transforming the material into the immaterial and the immaterial into the material through its cooption of the Hegelian dialectic.

As chapter one established, Eudora Welty's "Place in Fiction" announced her subscription to a parallel view with regard to fiction. She contends that "point of view is hardly a single, unalterable vision, but a profound and developing one of great complexity," adding that elaborate "vision itself may move in and out of its material, shuttle-fashion, instead of being simply turned on it, like a telescope on the moon" (795). Most of the stories collected in *A Curtain of Green* demonstrate that defiance of the tyranny of actuality, and illustrate Welty's shuttling between actuality and abstraction. This loose and assorted collection of seventeen stories shows the early orientation of Welty's artistic prejudices, which would guide her during much of her career. Welty's surreality of vision emerges repeatedly in her fiction when, as Suzanne Marrs observes, she engages the "exhilarating power of imagination" to "transform the world of Mississippi into her own fictional world—one removed from the randomness of daily experience, a world that would be shaped by and centered upon issues she deemed crucial" (*One Writer's* 16). Over the years, Welty's view of imaginative transformation and the strategies required to realize the principle would develop and intensify, but in this first volume of short stories she holds to her fundamental conviction that fiction's point of view, its frame, should glow, like her nightlight, illuminating the surreality of the waking life in dream and vice versa.

"A Memory" most conspicuously shows Welty's surreality in *A Curtain of Green.* Forming a centerpiece to the collection, it numerically marks the collection's halfway point, and metaphorically it emblematizes the typically Weltian strategy of reconciling scrupulously presented realistic and equally scrupulously presented non-realistic narration into a harmonious synthesis, a method that reflects her adoption of surrealist tenets. The story's title so obviously alludes to Dalí's *The Persistence of Memory* that the art lover in Welty could scarcely have overlooked the similarity—particularly since this painting had gained such fame. Both painting and story present a surrealist point of view in which conventional representational strategies dissolve before the mind's eye to expose a surreality of presentation privileging memory and elevating its imaginative quality in order to undermine space and time.

The story opens with the metaphor of the painter's frame by way of describing the process of artistic composition. "Ever since I had begun taking painting lessons," Welty records, "I had made small frames with my fingers, to look out at everything" (*Stories* 92). The small frames that this young girl by the lake creates anticipate the larger brimming frame of the theoretician in "Place in Fiction." Both young girl and mature artist attempt to control the rush of life through this painting device, which fragments the world and restricts the audience's point of view to the fiction writer's frame. As Danièle Pitavy-Souques points out, the "'picture' or 'representation' of reality" that the girl observes certainly does not have representational qualities of the kind identified with "realistic painting" ("Blazing Butterfly" 120). Literal recording of items surfacing in the frame does not make for interesting or surreal art. Surreality only obtains from the artist who, like the young girl, develops a "dual life" (*Stories* 93), and Welty's narratives consistently interrupt claims for realism by interjecting objects that generate moments of realistic uncertainty and anxiety. Narratives like "A Memory" duplicate the double reality we experience when we view an image like Dalí's *The Persistence of Memory*, a painting that gives rise to suspicions about its own duplicity. Objects rendered therein slide and soften unexpectedly, liquefy and refuse to observe their continuity with the other elements in the composition. Unreal scenarios assume a degree of photographic realism that baffles comprehension and foils rational processing, an experience that finds an almost identical parallel in the vein of surreal language that runs so deeply through Welty's art.

Halfway through "A Memory," for example, the following passage appears:

> As I lay on the beach that sunny morning, I was thinking of my friend and remembering in a retarded, dilated, timeless fashion the incident of my hand brushing his wrist. It made a very long story. But like a needle going in and out among my thoughts were the children running on the sand, the upthrust oak trees growing over the clean pointed roof of the white pavilion, and the slowly changing attitudes of the grown-up people who had avoided the city and were lying prone and laughing on the water's edge. I still would not care to say which was more real—the dream I could make blossom at will, or the sight of the bathers. I am presenting them, you see, only as simultaneous. (*Stories* 94)

Published early in her career, this paragraph highlights the essentially equivocal quality in the pictorial representation of materiality that endured throughout much of Welty's writing life. She gives a specific time, a specific weather condition, and—in her friend and in the brushing of the wrist—a specific subject and moment for contemplation. The figure of the needle emerges concretely, as do the children, the oaks, the sharply angled roof, and the prone and laughing adults. But despite the apparent clarity of its presentation, the scene's pretension to realism disintegrates because of the conflation of remembered thoughts of brushing with processing of the external scene. Welty intentionally equivocates here, assigning parity to the "reality" of "internal" and "external" circumstances such that their commingling creates a surreality. For readers, the metaphor of the needle occupies the same cognitive space as the children to whom the needle corresponds.

Similarly, the hand that brushes the wrist—a detail concretely presented although temporally removed—merges with supposedly externally framed objects, such as the trees, the roof, and the family of bathers. In the concluding two sentences, Welty reinforces what the paragraph has enacted: Any moment of perception necessarily integrates the actual and the abstract to create a hallucinatory surreality at the meeting of mind and matter.

This moment in the narrative and others like it handicap any sense of realism of the kind Ian Watt defines in *The Rise of the Novel*. Reality refuses objectification through the viewer's lens because the dream and the sight of the bathers collapse into a surreal pictorial unity. As quickly as Welty introduces items into view, she softens their outlines through subtle figural transformations. In this example, the children metamorphose into a needle that stitches thought to actuality, and neither children nor needle have a greater claim to truth. Welty matches and melds them, so that the viewer cannot have full confidence in the knowledge gained from envisioning the scene. Her description implies that from one viewpoint, the needle forms the children, and, from a second, that the children form the needle. Further, from a third viewpoint, the object presented may form a composite image. This kind of ambiguity in figural representation characterizes swaths of Welty's fiction. Like Dalí in particular—but also to some extent like other surrealists, such as Rene Magritte or Max Ernst—her art delivers fastidiously depicted double figurations of this sort, forcing a trick upon the eye, and throwing into question the identity of an object perceived.

The insight Welty provides here about the nature of surreal perception extends to many stories in *A Curtain of Green*, but not all the narratives demonstrate the inclination equally. For reasons unexplored here, but perhaps related to the apprentice nature of the volume, works such as "Lily Daw and the Three Ladies," "A Piece of News," "Why I Live at the P.O.," and "The Hitch-Hikers" show little of the influence that would come to mark so strongly the works that followed. The collection's title story, however, does not fall into this category. "A Curtain of Green," for example, reintroduces the theme of recollection, warning with its title that curtains screening painful memories cannot supply permanent protection from exposure. The protagonist, Mrs. Larkin, has lost her husband in a freak accident: A large chinaberry tree crushes him to death in his car. She reacts by trying to extinguish the pain of his absence behind curtains of green foliage in her garden, which "was a large, densely grown plot running downhill behind the small white house where she lived alone now." Welty's opening paragraph subtly directs the reader's response by providing some apparently simple details, such as the time, the season, and the state of the weather. The second paragraph, though, moves almost imperceptibly into a characteristic pictorial mode: "One day, almost as late as five o'clock, the sun was still shining. It seemed almost to spin in a tiny groove in the polished sky, and down below, in the trees along the street and in the rows of flower gardens in the town, every leaf reflected the sun from a hardness like a mirror surface" (*Stories* 130). Through the series of figural representations here, the objectified world of the first paragraph reveals itself as the product of a kind of hallucinatory vision. The surreal perspective acts to transfigure the details—such as the sun, the sky, the trees, the street, the flowers, and the leaves—and project them into dreamy arrays, presenting an evenly polished sky with the sun revolving mechanically in a groove, reflecting light on leaves transformed into hard, mirrored planes. These deliberately selected metaphors demonstrate the fiction's undermining of realist perspective by revealing the pivotal role representation plays. This particular depiction of the setting for Mrs. Larkin's moment of near emotional collapse complements the theme of the story because the hallucinatory imagery amplifies what Suzanne Marrs describes as the character's confrontation of the "dark irrationality of human experience" (*One Writer's* 6). To flee her sadness, she attempts to create order and space in curtains of green to hide her pain. That effort fails, proving seductive but hallucinatory.

The hallucinatory quality of the narrative builds cumulatively through the accretion of discrete textual examples, a tactic deployed in many of Welty's narratives. Early on, she shows Mrs. Larkin spotlighted by the sun, whose "intense light like a tweezers picked out her clumsy, small figure in its old pair of men's overalls rolled up at the sleeves and trousers, separated it from the thick leaves, and made it look strange and yellow as she worked with a hoe—over-vigorous, disreputable, and heedless" (*Stories* 130), observing the "flashing sky" through "dull and puckered eyes." Later, Mrs. Larkin's "sharp line" for a mouth indicates her silence. She never appears to speak, but she sees precisely in her mind's eye, "as if a curtain had been jerked quite unceremoniously away from a little scene" to expose a moment of high crisis: "There had been no warning. But there was the enormous tree, the fragrant chinaberry tree, suddenly tilting dark and slow like a cloud, leaning down to her husband" (132). Now, she camouflages herself behind her home's high walls, dwelling on her pain while hoeing the earth in the still garden where "The sun seemed clamped to the side of the sky," and where she feels observed "as though her loneliness had been pointed out by some outside force whose finger parted the hedge" (133). Perhaps she senses the gaze of the neighbors, who sometimes spy from their windows to locate Mrs. Larkin's "place in the garden, as they might have run their fingers toward a city on a map of a foreign country, located her from their distance almost in curiosity, and then forgot her" (132). When considered with the other pictorial metaphors deployed, this devastating final figuration, which summarily expresses the deepness of Larkin's hurt and the superficiality of her neighbors, demonstrates Welty's surreal sensibility. "A Curtain of Green" equates a garden with a map, a person with a disregarded city, the sun with a pair of tweezers, a spying force with a finger pointing the way to dejection. Mrs. Larkin's mouth is similarly reduced to a painter's line. Assembling these distinctive and unusual metaphors and dispersing them throughout the narrative creates for Welty a finely balanced surreality, at once diminishing physicality and reducing abstraction.

The textual folding of the material world into the surreal emblems that proliferate in "A Curtain of Green" repeats itself extensively in the collection as a whole. "The Whistle," another narrative preoccupied with loss and hardship, begins boldly, as if a dramatist issued a stage direction: "Night Fell. The darkness was thin, like some sleazy dress that has been worn and worn for many winters and always lets the cold through to the bones." Welty begins with a material impossibility: Darkness literally drops like a painted scene lowered onstage as a backdrop for the ensuing action. In an instant, however, the blackness changes shape. No longer a fallen backdrop, linear and implacable, it transforms into a flimsy dress that envelopes the home of the central characters, Jason and Sarah Morton, a pair of tenant farmers, whose

> farm lay quite visible, like a white stone in water, among the stretches of deep woods in their colorless dead leaf. By a closer and more searching eye than the moon's, everything belonging to the Mortons might have been seen—even to the tiny tomato plants in their neat rows closest to the house, gray and featherlike, appalling in their exposed fragility. (*Stories* 70)

The farmers lie cold, and readers feel as if they have entered the Mortons' deathly dream. As Ruth M. Vande Kieft observes, Welty "seems to be walking down a dark corridor opening doors on scenes and situations in which the characters are discovered in various painfully grotesque postures and actions induced by the brutal ironies of life" (66–67). Jason huddles "under the quilt in the long shape of a bean," while Sarah lies awake: "Her eyes seemed open too wide, the lids strained and limp, like openings which have been stretched shapeless and made of no more use." Night after night the couple freezes in the cold, "but no more communicative in their misery than a pair of window shutters beaten by as storm" (*Stories* 70). This series of reversals, in which observed details morph into surreal figural entities, demands that the audience suspend reading for plot and focus instead on the language's mode of presentation, a mode that invests as much truth in the linguistic/visual representation as it does in the object described. Besides minimizing the importance of what happens in a story like "The Whistle," Welty's choice of this surreal system of perspective diminishes the importance of motif and symbol in creating networks of meaning. Rather than reading for meaning identifiable through metaphoric events and em-blems, Welty requires that her audience be attuned to the subtleties of her surreal point of view, which folds dreams into waking apprehension.

She adopts that same surreal perspective in "Death of a Traveling Salesman," her first story, published in 1936. R. J. Bowman, a shoe salesman, literally arrives at the end of the road, a "petering-out path" (*Stories* 145) that runs adjacent to a ravine into which his car slides. The narrative begins inconspicuously and without apparent complexity: "R. J. Bowman, who for fourteen years had traveled for a shoe company through Mississippi, drove his Ford along a rutted dirt path" (144). However, Welty submits the de-clarative honesty of these first two lines to the paranoiac cast of mind that suffuses the whole narrative, one of Welty's stories "about troubled male wanderers" (Schmidt 49). Bowman feels angry, helpless, and fevered. "The sun," Welty writes, "keeping its strength here even in winter, stayed at the top of the sky, and every time Bowman stuck his head out of the dusty car to stare up the road, it seemed to reach a long arm down and push against the top of his head, right through his hat—like the practical joke of an old drummer, long on the road" (*Stories* 144). Here, Welty presents another story like "A Memory," in which a protagonist has trouble distinguishing between things objectively witnessed and subjectively imagined. On an-other occasion, Bowman meditates dilatorily on the number of hotel rooms he has occupied in his career and on the number of women in his life:

He could only remember little rooms within little rooms, like a nest of Chinese paper boxes, and if he thought of one woman he saw the worn loneliness that the furniture of that room seemed built of. And he him-self—he was a man who always wore rather wide-brimmed black hats, and in the wavy hotel mirrors had looked something like a bullfighter, as he paused for that inevitable instant on the landing, walking downstairs to supper. . . . He leaned out of the car again, and once more the sun pushed at his head. (144–45)

The context of the story does not clearly explain why Bowman would identify rooms inside rooms with women, or why he associates women with furniture. The story provides no answer to these mysteries, instead justifying their correspondence as the result of Bowman's mind, which for some weeks had endured a "long siege of influenza" (144). Another pos-sibility (especially allowing for the bullfighter, an icon of Spanish culture) remains: The collection of boxes, women, and furniture echoes Dalí's sur-real conglomeration of these elements in his *Venus de Milo with Drawers*, a statue whose meaning has some relevance for Bowman because it ex-presses, among other things, the mystery of feminine sexuality. Although Welty most probably would not have in person seen this most famous of all his experiments with bodies and furniture, this preoccupation with the "body fitted out with drawers was a recurring theme in Dalí's work as early as 1934" (Blum 123). She may, however, have run across the motif reprinted in magazines or newspapers, such as its appearance a few months after *Manuscript* published "Death of a Traveling Salesman." Cecil Beaton's ar-rangement of Schiaparelli suits, created in conjunction with Dalí, appeared in *Vogue* in September 1936 (132). Blum reports that "Beaton created a sur-real dream world for his photographs," showing one of two models "hold-ing up a copy of issue number 8 of the Surrealist magazine *Minotaure* (June 15, 1936), which featured a cover by Dalí of a minotaur with an open drawer in its chest, a lobster spilling from a hole in its stomach, and clawlike red fingernails . . . all themes that would make an appearance in Schiaparelli's designs" (132).

Lost, Bowman approaches a ravine but does not ask for directions from the strangers he spots there. Deliberate in composing the landscape and locating people in it, Welty employs language that continuously shapes the material into surreal pictorial vistas:

People standing in the fields now and then, or on top of the haystacks, had been too far away, looking like leaning sticks or weeds, turning a little

at the solitary rattle of his car across their countryside, watching the pale
sobered winter dust where it chunked out behind like big squashes down
the road. The stares of these distant people had followed him solidly like
a wall, impenetrable, behind which they turned back after he had passed.
(*Stories* 145)

Here, a curious dreamlike quality—retained, cultivated, and developed
over much of her career—emerges once again. Standing in the fields or on
haystacks, people take on the appearance of sticks or weeds attracted by
Bowman's rattling car. The driver seems to assume a position at the fixed
center of a world, which revolves with his consciousness at its core, perceiv-
ing chunking dust as "big squashes" and the stares of the locals as a solid
wall. As the narrative unfolds, the surreal figuring of elements multiplies
and accumulates, acting on the story's realistic surface texture, softening its
rigidity and internalizing its exteriority. After Bowman's car has careened
over the road's edge, he views it from above, seeing that "his car had fallen
into a tangle of immense grapevines as thick as his arm, which caught it
and held it, rocked it like a grotesque child in a dark cradle, and then, as
he watched, concerned somehow that he was not still inside it, released it
gently to the ground." The familiar pictorially presented detail intersects
with highly figurative language to produce a thickly visual presentation,
unexpectedly merging a car's unforgiving steel with the softness of the natural world and the sway of a loving parent. Encountering a house and the
woman who occupies it, he feels his "heart began to behave strangely. Like
a rocket set off, it began to leap and expand into uneven patterns of beats
which showered into his brain, and he could not think" (146). Bowman's
failing heart, which beats at the thematic core of "Death of a Traveling
Salesman," enjoys a temporary respite in this small home with its first room

enclosed in the gloom of yellow pine boards. He could see the other room,
with the foot of an iron bed showing, across the passage. The bed had
been made up with a red-and-yellow pieced quilt that looked like a map
or a picture, a little like his grandmother's girlhood painting of Rome
burning. (148)

And when Welty writes that Bowman "had lived a month in which nothing had happened except in his head," she seems to allude to her narrative

point of view, which refuses to formalize the exterior world except through impressions accorded her by Bowman's paranoia. Like Bowman's condition, which alternates between "heartbeats and dreams" and "fever and privacy," the narrative perspective travels to and fro, producing surrealism's synthetic reality made up of often odd and paradoxical juxtapositions. The pulse in his palm leaps "like a trout in a brook." His eye transfixes the woman of the house "as though she held the cord they were strung on" (149). The women's husband, Sonny, returns home through the half-light like a "white speck" that "floated smoothly toward her finger, like a leaf on a river, growing whiter in the dark" (152). And later, Sonny brings fire to light the lamp, turning the entire room "golden yellow like some sort of flower, and the walls smelled of it and seemed to tremble with the quiet rushing of the fire and the waving of the burning lampwick in its funnel of light" (154). Welty distributes this kind of visually charged and hallucinatory language throughout the story, contributing to the pervasive sense of Bowman's psychological instability and paranoia.

In another story, "Flowers for Marjorie," a similar collection of densely figurative and pictorial moments amasses to create a surreal atmosphere. A story about poverty, frustration, anger, and insanity, "Flowers for Marjorie" climaxes in Marjorie's murder by her husband, Howard. Born out of the desperation of the dark years of the Depression, Howard's deep psychological malignancy finds representational analogies in Welty's deployment of surreal metaphors and similes. Contemplating his lot, he snaps a toothpick from his mouth, and it lands "in the grass like a little tent." The clean and neat sight of the tent surprises Howard and the pigeons, which startle, making his eyes whirl "all at once, as though a big spoon stirred them in the sunshine. He closed his eyes upon their flying opal-changing wings." When he remembers Marjorie (whom he puts off thinking about), the "thought of her was like a wave that hit him when he was tired, rising impossibly out of stagnancy and deprecation while he sat in the park, towering over his head, pounding, falling, going back and leaving nothing behind it" (*Stories* 119). Howard's intense disaffection ultimately leads to his wife's murder, which he carries out with a butcher knife. After the stabbing, he notices "little white cloudy markings on her nails" and the blood pooling on her corpse, where "her lap was like a bowl" (124). This torrent of hallucinatory similes—typically Weltian in their precision, bold realization, and deftness—marks the opening and subsequent pages of the story, introducing the reader and enfolding him or her into a world in which atrocious acts, prompted by what Louise Westling characterizes as "unexpected masculine hostility" (*Eudora* 72), grow out of deeply buried psychological pathologies.[2]

Lethal pathologies preoccupy Welty in "Clytie," too. Bound to a life of servile drudgery, sibling cruelty, and confinement, Clytie Farr commits suicide in the most absurd way: She dashes her head though the "glittering surface" and into the "featureless depth" of a water barrel, from which her "poor ladylike black-stockinged legs up-ended and hung apart like a pair of tongs" (*Stories* 110). These blackly comical descriptions of Clytie's death conclude the story, but the surreal choice of simile to depict her parted legs continues the dreamy tone established at the narrative's opening: "It was late afternoon, with heavy silver clouds which looked bigger and wider than cotton fields, and presently it began to rain" (99). The hallucinatory imagery that sustains Welty's surreality describes an object and shapes its representation through the prism of the dream, so that the distinction between the legs and the tongs or the clouds and the cotton fields collapses. When townspeople see Mr. Tom Bates's boy, a local resident, they view a "face as clean-blank as a watermelon seed," but when Clytie sees him, she "observed grains of sand in his eyes and in his old yellow lashes, he might have come out of a desert, like an Egyptian" (102). What depiction of Tom Bates's boy should the reader trust? The empty face or the exotic guise of the outsider? Welty goes silent here, of course. But later on, she returns to the subject of faces when she transfers a series of faces onto other faces, overlaying them into composites to reproduce Clytie's distressing sense of psychic disorientation and disintegration:

Yes, in a sort of arbor hadn't she laughed, leaned forward. . . and that vision of a face—which was a little like all the other faces, the trusting child's, the innocent old traveler's, even the greedy barber's and Lethy's and the wandering peddler's who one by one knocked and went unanswered at the door—and yet different, yet far more—this face had been very close to hers, almost familiar, almost accessible. And then the face of Octavia was thrust between, and at other times the apoplectic face of her father, the face of her brother Gerald and the face of her brother Henry with the bullet hole through the forehead. . . . It was purely for a resemblance to a vision that she examined the secret, mysterious, unrepeated faces she met in the street of Farr's Gin. (105)

The assortment of faces Clytie superimposes over her own recalls the multiple similitudes Dalí's paintings of paranoiac and hallucinatory states present. Clytie clearly experiences paranoiac visions that repeat and converge with the faces she observes in the streets of Farr's Gin, but, as Peter Schmidt remarks, her "dreaming is continually interrupted by the demands that Octavia and the rest of her family place upon her" (28). Finally, crowded by visions of faces other than her own, she peers into the barrel's watery surface, which honestly reflects her haggard appearance and fragmented identity[3]. Confronted by the image, now stripped of its illusory cognates, she drowns herself.

Confrontation with aging is also a theme in "A Visit of Charity." When Marian, a young Campfire Girl, visits the old ladies home on the edge of town, she encounters unexpected hostility and aggression. Early on, Welty anticipates this cold reception when she describes the "prickly dark shrubs" guarding the home and the building itself, "which was of whitewashed brick and reflected the winter sunlight like a block of ice." The interior of this uninviting edifice is supervised by a white uniformed nurse who has "close-cut hair which stood up on the very top of her head exactly like a sea wave." Advancing beyond the nurse's desk, Marian feels "as if she were walking on the waves" created by the "loose, bulging linoleum on the floor." Given the dreamlike atmosphere generated by these descriptions, it comes as little surprise that "[t]here was a smell in the hall like the interior of a clock. Everything was silent until, behind one of the doors, an old lady of some kind cleared her throat like a sheep bleating" (*Stories* 137). More a frightening ordeal than a friendly visit, the trip results in Marian witnessing the two old ladies' spiteful bickering and in a room where the "window shade was down, and the only door was shut." Marian's imagination takes off when she looks at the ceiling imagining, "[i]t was like being caught in a robber's cave, just before one was murdered" (138). Welty introduces the quarreling and peevish women absurdly. One has a "bunchy white forehead and red eyes like a sheep," an "unexpectedly small and sorrowful" mouth "like a pet's" (139), and small lips which drop apart suddenly to reveal a "half circle of false teeth with tan gums" (141). The other woman points a "horny finger" and reaches her hand over to Marian, who reports that it feels "like a petunia leaf, clinging and just a little sticky" (140). Toward the end of the story, when Marian observes the first woman "very closely and plainly, and very abruptly, from all sides, as in dreams" (142), Welty may be relating the girl's dreamy delusional point of view as to her own when writing fiction. The story's surreal, perhaps even cubistic approach maybe what allows readers to view all sides of a scene at once: the haircut and the sea wave; the linoleum and the watery swells; the sheep's eyes and the women's eyes; and the aging finger and the sticky petunia leaf. These sets of parallels establish discontinuities such that an observer cannot easily reconcile one viewpoint with another.

The vicissitudes of aging also constitute a central theme in "Old Mr Marblehall," a story that relates the intricacies of an old man's double life, a life in which vivid dreams turn outward with such ferocity and persistence that they seem less fantasy than reality.[4] Mr. Marblehall of Natchez, Mississippi, leads parallel lives, forming the most prominent feature of his existence, the central motif of the story, and a deceit the neighbors least expect of this inconspicuous elderly gentleman. "He is just like other people to them," Welty says of the townspeople: "He could have easily danced with a troop of angels in Paradise every night, and they wouldn't have guessed. Nobody is likely to find out that he is leading a double life" (*Stories* 114). Of course, Mr. Marblehall's startling deception seems no less fantastic than an equally startling dance with the angels, and Welty alludes to his double life (a metaphor deployed most conspicuously in "A Memory") numerous times in the story. The narrator first directs the reader: "But there he is, quite visible, alive and old, leading his double life" (115); Mr. Marblehall imagines one of his sons writing "Papa leads a double life" (116) on the side of a fence; and in the last line of the story, the aged man contemplates the townspeople, "his old eyes watering and wild, imagining that if people knew about his double life, they'd die" (118). Mr. Marblehall's apparently quiet life illustrates a daring that Welty must have appreciated, for he lives at the surreal intersection of two realities. This seemingly "sheltered life" reveals a "serious daring" that "starts from within" Marblehall's mind (*One Writer's Beginnings* 948).

And Welty accents what starts from inside by integrating dream and waking realities through an assortment of surreal similes and metaphors, establishing a bedrock of dream imagery that underlies and unifies many of the stories collected in *A Curtain of Green*. Mr. Marblehall's first wife "is a large, elongated old woman with electric-looking hair and curly lips." Her marriage "has set in upon her nerves like a retriever nosing and puffing through old dead leaves out in the woods." She "dresses her hair like a unicorn horn" (*Stories* 111). And her son "has a monkey look, a very penetrating look" with "very sparse Japanese hair, tiny little pearly teeth, long little wilted fingers" (113). Marblehall's second wife, however, has none of his first wife's reserve or cold humor, although Welty presents both women with the same adroit deployment of fantastic imagery, lingering and emerging roundly before the mind's eye, producing what Noel Polk calls descriptions that "do not compute, that do not yield themselves completely even after repeated readings, even after repeated attempts to impose interpretation on them" ("Welty, Hawthorne" 560). The second wife screams at her neighbor, and she appears "funnier looking" than the first, resembling "funny furniture—an unornamented stair post in one of these little houses, with her small monotonous round stupid head—or sometimes like a woodcut of a Bavarian witch, forefinger pointing, with scratches in the air all around her." Welty vividly paints with words, rendering the woman "so static she scarcely moves" with a verbal image showing "thick cut shoulders" that lead the eye downwards "past her cylindered brown dress to her short, stubby house slippers" (*Stories* 115). Like a mechanical toy, she "rolls back into the house as if she had been on a little wheel all this time." Electric hair, unicorn horns, monkey looks, and funny furniture (an image that could well be used to describe Dalí's *Venus de Milo*) all come straight from surrealist imaginary, as does the second son's depiction of his mother. Surmising that she "was totally solid, down to her thick separated ankles," he contemplates her appearance "when she stands there on the porch screaming to the neighbors, she reminds him of those flares that charm him so, that they leave burning in the street at night—the dark solid ball, then, tongue-like, the wicked, yellow, continuous, enslaving blaze on the stem. He knows what his father thinks" (116). These visually exciting surreal episodes help maintain the story's absurdist dimensions.

Similarly, in "The Key," perception and reality collapse into a single surreal viewpoint, demonstrating Welty's long-held conviction that the observer's and the dreamer's frames actually intersect. Albert and Ellie Morgan of Yellow Leaf, Mississippi, wait for a train to ferry them to Niagara Falls. In the silence of the waiting room, a "little girl lay flung back in her mother's lap as though sleep had struck her with a blow," while Ellie sits "with a face as pink and crowded as an old-fashioned rose" and rests "there as tense and solid as a cube" (*Stories* 37). Next, Welty turns her comic eye on Albert, who waits beside his wife and looks

home-made, as though his wife had self-consciously knitted or somehow contrived a husband when she sat alone at night. He had a shock of very fine sunburned yellow hair. He was too shy for this world, you could see. His hands were like cardboard, he held his hat so still; and yet how softly his eyes fell upon its crown, moving dreamily and yet with dread over its brown surface! (38)

Superficially, the story focuses on the tensions that bear upon this couple's relationship. A young man drops a hotel room key, and Albert's retrieval of the object concentrates the narrative's energies on the marriage's difficulties, which seem to stem from Ellie's intractability and Albert's passivity. However, beyond these circumstances of plot, Welty points to the double life to which the above extracts refer. She describes the little girl, Ellie, and Albert in a manner such that the apparent realism of the portrayal deforms and transforms, suffusing the concrete with the destabilizing plasticity of a dream.

The idea of double perception also finds expression in the young man. His key comes to stand for the unlocking of the emotional sensitivity necessary for Albert and Ellie's marriage to succeed, and the stranger develops into a focal point for Albert's search of his interior life. "You felt a shock in glancing up at him," Welty writes of the man,

> and when you looked away from the whole yellow room and closed your eyes, his intensity, as well as that of the room, seemed to have impressed the imagination with a shadow of itself, a blackness together with the light, the negative beside the positive. You felt as though some exact, skillful contact had been made between the surfaces of your hearts to make you aware, in some pattern, of his joy and his despair. You could feel the fullness and the emptiness of this stranger's life. (*Stories* 42)

The mysterious man's aura serves as a counterpoint to Albert's meditations, and Welty illuminates a moment of imaginative identification through the coincidence between Albert's and the stranger's experiences. The closing of eyes and the opening of interior sight confer a synthetic reality on the moment, in which a double image appears, the negative beside the positive, recalling the doubleness of Mr. Marblehall. Albert's possession of the key, a "strange thing" that may resuscitate a "fish he had once spied just below the top of the water in a sunny lake in the country" (40) as a child, permits him to orient himself in a renewed relation to Ellie, whose "anxious, hovering body could wrap him softly as a cradle." But "that powerful sign, that reassurance he so hopefully sought, so assuredly deserved—that had never come. There was something lacking in Ellie" (44). Quarreling over the key, husband and wife miss their train north, and Albert, gloomily imagining his wife's disappointment, "dreamily reappraises" (Appel 19) the key's significance:

> And you knew how she would sit and brood over this as over their conversations together, about every misunderstanding, every discussion, sometimes even about some agreement between them that had all been settled—even about the secret and proper separation that lies between a man and a woman, the thing that makes them what they are in themselves, their secret life, their memory of their past, their childhood, their dreams. This to Ellie was unhappiness. (*Stories* 46).

Ellie's unhappiness, then, originates in her unwillingness to accord a separate, mysterious, and partially singular life to her husband. This allotment of himself—composed of the "secret life," of memories, of dreams, and of his childhood—prevents Ellie from acquiring complete knowledge of her husband. Her desire cannot be fulfilled because of the psyche's persistent subverting of rational knowledge through its incessant production of secrets, fantasies, and dreams.

Fantasies of escape and evasion also emerge as concerns in "Petrified Man." Gossiping women in a southern beauty parlor mostly advance the narrative of this freak show exhibit, a body slowly metamorphosing into stone in a kind of parody of the ultimately sexual surrealist obsession with soft things hardening and hard things softening. Eventually, the petrified man's condition proves false. Mrs. Pike, a friend of Leota the beautician, recognizes him for a phony and as a criminal on the run for "rapin' four women in California" (*Stories* 33). Unlike Mr. Marblehall, whose secret remains inviolate, Mr. Petrie suffers exposure and punishment. If, along with Mr. Marblehall, the young girl in "A Memory" represents an example of the successfully maintained double life, "Petrified Man" illustrates its failure. Mr. Petrie's evasion of responsibility for his crime lasts only while he can pull off the stunt and wear the disguise. In the end, these measures prove futile.

Despite this story's obvious black comedy, Welty seems to present a warning about the dangers of overinvesting in imagination—the double life's nightmarish flipside, if you will. Acknowledging dreams in waking experiences may promise discovery of new knowledge constructed on the foundation of surreal apprehension, but a thoroughgoing envelopment in dreams, to the exclusion of material life, leads to psychosis and catastrophe. Welty draws attention to the grotesqueness of such an exclusionary investment when she describes the freak show's display in a bottle of dead twins "joined plum together," with "two heads an' two faces an' four arms an' four legs, all kind of joined *here*. See, this face looked this-a-way, and the other face looked that-a-way, over their shoulder, see" (*Stories* 26). The heads seem to look past each other over shoulders and create a disturbing image of the double life expired and preserved as spectacle, cautioning against the jeopardy of extreme introversion. Death also confronts the rapist, a man whose erotic fantasy life causes him to act on his obsessions without constraint. Mr. Petrie's sexual violence results from an overvaluation of his fantasy, effecting a break such that "his head and mind ain't a joint" and causing his humanity to turn to "pure stone" (27).

The magic universe brought to town on the backs of trailers transporting the carnival has a special place in Welty's work. She draws heavily upon it in "Petrified Man" and many other places in her fiction. The fair provides a perfect setting for the introduction of surreal ideas, and stories like "Petrified Man" and its counterpart in *A Curtain of Green*, "Keela, the Outcast Indian Maiden," clearly derive from Welty's experiences as a junior publicity agent for the Works Progress Administration during 1936 (Marrs *One Writer's* 12), and from her other travels around Mississippi later in the decade. *Eudora Welty: Photographs*, a large compendium of photographs taken between the thirties and fifties and documenting a diverse array of subjects, shows a writer very much preoccupied with dreams as they found public expression in advertisements, parades, and circus acts. For example, one print of hers from the forties entitled *Hattie Carnegie Show Window* shows a New York shop front displaying a woman's mannequin mounted with the head of a cow, preening in its new dress. This obviously surrealist inspired advertising campaign had caught Welty's eye, but a look back through the collection reveals that anthropomorphic animals had long fascinated her. For instance, her numerous pictures of women and young girls posed for Jackson's Farish Street Baptist Church's "Pageant of Birds" parade illustrate her predilection for photographing subjects caught in moments of dreaming transformation. This interest is also illustrated in the pictures she took of various Mardi Gras players, both in New Orleans and in Nice, France, that show revelers metamorphosed into mythological figures, such as the grim reaper or Medusa, or otherwise disguised and dressed as if they

Hattie Carnegie show window/New York City/1940s. Reprinted by the permission of Russell & Volkening as agents for the author's estate. ©1989 by Eudora Welty.

had walked out of or into a dream. All of these surreal examples filtered into the fiction she would write over the years, but perhaps the best photographic evidence for her surreal sensibility comes from her pictures of sideshows lining the midways at state fairs.

Eudora Welty: Photographs reproduces a number of pictures taken in 1939, the same year that Dalí erected his surrealist funhouse in the middle of the amusement zone at the New York world's fair. *Carnival Work Crew* reveals four men seated at a dining table. One man is partially concealed, while two others appear to be laughing at a joke or perhaps at the notion that any photographer would want to capture their likenesses while they are eating. A third worker draws heavily on a cigarette, and the others smirk and smile suggestively, but the joke lies just out of reach. Another

Sideshow, State Fair/Jackson/1939. Reprinted by the permission of Russell & Volkening as agents for the author's estate. ©1989 by Eudora Welty.

photograph frames the entrance to an attraction called "Sex Mad," a plac-
ard nearby boldly announcing "Male and Female Creation of Life in the
Nude" and another promising "The Naked Truth," while men cluster inside,
their backs to the lens. About half of the images show customers entranced
by the fair's various spectacles. Some watch the sex show; some watch the
turning Ferris wheel; some marvel at a man thrown in circles in a steel
boat; some stand in line for tickets. Still others, mostly young boys, watch
the hypnotist and his young assistants, a trio of half-undressed women.
None of the fairgoers looks back at the camera. It is as if the attractions
have so thoroughly captured their attention that they have vanished from

view—just as Uncle Felix imagines he does when he gazes through the stereopticon in "Kin."

Some of the most compelling evidence of Welty's preoccupation with surrealist art, however, comes from the pictures she shot of folk art painted on large fabric signs advertising sideshows. No European avant-garde art hung in Mississippi during the thirties, but that shortcoming did not prevent Welty from photographing the folk art equivalent. These signs—and perhaps the traveling shows themselves—displayed cows, like the one Welty photographed in the New York shop front a decade later, transformed into humans or doubled to present "Siamese Calves" with "Two Bodies and 8 legs." "Twisto," the "Rubber Man," vies with the "Headless Girl" and the "Mule Face Woman," disfigured men and women Welty would draw upon, for example, when creating scenes in "Music from Spain" that introduce the surreal "side-show Emma" and Thelma, the "optical illusion" (*Stories* 487). In one photograph, a number of such signs seem to publicize a hypnotist's show. He stands at a microphone, enticing an audience of young boys to submit to his spell, while his assistants stand behind and a man dressed as a woman acts as if he levitates between two separated chairs. Drawn to the world of the circus, an arena of spellbinding diversions, Welty discovered a native habitat for things surreal and a treasure house of metaphors and images.

Out of this rich seam of dreams, she mined "Keela, the Outcast Indian Maiden" which, like "Petrified Man," concentrates on the life of a freak show geek in order to investigate the frequently illusory nature of perception.[5] Circus owners abduct Lee Roy, a crippled Texan, and transform him into Keela, the Outcast Indian Maiden, a sideshow attraction "supposed to be an Indian woman, see, in this red dress an' stockin's" (*Stories* 50). As part of his grisly act, Keela thumps an iron bar to scare onlookers, and decapitates, bleeds, and devours live chickens. Steve, a former announcer for the show, takes Max, a local bootlegger, to visit Lee Roy, who has escaped and now regards his sideshow experience fondly. He likes to entertain his family with tales "about de ole times when I use to be wid de circus—" (56). Whereas the dominance of Mr. Petrie's dream life brings destruction through petrifaction, Lee Roy rejects his alter ego and distances himself from Keela, who exists only as a character in an old story he tells his children. This narrative provides an antidote to the darkness of "Petrified Man" because Lee Roy finds refuge from the circus, itself a metaphor for a world of intoxicating excitement, marvels, magic, imagination, and illusion—but also exploitation and danger.

While liberty restores dignity to Lee Roy's life, the shattering of the circus illusion deeply unsettles Steve, who thinks "about it at night—that an' drums on the midway" (*Stories* 51) and has "[b]een feelin' bad ever since. Can't hold onto a job or stay in one place for nothin' in the world" (53). Once he hailed spectators and blew the "siren out front" and sold tickets to Keela's show, but now the excitement of the carnival has metamorphosed into the horror of an obsessive's dream (48).[6] The present of Welty's story returns Steve to the role of announcer for the show. She restages Steve's promotion of the attraction, but his hailing of Max, the only paying spectator, leads to a moment of ghastly revelation rather than happy illusion. Decades later, in *One Writer's Beginnings*, Welty would speculate that after concealing a secret, "one secret is liable to be revealed in the place of another that is harder to tell, and the substitute secret when nakedly exposed is often the more appalling" (857). Lee Roy's kidnapping and miserable treatment evokes Steve's sympathy, but pity for Lee Roy, who Max and Steve consider a "little clubfooted nigger man," is the hard-to-admit truth (*Stories* 48). The "more appalling" and psychologically devastating "substitute secret" resides in Steve's acknowledging his seduction by the illusion of Lee Roy/Keela, both man and woman. The young man's "troubled eyes" (50), his foolishness, and his madness originate in his failure to perceive accurately. "But I didn't know," Steve pensively reflects. "I can't look at nothin' an' be sure what it is. Then afterwards I know. Then I see how it was" (54). Welty here emblematizes the dilemma that confronts Steve, a man whose circus life, the life of the dream, collides with material reality in the figure of Lee Roy/Keela. Exposure to surrealism's double reality has badly damaged the ex-barker, and his attempt to educate Max to the hallucinatory condition of perception fails. "I don't hear anything," Max boasts. "I got a jukebox, see, so I don't have to listen" (50). The bootlegger makes a poor wedding guest. He tolerates Steve's rambling rhyme, but ultimately stops listening and turns the jukebox's volume up high.

Jukeboxes and drums lead thematically to "Powerhouse," a story about the transformative power of music, embodied in the title's hero. The story also concerns art's potential for the revising all kinds of boundaries—racial, sexual, social, and artistic. Although Welty writes the opening from the perspective of a racist observer, who introduces Powerhouse and his band through a series of noisome slurs, the passage ironically reveals and revels in the source of the pianist's magic. Nobody can categorize him, arrest his imagination, or minimize his energy, because "Powerhouse is playing!"

> He's here on tour from the city—"Powerhouse and His Keyboard"—"Powerhouse and His Tasmanians"—think of the things he calls himself! There's no one in the world like him. You can't tell what he is. "Nigger man"?—he looks more Asiatic, monkey, Jewish, Babylonian, Peruvian, fanatic, devil. He has pale gray eyes, heavy lids, maybe horny like a lizard's, but big glowing eyes when they're open. He has African feet of the greatest size, stomping, both together, on each side of the pedals. He's not coal black—beverage colored—looks like a preacher when his mouth is shut, but then it opens—vast and obscene. And his mouth is going every minute: like a monkey's when it looks for something. Improvising, coming on a light and childish melody—*smooch*—he loves it with his mouth. (*Stories* 158)

The spectator's panoply of insults actually works in reverse, diminishing the accuser, revealing his or her attraction toward the apparently maligned target, and elevating the victim so that he achieves a kind of invincibility through the manifold masks that he assumes. Welty does not extend the invective in the continuing descriptions of Powerhouse and his band, but she does retain the presentation of the musicians in language that surreally transfigures and multiplies them visually: "[Powerhouse] is in motion every moment—what could be more obscene? There he is with his great head, fat stomach, and little round piston legs, and long yellow sectioned strong big fingers, at rest about the size of bananas." He appears to be "going all the time, like skating around the skating rink or rowing a boat" (158). Welty presents the performers dynamically, and as traveling magicians rather than musicians, both monstrous and marvelous. "Watch them carefully," she urges, "hear the least word, especially what they say to one another, in another language—don't let them escape you; it's the only time for hallucination, the last time" (159). Just like magicians, the players create illusions for the delight of the audience, and Welty generates a parallel set of surreal illusions in the representation of her heroes: Powerhouse looks over the end of his piano "as if over a cliff" (160); his "head rolls and sinks like a weight between his waving shoulders" (160–61); a "bubble shoots out on his lips like a plate on a counter" (161); he "holds his hands out and turns up the blanched palms like sieves" (163); he conjures and makes a coin "vanish like a magician" (164); and his "face looks like a big hot iron stove" (166), displaying a "vast oven mouth" (168). Moreover, the drummer spins his musical web over the drums "like a spider" (162), and the clarinet player, Little Brother, "takes a step forward when he plays and stands at the very front, with the whites of his eyes like fishes swimming" (160). Later, he lays down his clarinet "like a precious vase," and "looks like an East Indian queen, implacable, divine, and full of snakes" (162). During an intermission in the performance, the band retires to the ironically named "World Café," an eatery in "Negrotown" (163) where the band members drink beer as "their eyelids come together like curtains." Powerhouse takes this opportunity to show his gift for narrative, relating the tensions between him and his distraught wife, who saddens when he goes on the road and listens intently for his footfall "till her ears and all grow out like old music-box horns but still she can't hear a thing" (165). The subtle and gradual accumulation of these surreal images reinforces a less subtle point Welty makes in this story about the liberty and beauty found in musical expression, and about the role artists play in disturbing apparently settled categories. As an artist, Powerhouse parallels Welty: Both create stories—although in different media. Like Prospero in *The Tempest*, both occupy the role of magician, capturing whoever washes up on their island in their pleasing hallucinations.

One might easily identify Welty with any number of characters in *A Curtain of Green*. A survey of the collection reveals many who lead double lives, in actuality or through the dual reality of their condition as observers watching life through their own particular frames. "A Worn Path," the narrative that brings *A Curtain of Green* to an end, perhaps presents the writer in metaphorical form. Welty's depiction of Phoenix Jackson reveals an element of self-portraiture. Picturing Welty as the Jackson phoenix doesn't require much imagination, particularly given her choice of myth: a bird that demonstrates an eternal duality, perpetually reinventing itself and shape shifting while retaining a singular identity. The phoenix thus serves as an apt metaphor for the paradoxically constant and inconstant condition of surreal perception. In "Is Phoenix Jackson's Grandson Really Dead?" an essay published during the 1970s, Welty parallels old Phoenix with fiction writers. "Like Phoenix," she suggests, "you work all your life to find your way, through all the obstructions and the false appearances and the upsets you may have brought on yourself, to reach a meaning—using inventions of your imagination, perhaps helped out by your dreams and bits of good luck" (817–18). As its title seems to imply, this short essay deters readers from reading exclusively for the plot that follows Phoenix's treacherous journey to Natchez to collect medicine for her ailing grandson. Instead, Welty urges a focus on Phoenix's journey, not on whether she makes a safe return trip, or whether the grandson lives or dies. These considerations miss the point. Instead, Welty states, the "errand of love" forms the nucleus that she created from the singular observation of a "solitary old woman like Phoenix." The author recalls studying the woman who appeared in the "middle distance" and walked "her way across my line of vision" as if into and over the frame of the narrative, to emerge fictionalized and transfig-ured on the other side (816). The characteristic emphasis on sighting the woman for the purposes of fiction continues as Welty declares:

[H]er going was the first thing, her persisting in the landscape was the real thing, and the first and the real were what I wanted and worked to keep. I brought her up close enough, by imagination, to describe her face, make her present to the eyes, but the full-length figure moving across the winter fields was the indelible one and the image to keep, and the perspective ex-tending into the vanishing distance the true one to hold in mind. (816–17)

As always, Welty chooses her language carefully; she aims to find a sort of paradoxical language that portrays Phoenix as visually going or staying in motion while keeping her static and anchored in the landscape. That sort of writing enters the realm of the surreal.

A reading of the story shows that Welty does accomplish what may seem contradictory. The slow pace of Phoenix's toiling almost arrests her motion, but still she indefatigably advances toward Natchez. The first paragraph of the narrative introduces Phoenix "coming along," as if she has emerged magically from a dream and may return at any moment: "She was very old and very small and she walked slowly in the dark pine shadows." Moreover, Welty depicts her character curiously, "moving a little from side to side in her steps, with the balanced heaviness and lightness of a pendulum in a grandfather clock." In the next paragraph, she defines Phoenix further, noting dreamlike eyes which "were blue with age" and skin which "had a pattern all its own of numberless branching wrinkles and as though a whole tree stood in the middle of her forehead, but a golden color ran underneath, and the two knobs of her cheeks were illumined by a yellow burning under the dark" (*Stories* 171). Throughout the story, Welty transfig-ures Phoenix in such surreal descriptive moments, as when sweat glistens in the old woman's wrinkled skin "like a bright net" (177). As she waits for her grandson's medication, Phoenix sits "silent, erect and motionless, just as if she were in armor" (178). The walking, swaying, dreaming, and glowing sets her in motion, but configuration as a clock pendulum, a golden tree, a net, and a suit of armor surreally arrests Phoenix, conferring on her a mythic status.

The hallucinatory mode of representation extends beyond the narrative's depiction of Phoenix metamorphosed into surreal objects that surprise and disarm with the unexpectedness of their juxtaposition. Beyond these surreal transformations, the story foregrounds her path through a delusional dream world that reveals Phoenix's paranoia. Like a dreamer, she navigates the pitfalls and the pleasures of a dreamscape, and all readers can identify with the peculiar terrain and circumstances of this familiar worn path. Not quite herself, Phoenix marches "like a festival figure in some parade" (*Stories* 172), and the country through which she passes has a strange, ethereal and sometimes forbidding atmosphere. "Big dead trees, like black men with one arm, were standing in the purple stalks of the withered cotton field" (173), as she follows the track "through the little strings of trees silver in their dead leaves, past cabins silver from weather, with the doors and windows boarded shut, all like old women under a spell sitting there" (174). As she walks on, approaching the town, "[t]he shadows hung from the oak trees to the road like curtains" (176), and when she arrives at the doctor's office, a "tower of steps" dwarfs her (177). Clearly, Phoenix's state of mind does not distinguish between material circumstance and imagination. Suspicions of this permeability caused readers of the story (Welty responds to them in the essay introduced above) to fret over the death or perhaps even the existence of Phoenix's grandson. In the story, though, Welty seems preoccupied only with presenting the life-prolonging and enriching power of this woman's imaginative/delusional life. Phoenix has a highly elaborate and fantastic sensibility. Welty has Phoenix chide herself, "My senses is gone. I too old" (173), but her illusion of a fantasy life remains intact and active. Hallucinations visit Phoenix periodically. A young boy offers her a slice of marble cake, but "when she went to take it there was just her own hand in the air" (172); she passes through a field of dead corn that whispers to her; she perceives a scarecrow as a "man dancing in the field" (173); she falls into a ditch where a "dream visited her, and she reached her hand up, but nothing reached down and gave her a pull." When Phoenix apparently mistakes abandoned cabins for women sitting spellbound, she remarks, "I walking in their sleep" (174), as if designating herself a sleepwalker travelling the liminal path plied by all surrealist artists.

Few would contest Michael Kreyling's judgment that even "though some descriptive categories do help in relating the stories in *A Curtain of Green* to each other, these seventeen stories simply refuse to be categorically arranged" (*Eudora Welty's* 5). Nonetheless, his reading of the collection does advance a general claim that the fiction in this volume shows Welty probing life's enigmas. Although these "stories are varied and different," the "effort toward connection through an exploring technique unifies the stories" (15). My analysis of the collection concurs inasmuch as the narratives do show Welty confronting the mysteries of human experience—but through a particular frame of reference, the paradigm of surrealism. The language she uses in *A Curtain of Green* continuously reveals the irrational as it intersects with the rational, and the paranoia that invests the apparent neutrality of realistic perspective. Not only does Welty thematize the duality of surreally derived knowledge by her depiction of the various double lives on display in the collection, she duplicates and reinforces that duality, that discrediting of realistic narrative, with similes and metaphors that reproduce paranoia, often as a facet of her own narrative voice. Surreality, then, forms a condition of perception not limited to her characters as they populate the stories. She frequently narrates the double life of the sleepwalker, as it were, from an identical viewpoint. In *The Wide Net*, the subject of the next chapter, Welty maintains her surreal convictions, which only deepen and continue to shape her work in fundamental ways.

3

DREAMING POURED CREAM CURTAINS IN
THE WIDE NET, AND OTHER STORIES

Robert Penn Warren's landmark 1944 defense, "The Love and the Separateness in Eudora Welty," still occupies a central position in criticism devoted to the study of Welty. Bristling at Diana Trilling's harsh assessment of *The Wide Net* in her 1943 review in the *Nation*, Warren defuses the accusations leveled at Welty's excessive style and obscurity. He does so by advancing his thesis that despite the fact that *A Curtain of Green* and *The Wide Net* showed a "good deal of the falsely poetic" (21) and some "hocus-pocus" (27), both works fundamentally conform to a pattern derived from a conscious method and a developing narrative technique that provides for the realization of the author's ideas. For Warren, the "fact of isolation" (22) creates the "basic situation" of Welty's writing: "The drama which develops from this basic situation is either of two kinds: first, the attempt of the isolated person to escape into the world; or second, the discovery by the isolated person, or by the reader, of the nature of the predicament." This influential essay has shaped the critical response to Welty and for good reason. Warren illuminates a key preoccupation of Welty's: how to minimize the cost and maximize the gain that life's isolation and intimacies afford. Although Warren basis his opinion only on "two volumes of stories" (21), the situations he alludes to and the ideas he finds examined in the narratives remain a useful guide to Welty's output—particularly that of the thirties, forties, and fifties.

Like any critic of generous spirit, Warren strives to express the purpose, meaning, and quality of his subject's art, while minimizing distortion and avoiding the danger of misrepresentation. And, in this seminal essay, he comes closest to achieving that end when he reports on Welty's writing philosophy:

It is a method by which the items of fiction (scene, action, character, etc.) are presented not as document but as comment, not as a report but as a thing made, not as history but as idea. Even in the most realistic and reportorial fiction, the social picture, the psychological analysis, and the pattern of action do not rest at the level of mere report; they finally operate as expressive symbols as well. (27)

Here, Warren marginalizes documentary presentation and diminishes the degree to which Welty's fiction supplies a realistic account of events that rests "at the level of mere report." In the first instance, Warren places emphasis on her method of presenting reality, a subject on which she would dwell at length in "Writing and Analyzing a Story" and "Place in Fiction," two essays from the fifties that are central statements of her writing practice. In the second instance, he accents the picture, the analysis, and the pattern as operating like "expressive symbols." Since Warren's remarks appeared, legions of critics, armed with New Criticism's theoretical bias toward constructing well-wrought urns, have written about Welty the Anglo-American modernist, a writer whose narratives reach an almost metaphysical unity in their dispersal of symbol, myth, and motif, creating symbolic networks of allusion and reference.[1] However, the stress placed on Welty the symbolist and her primary progenitors in the English-speaking world, W. B. Yeats and T. S. Eliot, obscures our view of Welty the avant-garde surrealist, a characterization Warren gestures towards with his analysis of her treatment of objects and the form their representation takes.

In fact, the gesturing and reaching toward surrealism that Warren's article shows may originate in Trilling's review, at least half of which is devoted to establishing and exploring a parallel between Welty and surrealism's commercial exploitation by Dalí. Reaching a peroration, Warren observes, "If anything, the dreamlike effect in many of the stories seems to result from the author's undertaking to squeeze meaning from the item which, in ordinary realistic fiction, would be passed over with a casual glance" (28). Rarely casual, Welty creates totally believable fictional worlds layered with strikingly unexpected and fantastic imagery obtained from her adoption of an essentially surrealist viewpoint. Like the narratives in *A Curtain of Green*, the stories of *The Wide Net* demonstrate surrealism's influence not only in terms of choice of subject but in matter of style.

"A Still Moment" offers a starting point here, because this dense, complex, and dark story profoundly inquires into how artists treat their raw materials, a critical consideration for revealing the surreal point of view. The narrative opens in medias res. Lorenzo Dow, an itinerant Methodist preacher, speeds on his horse toward an evening revival meeting, where he hopes to save the sinners who fill the campground "like the sky with the stars" (*Stories* 230). Soon, James Murrell, the outlaw and Natchez Trace bandit, joins him, for Murrell intends to murder Dow and make the preacher the newest addition to his pantheon of unsuspecting victims. Soon, the two travelers halt beside a "great live-oak tree" (232) and John James Audubon, the naturalist and painter, mysteriously appears. One man searches for souls, another for victims, and another for birds; suddenly, Audubon's search ends when a "solitary snowy heron" alights to "feed beside the marsh water" (235). The men's varying interpretations of the heron's appearance, their "three attitudes of looking at life" (*Comment* 20), form the heart of this story, one Welty greatly treasured.

The events take place against the backdrop of the Natchez Trace, the ancient trail that for hundreds of years served as the "migratory route for animal populations and for the indigenous peoples" and, latterly, "became, at the turn of the nineteenth century, the major overland route for emigrants from the trans-Allegheny east to the new territory of the lower Mississippi" (Kreyling *Understanding* 51). All the stories collected in *The Wide Net*, except "The Purple Hat," share the common ground of the Trace, which forms a thread tying the collection together. In Welty's essay, "Some Notes on River Country," she contemplates the deeply felt "sense of place" she experienced in the scattered and sometimes deserted settlements that dot Mississippi's frontier bordering the great river. "A Place that ever was lived in," Welty's opening declares, "is like a fire that never goes out" (760), and in *The Wide Net* she rekindles that fire as it smolders in the Trace, revealing paths in the darkness and connecting individual to individual, family to family, community to community, the past to the present, and the real to the surreal.[2] This magical conduit recalls Phoenix Jackson's worn path to Natchez because Welty identifies both tracks through the wilderness with the imagination, dreams, and the irrational as well as with peril, fear, and desperation.

Told from Dow's perspective, the story's opening immediately evokes the Trace as a locale of mystery and magic:

It was the hour of sunset. All the souls that he had saved and all those that he had not took dusky shapes in the mist that hung between the high banks, and seemed by their great number and density to block his way, and showed no signs of melting or changing back into mist, so that he feared his passage was to be difficult forever. The poor souls that were not saved were darker and more pitiful than those that were, and still there was not any of the radiance he would have hoped to see in such a congregation. (*Stories* 228)

This richly visualized description of the Trace's haunting mists exemplifies Warren's contention that ideas or comments advanced in Welty's narratives counter the view of fiction as documentary or fiction as "mere report" (27). The early presentation of the Trace exposes it as a place where the immaterial takes shape in concrete form: Saved and damned souls mass, neither dissipating nor melting, but wreathing the Trace to create obstructing, shady forms. The misty yet substantially rendered souls almost bar Dow's passage, and they create a ghostly congregation shown in varying degrees of light. In this passage, so characteristic of her style, Welty represents the Trace by densely layering detail, generating depth and definition in order to fold documentary reporting into surreal apparitions in order to delight and disorient. Later, when Audubon views the Trace, he experiences that same sense of wonder:

Coming upon the Trace, he looked at the high cedars, azure and still as distant smoke overhead, with their silver roots trailing down either side like the veins of deepness in this place, and he noted some fact to his memory—this earth that wears but will not crumble or slide or turn into dust, they say it exists in one other spot in the world, Egypt—and then forgot it. (*Stories* 233)

Again, Welty imparts a palpable sense of place through the use of figurative language to subvert the materiality of the scene. She transforms the Trace, the cedars, the smoke, the roots, and the earth into a magical domain of azure wisps of vapor, metallic veins that deeply delve, and exotic earth that tells of Egypt. Moreover, the passage anticipates Audubon's destruction of this magic.

Imagining a meeting between these three men permits Welty to juxtapose their various relations to the world. "In this story," Ruth M. Vande Kieft perceptively writes, "three men try to wrest final meanings out of life from three different points of view" (20). Dow interprets events in the natural world as signs sent from God. He believes in God's providence, securing him from the Trace's threats, such as when he escaped Indian raiders by putting "his head to the horse's silky mane" so that a "bullet meant for him would endanger the horse and make his death of no value." In this instance, a moment of surreal transformation, Dow turns "half-beast and half-divine, dividing himself like a heathen Centaur," and, in the past, he has similarly avoided death by metamorphosing into a roaring tiger, an alligator blowing "savage bubbles" (*Stories* 229), and a dead man. These evasions confirm the righteousness of his faith and affirm the authority of his vision. James Murrell acts according to an absolute vision, too: "Destroy the present!" and the "living moment," so the "man that lives in it must die before you can go on" (231). He rides the Trace abiding by this conviction, having contempt for the world and planning to subject Dow, like all of his victims, to his rage.

Welty brings these personalities into coincidence in order to explore their discrete envisioning of, and subsequent acting on, the world of the Trace. Dow and Murrell, Vande Kieft observes, "are like brothers seeking light" to illuminate human mystery. As she observes, "Evangelist and murderer, soul-saver and destroyer, seem to become as one" (21). Unlike Audubon, however, neither of these men assumes the role of artist in his journey to uncover life's mystery. This role she allocates to Audubon. Through the still moment of the heron's beauty, which transfixes the men, she examines the artist's responsibility to represent his or her subject accurately, heedless of the illusion created by mimetic representational devices. Audubon, the Enlightenment naturalist and naturalistic painter, grossly violates Welty's philosophy as she outlines it in "Writing and Analyzing a Story" and "Place in Fiction." He explores the Natchez wilderness in a bold attempt to disprove the "wildly varying" descriptions of birds he believes the townspeople invent, and he holds adamantly, like Dow and Murrell, to his conviction that such mysterious fancies "would be disposed of and shamed by any man's excursion into the reality of Nature" (*Stories* 234). For Audubon, nature must submit its variation to uniformity, as expressed in his method of drawing birds by shooting them and then arranging the body "before me by means of wires" in order to copy "with a closeness of *measurement* that I hope will always correspond with *nature* when brought into contact" ("Audubon" 754). Clearly a man of his time, Audubon intends that his efforts to "acquire a thorough knowledge of birds" contribute to the advancement of knowledge generally, and that his pictures please "every person" as well as the "scientific classes" (753). With the other men, Audubon observes the heron in the distance and meticulously assesses its aspect, appearance, and behavior: "When it feeds it muddies the water with its foot.... It was as if each detail about the heron happened slowly in time, and only once. He felt again the old stab of wonder—what structure of life bridged the reptile's scale and feather? That knowledge too had been lost" (Welty *Stories* 236). As a result of his obsession with the literal recording of the subject's anatomy, Audubon's art obliterates the material that inspires the painting. "A Still Moment" stages this gratuitous act in order to show that the naturalist's motivations lead him to a greatly diminished knowledge of life because he seeks enlightenment by effacing his object. Audubon's fastidious eye and equally exacting naturalistic representations lead to a shrinking rather than an enlargement of knowledge, misrepresenting the duality of perception.

The heron's sudden alighting astonishes, overwhelms, and affects the men variously, but Audubon's decision to shoot the bird destroys the plenitude of the moment, illustrating the pointless sterility of his project to "record all the life that filled this world" (Welty *Stories* 236).[3] Welty presents the naturalist as a man driven to uncover secrets, not only about his own "mysterious origin," but about his desire for revelation through "endless examination" of "every bird" and "every serpent that shone underfoot." However, such "discoveries" meant for betterment of scientific knowledge prove futile because his art denies the dialectical condition of human experience. His essay at understanding his interior life leads him exclusively outwards, so his art fails to accommodate subjectivity. "Some men's eyes," Welty proclaims, "persisted in looking outward when they opened to look inward, and to their delight, there outflung was the astonishing world under the sky" (237). Audubon attempts to control materiality by taxonomizing it, stilling its motion with the gun and the painter's brush, tools "A Still Moment" presents as synonymous. "The gaze that looks outward must be trained without rest, to be indomitable" (238), Welty declares. When Audubon sights the heron, he dreams narcissistically of the indomitability of his gaze, "with his mind going to his pointed brush, it must see like this, and he tightened his hand on the trigger of the gun and pulled it, and his eyes went closed." Here, Welty collapses the moment of the trigger pulling and the moment of the brush representing into a single instance indicative of Audubon's blind arrogance. Danièle Pitavy-Souques, too, argues for this equation when she claims that the killing "shows how representation involves a fracture," noting that Welty "acknowledges the presence of an absence through the symbolism of the dead bird used to represent a live one" ("Blazing Butterfly" 126). In opposition to Audubon's naturalistic mode of presentation and to the fracture that it reveals, Welty attempts to show the bird's living beauty.

The depiction of the snowy heron Welty supplies in the narrative foregrounds her surreal point of view, which aims at retaining in her representation what Audubon's naturalism cannot picture. She reproduces the bird's life, its beauty, and its doubleness, all combined in a still moment that pulses dialectically between arrested motion and activity: "Fixed in its pure white profile it stood in the precipitous moment, a plumicorn on it head, its breeding dress extended in rays, eating steadily the little water creatures." And, a few lines later, she notes the bird as it appears to the three men: "But before them the white heron rested in the grasses with the evening all around it, lighter and more serene than the evening, flight closed in its body, the circuit of its body closed, a bird seen and a bird still, its motion calm as if it were offered: take my flight. . . ." (*Stories* 236). Welty assiduously composes the presentation of the heron in her brimming frame: The bird stands motionless, fixed, and crisply silhouetted in the same representational moment as it feeds steadily, commanding the evening light to illuminate its tranquility. Her narration, in essence, visually represents the bird through a series of paradoxes: still and active, serene and voracious, grounded and in flight, closed and exposed, observed and yet dreamed.

In contrast to Welty's literary depiction, Audubon's still life representation ultimately distresses and disappoints him because it fails to duplicate his experience of the bird as he sees it. Gail Mortimer also interprets Audubon's killing in "A Still Moment" from this troubled perspective when she points out, "[H]e commits this act despite the fact that his experience has taught him that his art cannot, even in his own eyes, fulfill his vision of nature's beauty" (71). While Audubon reproduces the heron in minute detail and with strict adherence to the precepts of naturalistic presentation, the picture still dissatisfies:

> It was undeniable, on some Sunday morning, when he turned over and over his drawings they seemed beautiful to him, through what was dramatic in the conflict of life, or what was exact. What he would draw, and what he had seen, became for a moment one to him. Yet soon enough, and it seemed to come in that same moment, like Lorenzo's horror and

the gun's firing, he knew that even the sight of the heron which surely he alone had appreciated, had not been all his belonging, and that never could any vision, even any simple sight, belong to him or any man. He knew that the best he could make would be, after it was apart from his hand, a dead thing and not a live thing, never the essence, only a sum of parts; and that it would always meet with a stranger's sight, and never be one with the beauty in any other man's head in the world. (*Stories* 239)

This devastating moment of clarity acknowledging Audubon's failure to standardize nature's seeming endless diversity indicates why Welty selected the story's title. The laws of representational painting preclude the reproduction of the contradiction inherent in perception, which detects both the stillness and the momentum of experience. The words of the title, "A Still Moment," encapsulate the paradox that surrealist theory emphasizes. Through its free combining of apparently oppositional elements in a composition, surrealism provides for a synthesis of the kind Welty depicts in the heron, which curiously and marvelously shimmers in its stillness, yet remains still in its movement. In stark contrast, Audubon's presentation of the bird only created a "sum of parts," vitiating the heron's vital beauty (239).

Although "A Still Moment" does not open *The Wide Net*, its far-reaching indictment of Audubon and the tradition of representational art he symbolizes surfaces again and again in the collection. In a 1942 letter to her agent, Diarmuid Russell, Welty defends her broadly anti-representational technique from detractors such as Edward Weeks at the *Atlantic*, who had rejected "A Still Moment." She categorically denies the story is symbolic, claiming, "I wanted it to state literal facts, but since the facts were about character & experience in themselves the terms I used sounded as if they were symbols." Writing against ingrained reading habits, which searched for a story's meaning in the distribution of symbols embedded in the fabric of plot, Welty's innovative fiction advanced along another path, diminishing the complexities of plot in favor of revelations yielded through style and point of view. "In this case," Welty says of "A Still Moment," "the literal seemed to me more wonderful than the symbolic. I think often it is more wonderful, for it takes its place in a higher organization of knowledge than most symbolism" (qtd. in Kreyling *Author* 86). Here, she points to the heron's literality as central to the story's organization. Rather than adopting the symbolist theory of T. S. Eliot or W. B. Yeats as a guide for interpreting the heron's mysteries, she elevates the knowledge derived from apprehending the bird in its environment. This epistemology, which grounds itself in both the literal and the abstract, reveals the heron as an example of a "higher organization of knowledge" contingent upon the varieties of perception found within a perspective such as surrealism (86).

The stories of *The Wide Net* demonstrate an intensification and an entrenchment of Welty's primary assumption that representation should present the observer's perspective as much as it does the material represented. And, as Welty's investigation of perception and its treatment in fiction develop, she cultivates a more nuanced, knotty, and figurative narrative mode that increasingly minimizes the significance of plot as a narrative device for conveying meaning. In *Author and Agent*, Michael Kreyling concludes that for Welty, plot begins to take a back seat, and that the "new logic" (82) of the Natchez Trace stories reacts to the madness of World War Two. Kreyling goes on to say:

> And yet her stories seemed to require rebellion, a new technique of narration, a new configuration of gesture and meaning attuned to the heart, not to the logic of events-in-the-world (plot). Plot, as a symbol of enlistment into conventional understandings of the world, was more expendable than ever before now that the world presented war as its logic. (82–83)

As an assessment of artistic revolt against history's somber tide, Kreyling's judgment of Welty's fiction echoes Maurice Nadeau's contention that surrealism's revolutionary agenda emerged from the disaster of World War One (44–45). When confronted with catastrophic war, Welty and the surrealists fled to their dreams and the power of the imagination to transform creation before it could round and devour them. Just as Kreyling indicates, *The Wide Net* illustrates an author obsessed by the potency of dreams and the hallucinogenic condition of perception; however, these surreal preoccupations have antecedents in *A Curtain of Green*. If the "new logic" seems new (82), it rises to prominence out of Welty's long-standing fascination with dreaming and waking realities.

This narrative insistence in "A Still Moment" on thematically and stylistically integrating the abstract with the concrete also finds expression in "The Wide Net" and "The Purple Hat." Many critical readings of the former point to the story's reliance on Celtic, Classical, and local Mississippi legend in recounting a comic tale of boyish adventure and adult responsibility. The latter narrative, in which Welty tells a ghost story about a mysterious woman who refuses to die, is a contribution to the Gothic genre. Despite obvious differences in tenor and genre, both stories demonstrate the author's surreal blending of the rational with the irrational and the marvelous with the ordinary.

Following the lead of Ruth Vande Kieft, most critics have analyzed *The Wide Net*'s title story primarily by focusing on plotline.[4] William Wallace Jamieson punishes his newly pregnant wife, Hazel, by spending an evening out, "cuttin' up" with old friends (*Stories* 210). When he returns the next morning, Hazel has vanished, leaving only a letter informing him that she has drowned herself in the Pearl River. Panicked, Wallace gathers a team of cohorts to drag the river for Hazel's body. However, they find no body. Hazel has fooled her husband, who eventually returns home, where the warring couple reconcile. Kreyling has keenly observed that the Welty of *The Wide Net* "was beginning to deal, consistently story by story, with the world-out-there as a porous phenomenon permeated by the feeling self" (*Author* 85–86), and that "[c]onventional narration of event-to-event, with its conventional logic and conventional assumptions about the self and history, could not serve this vision" (86). But other critics persist in reading the narrative for the significance of the events, rather than reading for representational strategies and what Welty suggests about the necessity of innovative fictional techniques for interweaving the world-out-there with the world-in-here.

Commentators have typically drawn attention to the story's allusion to mythologies, both ancient and modern. In fact, critics' emphases on the mythological allusions that Welty supplies in many of her stories have affirmed for many her modernist sensibility in the tradition of French symbolism, while excluding her modernist sensibility in the tradition of the avant-garde. In the former kind of reading, the mythological carries significance and meaning, attaching to and thickening the plot lines, so that allusion and plot together form the central ground for critical appraisal. Meanwhile, point of view and feeling, which in Welty's eyes "carr[y] the crown" above the other elements of fiction are slighted ("Place in Fiction" 781). Despite the historic pinpointing and unpacking of Welty's symbolic universe, no one has advanced a full interpretation of the story's most obvious motif, the same emblem that presides over the whole collection: the wide net itself.

Alfred Appel's 1965 study, *A Season of Dreams: The Fiction of Eudora Welty*, contemplates the net as a "metaphor for experience," but his analysis concentrates too narrowly on the intricacies of Wallace's feelings for Hazel. More broadly, the image symbolizes the fiction's fundamental mode of presentation that this study defines as surreal. Appel views the net as "unselective," ensnaring "anything in its path" (69), yet the story may actually demonstrate the reverse, as the net fails to trap its intended treasure, Hazel. Rather than a net that scoops up everything in its path, Welty's net acts more like a filter, screening the water and collecting only particles of the life that throngs the river. For example, the largest creature in the river, the King of Snakes, curiously eludes successive dredgings. Perhaps Welty deploys the net not as a metaphor for all-ensnaring experience, but as an image expressing her surreal point of view, a perspective that accents experience's partiality, its uneven filtering of life's river, and its investment of perception with a hallucinogenic or paranoiac aura. The wide net, then, parallels Welty's brimming frame metaphor, which sorts experience by simultaneously excluding and erasing while selecting and foregrounding. Similarly, the author's wide net behaves like a frame in that it captures, collects, and presents for inspection only fragments of life's giant panorama.

"The Wide Net" clearly illustrates Welty's positioning of her frame so as to undertake surreal envisioning when she describes characters and the environment through which they pass. For example, one of Wallace's fellow dredgers, a young boy named Brucie Rippon, bends "readily under William Wallace's hand-pat, and gave him a dreamy look out of the tops of his round eyes which were pure green-and-white like clover tops" (*Stories* 208). When Brucie shows his brother, Grady, a red thread plaything, a "look of helpless and intense interest gathered Grady's face like a drawstring—his eyes, one bright with a sty, shone pleadingly under his white bangs." Surreal depictions of the team subsequently yield to dreamy descriptions of the team's movement, following the "Old Natchez Trace" (211) that took "them through the deep woods and led them out down below the Pearl River, where they could begin dragging it upstream to the point near Dover." During their soporific progress toward the river, this ragtag assemblage spies a "long freight train" which, like themselves, "seemed like a little festival procession, moving with the slowness of ignorance or a dream, from distance to distance, the tiny pink and gray cars like secret boxes." Grady counts the "cars to himself, as if he could certainly see each one clearly, and Brucie watched his lips, hushed and cautious, the way he would watch a bird drinking." Arriving at the river's edge, everyone suddenly halts, as if stunned by the Pearl's broad majesty stretching out under the fall sunlight.

Doc, a loquacious local of unspecified authority and owner of the net, meditates on the scene as the others go silent: "[T]oday, in October sun, it's all gold—sky and tree and water. Everything just before it changes looks to be made of gold." Doc's sentiments concur with and perhaps color Wallace's assessment of the river's glow. The latter views the river's goldness and identifies its hue with the complex of feelings he has for his wife, who metamorphoses into the precious metal before his eyes: "[H]e thought of Hazel with the shining eyes, sitting at home and looking straight before her, like a piece of pure gold, too precious to touch" (212). Cold, inert, and impenetrable, Hazel appears at a distance, too remote for Wallace to reach, but the magic of the moment contains the hope of renewal and transfiguration.[5] No longer gold, the "river was glimmering, narrow, soft, and skin-colored, and slowed nearly to stillness. The net that was being drawn out, so old and so long-used, it too looked golden, strung and tied with golden threads" (212–13).

Welty's fictional transformation of the scene into a surreal fantasy for her audience finds an analog in Wallace's deeply puzzling reaction to the vista. Despite having fished in the river "all his life," he no longer knows it, and the others look "at him as if he were crazy not to know the name of the river." To Wallace, the river presents a profound and alluring mystery, the "same as if it were some great far torrent of waves that dashed through the mountains somewhere, and almost as if it were a river in some dream, for they could not give him the name of that." In a Dalínian superimposing of image on image, Welty presents the still, golden river before Wallace as continuous with the dashing torrent, coextensive with the river in the dream, and synonymous with the river below the bank, which appears "transparent and yellow like an old bottle lying in the sun, filing with light" (*Stories* 213). Neither Wallace nor the reader can identify the river's defining quality, because Welty's surreal portrayal of the scene refuses such compromise. The wide net has swept the vista, conferring on it a multiplicity of visions whose edges soften and blend to present a "pleasing and finished surface to the eye" (Welty "Place in Fiction" 784), an illusion admitting no faults that may fracture the surface of the story's surreal integument.

The hallucinogenic rendering of features observed within the frame or collected in the artist's net reveals Welty's debt to the style of surrealist artists. Consistent with Dalí's theory of paranoia-criticism, for example, she systematizes the confusion of the dream as it presents itself to the cold light of day, and her fiction testifies to the ordering power of the irrational in everyday living. In "The Wide Net," the river occupies a central position because it serves as the site for Welty's bending of material "reality" into the flow of the dream and abstract thought. The river obviously represents the river of life that the wide net surveys, and it also creates occasions for the story's characters to confront their emotional obsessions and fears. Like Wallace, Grady Rippon finds something unexpected and mysterious in the water: The river claimed his father, who returns to him now as a ghost. "Grady's inflamed eyes rested on the brown water," Welty records, "Without warning he saw something . . . perhaps the image in the river seemed to be his father, the drowned man—with arms open, eyes open, mouth open. . . . Grady stared and blinked, again something wrinkled up his face." The language figuratively merges Grady's eyes with the water's opaque plane; the liquid enables and disables sight, leaving the observer vacillating and in mystery. While the Pearl enchants Grady as he peers into it, Wallace dives into its depths to resolve his difficulty with his wife's pregnancy. He doesn't find Hazel in the "deepest place in the whole Pearl River" (*Stories* 217), but returns to the surface "in an agony of the blood and of the very heart, so woeful he looked." Despite the great heroism of Wallace's dive, Hazel still eludes him. After accomplishing such a huge feat, he surfaces only with a "little green ribbon of plant" (218), a modest laurel indeed.

That Wallace emerges from the depths of the Pearl River without treasure, agonized and confused, indicates that his journey toward peace and reconciliation with his wife is not over. His narcissistic absorption in his own fantasy of himself as an untouchable river god prevents him from compromising with Hazel, who refuses to tolerate his tantrums. Nonetheless, his failure to locate Hazel's body, despite his best efforts, has begun to make him question his superiority, even though, amongst his band of dredgers, he continues to act the braggadocio, vaunting his in-flated sense of masculinity in a near-naked, homoerotic display of virility. In a much commented upon scene critical to the narrative, Wallace enter-tains his comrades by dancing crazily, hooking a large catfish to his belt buckle and going "up and down so that they all hollered, and then tears of laughter streaming down his cheeks made him put up his hand, and the two days' growth of beard began to jump out, bright red" (*Stories* 219). Along with other critics, Peter Schmidt rightly interprets this performance as a virility dance celebrating the "phallic power of fathering and own-ing, as if the dance (and the all-male fertility ritual of the river-dragging) creates his beard, his manhood" (139). Despite the hilarity of the scene, the bearded dancer obliquely expresses a form of masculinity in crisis, a recurrent theme in the work of Dalí often represented by his recurring self-portrait, the Great Masturbator.[6]

Dalí recycles this iconic image of his highly stylized head repeatedly. It develops into a stock feature of his repertoire, appearing again and again in various incarnations—not least as part of his *The Persistence of Memory*. His biographer, Ian Gibson, describes the symbol as a "waxy-complexioned head with closed eyes, long lashes, prominent nose and a giant locust glued to the spot where there should be a mouth" (256).[7] Moreover, the head "represents Dalí as compulsive masturbator," "soon to find its maximum expression in *The Great Masturbator*," a painting that presents the giant head positioned horizontally, balanced on its nose, with closed eyes which "indicate that the masturbator, oblivious to external reality, is only concerned with the erotic fantasies being played out in the theatre of his mind" (257). Robert Radford, too, reports that Dalí's 1929 painting represents the artist's "major work on this theme" of onanism (123). As Gibson contends, the unconscious head suggests a mind turned inward toward a narcissistic fantasy life of the kind that Welty presents as dangerous in "Petrified Man" and as a potential threat in "The Wide Net." Dalí's representation of his head—also partially petrified through its incorporation of a rocky bluff[8]—expresses the guilt and fear that masturbation engenders because of its social censure. Yet Dawn Ades observes that the alternative to autoeroticism for the painter, "sexual relations with another," had "its own attendant threat of impotence" (75). During this period in his life, Dalí met and fell in love with his future wife, Gala. He foresaw a sexual union, but he "had never had a full sexual relationship with a woman" (76) and remained "locked in the auto-eroticism and masturbation of the previous years." *The Great Masturbator* reports on this tension in the artist's life through its presentation of a "couple embracing among the rocks of Cape Creus" (Gibson 283). The dilemma that confronts Dalí in his first deep relationship with a woman, and which he memorializes so publicly in this and several other paintings on the subject, matches William Wallace's predicament in "The Wide Net." A fulfilling sexual and emotional union with another requires the attenuation of and/or sharing of narcissistic fantasies. Welty's narrative line exposes this difficult set of relations and choices. In order to reach a mutually enriching settlement with his wife, William Wallace, the Great Masturbator, must acknowledge the limitations of his autoeroticism and redirect his libido toward Hazel.

To enact this reorientation, Welty stages Wallace's confrontation with and defeat of his narcissism in staring down the King of Snakes, an apt evocation of his masculine egoism. She presents the threatening snake as almost hailed by Wallace's sweaty display with the catfish. Its "old hoary head" lifts from the river's surface and its "long dark body" appears undulating, "loop after loop and hump after hump," as it spreads out "all across the river, like a necklace." Wallace stares "back at the King of Snakes with all his might" and deters the creature, sending it out of sight. As if signaling his triumph over the monster and his ongoing transformation, "thunder like a stone loosed and rolled down the bank," while in the eastern skies the troop view "gray, pink, and blue" clouds, appearing in a dreamy formation of "familiar castles" and "round towers" that soon grow black and issue thunder (*Stories* 219). Before long, the rain pelts the team fiercely, and Welty describes its dramatic onset as a "huge tail" that "seemed to lash through the air," lacerating the river and leaving a "wound of silver" (220). Beyond such familiarly presented surreal details, these hallucinogenic scenes emphasize Wallace's purgation and renewal, as the rain washes over the men and imparts purity to Dover, the town to which they now travel. The town looks "somehow like new" (221), as the afternoon heat drapes "everything like shiny mosquito-netting" (221–22), ensuring a pristine moment free from contamination.

Before reaching home, Wallace looks down from a hill at an "old white church glimmering there at the crossroads, far below" (*Stories* 225). He, too, stands at a fork in the road, and Welty supplies this deeply reflective moment to foreground Wallace's transition from immortal river god to mortal under the gods. From a nearby chapel, the music of the Sacred Harp Sing drifts by him:

> He stared away as if he saw it minutely, as if he could see a lady in white take a flowered cover off the organ, which was set on a little slant in the shade, dust the keys, and start to pump and play. . . . He smiled faintly, as he would at his mother, and at Hazel, and at the singing women in his life, now all one young girl standing up to sing under the trees the oldest and longest ballads there were.(225)

This poignant instant marks Wallace's acknowledgement of his fallibility. Despite the magnitude of his effort, he failed to retrieve Hazel's body from the abyss of the Pearl River, and this vision on the hilltop shows him the reason he came up empty handed: Grasping for one woman inevitably entails reaching for a multiplicity. Like the glimmering church, the multiply figured women may vanish, leaving him bereft, and his faint smile registers this miserable potential. Now, his puerile cockiness has disappeared, and the story leaves Wallace leavened with sobriety, more modest and largely sympathetic.

If "The Wide Net" humanizes its protagonist, "The Purple Hat" leaves readers questioning its protagonist's humanity. The woman who wears the hat occupies the central role in this story within a story. An armed guard, who a works for the Palace of Pleasure, a gambling hall in New Orleans, recounts to a barman and a young customer his sightings of a mysterious woman over a span of thirty years. She sports a strange hat variously described as "great and ancient and bedraggled" (*Stories* 269), as revealing a "jeweled hatpin" (273), and as "quite a hat. A great, wide, deep hat such as has no fashion and never knew there was fashion and change. It serves her to come out in winter and summer. Those are old plush flowers that trim it—roses? Poppies? A man wouldn't know easily. And you would never know if you only met her wearing the hat that a little glass vial with a plunger helps decorate the crown" (271). She seduces men for their money, and the guard has witnessed her death and resurrection twice. The title of this "playful ghost story" (Bunting 63), as Welty called it, recalls any number of Edgar Allan Poe gothic short stories,[9] such as "The Black Cat," "The Purloined Letter," or "The Cask of Amontillado," in which the author announces the presiding symbol of the narrative in the title. In a literary gesture to Poe, Welty plays with this convention, deploying the purple hat as a motif signaling the femme fatale's darkly seductive manner. The hat assumes the role of fetish for a lover to caress and carries the notion of addiction in its vial, plunger, and poppies. Kreyling supports this view, arguing that the alluring hat, when placed on the woman's lap, indicates a "clear zone of sexual symbolism" (*Understanding* 71). "The Purple Hat" is not the first story Welty had written about women destroying men. The protagonist recalls Elsa, the dangerous lover who drives her husband to madness in "Retreat," and also evokes Schiaparelli, one of Welty's favorite personalities from the thirties and forties, famous for her surrealist experimentation with women's clothing, accessories, and headwear. Unlike Chanel, Schiaparelli saw dressmaking "as an art" rather than "as a profession" (Blum 10), and her "famous collaborations with the artists Salvador Dalí and Jean Cocteau during the late thirties changed the face of fashion.

No longer was a dress merely a dress or a hat just a hat" (121). Reading this story in the context of designs by Schiaparelli (which Welty would have seen frequently in the leading fashion magazines of the day), provides further evidence of Kreyling's assertion about the hat's symbolism—especially given Schiaparelli's interpretation of Dalí, which produced "fashion designs, which could also carry alternate meanings. Thus a shoe was not a shoe but a hat" (142), and Tristan Tzara's notion, predicated on her hat designs, that "contemporary women's hats resembled female genitalia—a subconscious transforming of women's desires into clearly readable symbols within the realm of fashion" (122). Stories like "Retreat" and "The Purple Hat" redefine women like those depicted in many of Poe's tales, such as "The Black Cat," "Berenice," and "Ligeia," in which men fixate on women who are passive icons of death, disease, and decomposition. Through the model of modern femininity established by a woman like Schiaparelli—at least one incarnation of the New Orleans ghost—Welty critiques received ideas about gender roles.

That Welty's surrealist vision should deepen in appropriating ideas from the world of fashion and by modifying the machinery of gothic convention makes sense. In 1924, years before the publication of Welty's 1942 story, André Breton's "Surrealist Manifesto" located surrealism in the context of the English gothic tradition, a much earlier cultural formation that also privileged inquiry into the magical and the marvelous. The manifesto excoriates the dull and predictable realism that Breton associates with the majority of contemporary fiction writers who, in their "generous supply of novels" (6), have perfected a "purely informative style" (7). Breton ridicules the novelist who dulls brains "by the incurable mania of wanting to make the unknown known, classifiable," condemning the kind of fiction that "reinforces the reign of logic," which demeans life's dreams and imaginative activity (9). Only the classic gothic novel satisfies Breton's thirst to undermine logic's reign, and he exalts Matthew G. Lewis's *The Monk* as "admirable proof" that "only the marvelous is capable of fecundating works which belong to an inferior category such as the novel" (14). In addition to citing Monk Lewis as a historical ally, Breton presumptuously claims the Marquis de Sade and Poe for surrealism, adding the latter, among many others, to a long list of surrealism's supposed progenitors, as a "surrealist in adventure" (26–27).

Welty did not read or speak French well enough to have closely read Breton's various manifestoes, even if they were available in the United

States. Nonetheless, she, like Breton, instinctively embraced the marvelous, as it animated fairy tales and legends. In "The Purple Hat," surreal and gothic features combine to produce an investigation of extra-material phenomena. In her study of Welty and Gothicism, Ruth D. Weston reads the story as creating a "gothic space in codings recognizable to readers familiar with gothic conventions: a marginal zone somewhere between imagination and reality (a neutral territory), ghostly apparitions, and the hint of implicit and repeated violence that haunts a place" (*Gothic Traditions* 34). Her allusion to a "marginal zone" that merges "imagination and reality" refers to the fidelity between her notion of "gothic space" and Breton's formulation of intersections between dream and waking realities.

To offer a surreal interpretation of "The Purple Hat," however, furthers the gothic reading of the story. Weston's analysis builds upon Vande Kieft's early observation that realism and supernaturalism share space: The narrative "comes close to pure Gothic supernaturalism, despite its realistic frame setting of a New Orleans bar" (40). Weston does not stray too far from her touchstone, Vande Kieft, in her treatment, emphasizing the story's shortcomings and Welty's own harsh assessment of it.[10] For Weston, the story "seems only marginally magical and mysterious" and suffers a "failure of atmosphere" (34), yet both commentators, holding to the notion of supernaturalism embedded in realism in the tale, overlook Welty's presentation of the "reality" of the story as neither one nor the other. Vande Kieft's and Weston's contentions suggest that the narrative separates its realism from its supernaturalism, and that the realistic frame—the New Orleans bar—encloses and contains the supernatural tale. Another perspective might, however, show a more radical side: The irrationality and paranoia of the ghost story bleeds from its edges and into the present moment, subverting the realistic frame and showing that the two narratives form a contiguous whole, with the illicit ghost nested inside its supposedly rational and realistic outer shell.[11]

Welty begins revealing the inseparability of the two narratives by inserting a series of surreal similes to unravel the story's "realistic" fabric. The action begins in a bar, but Welty quickly morphs the "quiet little hole in the wall" bar into a "mouse-hole" (*Stories* 268), which the strange sunlight—curiously watery, reflecting, and still—illuminates. In this "realistic frame setting of a New Orleans bar" (Vande Kieft 40), a bartender serves. Welty draws him surreally, like an absurd cartoon: His "mouth and eyes curved downward from the divide of his baby-pink nose, as if he had combed them down, like his hair."[12] The tranquil, dreamlike atmosphere develops cumulatively and subtly as she presents each detail of the barroom scene, such as the stools, "black oilcloth knobs, worn and smooth and as much alike as six pebbles on the beach" (*Stories* 268). The armed guard who works at the gambling hall enters and sits on a "black knob," and "[f]or a moment his eyes seemed dancing there, above one of those hands so short and so plump that you were always counting the fingers . . . really helpless-looking hands for so large a man." A young man sitting close by stares at the guard "without much curiosity, looking at the affable face much the way you stare out at a little station where your train is passing through," and the large man begins his ghost story, which the rolling thunder punctuates. Welty observes that "they seemed to inhabit the world that was just beneath the thunder. The fat man let it go by, lifting his little finger like a pianist" (269). These surreal similes challenge the conventions particular to realistic narratives, and Welty disperses them in the frame *and* the story within.

Describing his surveillance of the gambling tables from a gantry suspended high in the Palace of Pleasure's dome, the guard remarks with a painter's eye upon the red carpet, which "changes and gives off light between the worn criss-crossing of the aisle like the facets of a well-cut ruby." Welty furnishes a counterpoint to the glinting carpet in the "ruby ring" that the guard wears on his "little finger." As if by slight of hand, she transforms his red stone into an image whose interior stages the action in the Palace of Pleasure, so that the gem reveals "[t]he tables and chandeliers" deep below his vantage point. These shapes form the hall's interior, which Welty now designates as "[l]ife in the ruby," rather than the life that contains the stone (*Stories* 270). Like the bar that assumes the appearance of a mouse hole, the gambling room appears as a projection seen through a stone evocative of the narrative's focus on desire. The bar merges with the Palace of Pleasure and vice versa, a superimposition reinforced by additional absurdist similes. Seen through the lens of the ruby, the woman with the hat has a face that "spreads over such a wide area. Like the moon's. . . . Much as I have studied her, I can only say that all her features seemed to have moved further apart from each other—expanded, if you see what I mean" (273). When she gets stabbed, "[t]he old creature, who had been winning at that, simply folded all softly in on herself, like a circus tent being taken down after the show" (273–74). Moreover, beyond these colorful similes, the two apparently discrete stories intertwine in the figures of the two drinkers.

The story inside the frame escapes its boundary through the older man and the younger man who sit at the bar. The guard persists in trying to rationalize his uncanny observations, but he fails to illuminate these dark and shadowy events. His narration aims at sharing the story and countering the mystery through recitation, yet the story within the story resists and retains its secrets and paranoiac atmosphere, as Welty embodies them in the agitated young man. Kreyling rightly points out that Welty "scarcely strays" from the "gothic ghost story" formula, and that the "young man at the bar is the old ghost's most recent human lover—perhaps her most recent murderer too" (*Understanding* 70). Indeed, the young man outside the frame seems to coincide very closely with the young man within, and Welty clearly presents them as cognates. Unlike the bartender, who listens as if enrapt, the anonymous young man at the bar seems provoked by the older man's cautionary tale, and acts nervous, fidgeting and kicking his feet around under the bar seat throughout the telling. Welty describes him as "unshaven," and as having "shaky hands," and looking "fearfully" (*Stories* 268). When the guard introduces the woman as a ghost, the younger man motions for more alcohol, which he continues to down distractedly, before turning wildly and impertinently asking the guard, "Who are you?" (270). The "drained," "expressionless," and pallid face of the man perhaps indicates his terror at re-experiencing events related by the guard (271). Ultimately, neither guard nor barman nor the young man succeeds in unraveling the knotty mystery of the account by submitting it to the scrutiny of recitation. Through the two customers, young and old, "The Purple Hat" demonstrates the permeability of the supposedly realistic frame to the terrifying excesses of nightmare.

"Asphodel," too, reveals the inseparability of the observer's world from that observed. Like "The Purple Hat," "Asphodel" contains a story within a story and refuses to draw a hard line between imagination and actuality. The frame of the story recounts the adventure of three old women, Cora, Phoebe, and Irene, who picnic in the lee of Miss Sabina's marital house, Asphodel. Miss Sabina's arranged marriage to Asphodel's philandering owner, Don McInnis, disintegrates under the pressure of infidelity and the strange deaths of all their children. Ultimately, Miss Sabina repudiates her husband and his lover, then burns Asphodel, leaving only a charred shell, a ruin that Marrs observes recalls "Mississippi's Windsor," a grand nineteenth-century plantation house that also burned (*One Writer's* 64). The events of Miss Sabina's life, related by the "Greek chorus" of the three women (Vande Kieft 46), form the narrative interior to the frame. Although the story is set in the nineteenth century, its style and open structure reflect the artistic preoccupations of the twentieth—especially when the interior narrative transgresses the frame's edge and continues out of the past and into the present moment as Don McInnis unexpectedly chases the party from his grounds.

Welty's deployment of surreal similes and figurative language in both the frame and the narrative it supposedly contains works to undermine the framing device, as in "The Purple Hat." The story opens simply enough with a description of the weather, the time, and the shape of things seen. "It was a cloudless day," Welty begins, "a round hill where the warm winds blew. It was noon, and without a shadow the line of columns rose in perfect erectness from the green vines." The imposing edifice of Asphodel confronts the party as it approaches: "It was a golden ruin: six Doric columns, with the entablature unbroken over the first two, full-facing the approach. The sky was pure, transparent, and round like a shell over this hill." At this early textual juncture, Welty diverts her reader's gaze from the general scene and toward the small detail of the cracked stone façade that meets the women's eyes. This fissure symbolizes a larger, more significant break in the story's fabric. Specifically, the imperfection suggests the frame's discontinuous surround, which permits the narrative's constant oscillating movement between the past and the present, the living and the dead, the actual and the fictional, and the material and the dream. "Asphodel" shows such categories to collapse when it provides moments of the "solid world" softening into dreams. Welty charges discrete moments of visual apprehension with a hallucinatory energy: The women stand before the entablature and look "modestly upward to the frieze of maidens that was saturated with sunlight and seemed to fill with color, and before which the branch of a leafy tree was trembling" (*Stories* 241). In this liminal place, forbidden to women by Miss Sabina, they indulge their imaginations in a steamy tale of sex, lust, and disavowal. Nearing the house, they cross into Asphodel's demesne as if into a dreamland. Over a stream they hop, ignoring a "no trespassing" sign. Then they look back upon their horse, a stallion whose "mane flutter[ed] in the light" and whose "tail flaunted like a decoration he had only just put on." Having unpacked their provisions, the women relax and recline "beside the warm and weighty pedestal. Above them the six columns seemed to be filled with the inhalations of summer and to be suspended in the resting of noon" (242). The egregiously phallic pillars excite the women, who sublimate their arousal by diverting it into storytelling. Ostensibly, they speak of the past and Miss Sabina, yet in the telling, and in the location they have chosen for their narration—beneath Keats's eternally untouched and eternally pursued maidens frozen in stone—they reveal their own frustrated desires.

Welty's construction of Miss Sabina's story inside the frame intentionally compromises the surrounding frame's integrity. The gradual accumulation of dreamy textual details fractures the partition supposedly containing the interior narrative. Desire's always-attendant temptations and entanglements stand at the thematic core of the recollected story, but this theme reasserts itself continuously in the present moment, as if seeping through tears in the dividing seam. For example, the Natchez Trace, which links Asphodel to Miss Sabina's ancestral home, creates a conduit for the channeling of erotic desires. Welty presents absolute chastity and its obverse, free sexual expression, as extremes symbolized by the two houses "separated by a long, winding, difficult, untravelled road—a curve of the old Natchez Trace— situated almost back to back on the ring of hills, while completely hidden from each other, like the reliefs on opposite sides of a vase" (*Stories* 242–43). Kreyling observes, "This situation suggests that in reality such opposites are part of the whole, and that someone who could see all sides would realize that" (*Eudora Welty's Achievement* 23). While Miss Sabina may have refused to acknowledge her dreams and desires, the three picnicking women, pressing at the red "pomegranate stains on their mouths," revel in their steamy dramatization (*Stories* 242).[13]

Acting as a chorus, they draw the concealed side of the vase into the open, and demonstrate memory's potency by creating a shared moment of titillating intrigue. "The three old maids," Welty writes, "who lay like a faded garland at the foot of the columns, paused in peaceful silence. When the story was taken up again, it was in Phoebe's delicate and gentle way, for its narrative was only part of memory now, and its beginning and ending might seem mingled and freed in the blue air of the hill." The old maids' collaborative recitation unhinges the narrative from history, finding a new context for it in the present moment. In their languid state, they openly admit to desiring Don McInnis, who "had the wildness we all worshipped that first night, since he was not to be ours to love" (*Stories* 244). As their tale unfolds and spreads itself into the moment, it acts on Asphodel's columns, which seem to lose their solidity: "The prodigious columns shone down and appeared tremulous with the tender light of summer which enclosed them all around, in equal and shadowless flame. They seemed to flicker with the flight of birds" (246). Here, Welty's presentation of setting works to destabilize the "solid world" of the story's opening, and deep-seated feelings imbue her descriptions (241); in this example, desire saturates the shared recollection, bathing the lethargic women in gentle, dematerializing streams of reverie-inducing light.

In counterpoint to the women's sustained erotic fantasizing, Miss Sabina emerges as the enemy of dreams, memory, and narratives that resuscitate the past in the context of the present. Scorned by her husband, whom she has repudiated, she rules the town with an iron fist. "Her power reached over the whole population," Cora recalls, "white and black, men and women, children, idiots, and animals—even strangers. Her law was laid over us" (*Stories* 246). Although Sabina's law appears to police all under her purview, she refuses to enter the post office, which she strangely abhors, calling it a "dirty little room." Phoebe, who like the other women collects her mail at the office, observes that the room is outside of Sabina's "domain," for "there we might still be apart in a dream, and she did not know what it was" (247). Commentators tend to interpret Sabina's ultimate desecration of the post office as a confrontation with the "outside world" (Vande Kieft 47), "modern life" (Appel 87), the "world outside" (Kreyling *Eudora* 23), or "isolation" (Mortimer 115), but the post office might also symbolize Miss Sabina's confrontation with the world inside. The chorus of women narrators identifies the post office as a dreamy refuge from Sabina's tyranny, but when her wrath finally comes down on the post office, she destroys all the letters there. Some she wildly tears, and others she bestially devours. She assumes the post office distributes love letters, and Sabina "never got a letter in her life" (*Stories* 248). Starved of love and embittered by her husband's infidelity, Sabina's frustration, rage, and death in the post office derive from her self-examination in a scene that illustrates Welty's drawing of letters and desire into coincidence. The three women's story—part fact and part fabrication—restores desire through the assembling of letters they use to construct their narrative.

If the circulation of surrealist imagery inside and outside of the frame fails to perforate any neat line of demarcation between scenes, the sudden appearance of Don McInnis at the denouement boldly demonstrates Welty's position that the strength of good fiction resides in its power to create interventions in time and so suture past frames of action to present frames. The three women believe their story safely contained by history and sealed with Sabina's death and, through the telling, they expect its danger to have been abrogated. "Here in the bright sun where the three old maids sat beside their little feast," Welty remarks, "Miss Sabina's was an old story, closed and complete. In some intoxication of the time and the place, they recited it and came to an end." Or so they think—when a fracture in the story's surrounding frame, introduced and deepened by Welty's deployment of surrealist rhetoric, provides for a final flurry of excitement.

The maids lie languorously stretched out, while "[a]bove them like a dream rested the bright columns of Asphodel, a dream like the other side of their lamentations." Purportedly a lament for Sabina's death, the lament's flipside, their erotic narrative, invokes Don McInnis, who steps out "into the radiant light," when he "stood motionless as one of the columns, his eyes bearing without break upon the three women, he was as rude and golden as a lion. He did nothing and he said nothing while the birds sang on. But he was naked" (*Stories* 249). The timid women scatter when confronted boldly by the man their story valorizes and has apparently summoned. From a safe distance, they look back at the ruin, but McInnis has disappeared or has perhaps transformed into the "thriving heard" of goats that now throng among the upthrust columns (250).[14] Rudely awakened from her reverie and roughly returned to the world where authority polices desire, Cora twice threatens McInnis with prosecution. In contrast, Phoebe chuckles, because "she seemed to be still in a tender dream and an unconscious celebration—as though the picnic were not already set rudely in the past, but were the enduring and intoxicating present, still the phenomenon, the golden day" (251). The last line of "Asphodel" pointedly reminds readers that this narrative does not reach a terminus. Phoebe doesn't revoke memory; she carries the dream of the past inside her, over the stream, by the "'No Trespassing' sign" (249), and out of the frame. In her mind, at least, the narrative revealed the winding of separate strands into a single thread, one that also illustrates Welty's synthesizing of and enmeshment of the story within the story and the dream within the waking mind.

The continuity that Welty demonstrates between apparently discrete narrative frames stuns the picnicking party in "Asphodel." Bearing his asp, Don McInnis crosses the threshold dividing the story's dream from its material circumstances. This act causes the women to flee the estate in disarray, their picnic abandoned. But Welty's other stories in *The Wide Net*, "At the Landing," "First Love," "The Winds," and "Livvie," also traverse the liminal expanse at the frontier of dreaming and waking realities. These narratives, however, achieve that discovery through the eyes of children or artless adolescents, and the surreal inquiry into the ambiguities of experience thereby assumes a more supple and nuanced rhetorical strategy. For example, none of these four narratives employs a framing device to mark the meeting of fiction and fact. Instead, Welty subverts the "solid world" (*Stories* 241) by presenting the narrative from a young person's point of view, amenable to the marvelous and the irrational, rather than one that steals away from it in fear, like the maids of "Asphodel."

The large number of children and young, inexperienced adolescents and adults who feature prominently in Welty's fictional universe attests to her preoccupation with the remarkable inventiveness of young minds. This theme in her work reasserts itself continually, because the child's mind reluctantly concedes its capacity for wonder and vehemently resists capitulation to the cynicism of adulthood. Like Welty, in his first "Surrealist Manifesto," André Breton recognized the necessity of restoring childlike appreciation for the magic of life. Indeed, the manifesto's opening paragraphs recommend a radical reassessment of adult consciousness, directing the reader to turn "back toward his childhood," where the "absence of any known restrictions allows him the perspective of several lives lived at once" (3). Moreover, toward the polemic's end, Breton returns to childhood in his peroration, proclaiming that the mind turned toward surrealism "relives with glowing excitement the best part of its childhood" (39):

> From childhood memories, and from a few others, there emanates a sentiment of being unintegrated, and then later of *having gone astray*, which I hold to be the most fertile that exists. It is perhaps childhood that comes closest to one's "real life"; childhood beyond which man has at his disposal, aside from his laissez-passer, only a few complimentary tickets; childhood where everything nevertheless conspires to bring about the effective, risk-free possession of oneself. Thanks to surrealism, it seems that opportunity knocks a second time. (40)

For Breton, adult life leads the imagination astray by impoverishing its fecundity and by leaving imagination integrated yet separate from its material environment. Through recuperated memories, the surrealist revolution promises a restoration of that lost inventiveness.

Similarly, Welty's fiction ministers to that absence. Like Breton, she instinctively understood the importance of a rich imaginative life to acquisition of revolutionary knowledge. If embracing the surreal revolution provided a second opportunity for Breton, Welty's fiction also furnishes an opportunity for renewal through memory. For example, in her 1984 memoir, *One Writer's Beginnings*, she contemplates a moment of childhood learning through the metaphor of painting. In particular, she recollects an art lesson devoted to sketching a still life:

> In a children's art class, we sat in a ring on kindergarten chairs and drew three daffodils that had just been picked out of the yard; and while I was drawing, my sharpened yellow pencil and the cup of the yellow daffodil gave off whiffs just alike. That the pencil doing the drawing should give off the same smell as the flower it drew seemed part of the art lesson— as shouldn't it be? Children, like animals, use all their sense to discover the world. Then artists come along and discover it the same way, all over again. Here and there, it's the same world. Or now and then we'll hear from an artist who's never lost it. (*Stories* 847)

Here, Welty's conceptualizing of childhood as a period of imaginative growth, surprise excitements, and magical discovery parallels Breton's emphasis on youth's importance to surrealism. To the young mind, as yet unintegrated and not led astray, the pencil and the flower it depicts share an identical perfume. That the young Welty considers this coincidence a part of the instruction and critical to artistic technique reveals the similarity of her guiding principles to Breton's as he presents them in the "Surrealist Manifesto." For both, restoring the imaginative play and the self-possessing freedom of childhood to jaded minds can stay—perhaps even revoke—the onset of adult cynicism and disaffection.

Despite the personal freedom and enrichment that Welty's advocacy of imagination promises in *The Wide Net*, she also shows imagination's contamination and dissolution. One of the darkest and bleakest of all Welty stories, "At the Landing," closes the collection. Completed in the summer of 1942 (Kreyling *Author* 92), after the other tales that appear in *The Wide Net*, it focuses on Jenny Lockhart, an ingénue whose concealment from life (she is immured in her grandfather's house and trapped under his watchful gaze) provokes her search for knowledge and leads to her sexual exploitation and defilement. Billy Floyd, an itinerant fisherman, roughly courts Jenny and ultimately rapes and abandons her. At the narrative's denouement, Jenny searches for him, but this quest only leads to other fishermen, who take turns with her and leave her in a grounded houseboat, a potent image of scuttled domestic dreams. A story that has provoked sharp disagreements among critics,[15] "At the Landing" troubled its author, too. Welty reported to her agent, Diarmuid Russell, "The story has been something of a trouble to me and may be bad," adding "Maybe it should be thrown away" (qtd. in Kreyling *Author* 92). Russell read the manuscript, ignored Welty's misgivings, and wrote back saying that he thought the story good. He felt that she sustained the story's mood well, and that "with greater length a certain shadowiness might have disappeared" (qtd. in Kreyling *Author* 92). He immediately qualifies his insights, though, with a revealing coda: "However that's just a thought and the Russells in summer aren't much for thinking but for sleeping in the sun and whiling away time dreamily" (92–93). Perhaps Russell's time in the sun created the right mindset for his enthusiastic reception of the story that Welty fretted over and eventually repudiated as a failure.[16] Despite her harsh judgment, Russell's assessment of the story's consistent mood and shadowy aspects (and the dreamy conditions under which he reviewed it) emphasize the story's great strength: its refusal to starkly partition experience into opposed and competing categories.

Welty's mode of representation in "At the Landing" effortlessly synthesizes interior and exterior states, frequently fusing them into singularities through a flood of surrealist-inspired imagery, which she lets swell. The story opens at night and in the midst of a dream, Jenny's grandfather's dream predicting The Landing's flooding and Jenny's fouling by Floyd (William Wallace's savage double and Don McInnis's cognate), who appears in the old man's nightmare with a catfish that "has gone loose and free" (*Stories* 291). Through Floyd, who appears inside and outside the dream's frame, Welty presents the reverie as an extension of the setting from which the dream supposedly emerges. The grandfather, both asleep and awake, brings the dream to his granddaughter, who gently returns him to his bed. There he lies in the "moonlight, which moved and crept across him as it would a little fallen withered leaf, and he never moved or spoke any more, but lay softly, as if he were floating being carried away, drawn by the passing moon; and Jenny's heart beat on and on, sharp as birdsong in the night, under her breast, until day" (292). Opening the story with the recitation of a somnambulist introduces readers immediately to the liminal world of The Landing, a location that Vande Kieft designates the "taking-off place" (28). The imaginary description of the grandfather's sleeping and death contributes to the presentation of The Landing as a locale much like the nearby Natchez Trace, where the materially presented undergoes hallucinogenic transformation. The grandfather's body shape shifts under the strangely moving moonlight and floats—now a leaf, drawn by the moon's gravity—while Jenny's heart beats sharply, as if she has witnessed the mysterious change and anticipates the freedom his death delivers.

Welty's perfectly measured narration succeeds in advancing the action of the story while suspending its literality, her prose shuttling between abstraction and actuality to reproduce the uncanny and intensely visual experience of a dream. Her creation of surreal settings as backdrops for the characters' actions proceeds from the story's opening dream sequence. The continuing deployment of dream imagery, after the grandfather's death, creates an equivocal literary effect that makes it impossible to distinguish where—or indeed if—the dream ends. For instance, Floyd appears as a figure in the dream, heralding the flood, and as a figure beyond its frame, travelling through town:

> Under the shaggy bluff the bottomlands lay in a river of golden haze. The road dropped like a waterfall from the ridge to the town at its foot and came to a grassy end there. It was spring. One slowly moving figure that was a man with a fishing pole passed like a dreamer through the empty street and on through the trackless haze toward the river. The town was still called The Landing. The river had gone, three miles away, beyond sight and smell, beyond the dense trees. It came back only in flood, and boats ran over the houses. (*Stories* 292)

Welty depicts The Landing, here, as a ghost town without a purpose. Oddly, inhabitants still remain, despite the river's migration and the danger posed by flooding. The Mississippi has retreated to leave only a channel of "golden haze" passing under the bluff, and the road appears to be unexpectedly dropping from the ridge to the town, like a cataract. Strangely, haze creates water, and water creates tarmac in this scene. The description of the sleepy town, its environs, and its lothario, Billy Floyd, supposedly contrasts with the dreamy texture of somnambulist's narrative, but the surreal style of representation (and particularly Floyd's doubling) voids any separation. Welty's obvious conflation of dreaming and waking states broadly extends throughout the story, forming a surreal vein of images. She thus parallels Breton's abiding aim to resolve "dream and reality, which are seemingly so contradictory, into an absolute reality, a *surreality*, if one may so speak" ("Manifesto" 14).

The folding of literally presented objects into the surreal context of her fiction describes the author's predominant strategy in "At the Landing." Mary Hughes Brookhart and Suzanne Marrs develop a parallel argument in their "More Notes on River Country." Commenting on Welty's choice of location for the story, they declare that she "had not only chosen, but had also added to, altered, and omitted details from an actual place in order to create the locale of her story, a locale both credible and thematically significant" (83). This insightful collaborative essay draws a set of correspondences between The Landing, as the narrative depicts it, and Rodney's Landing, the Mississippi town upon which Welty based her descriptions. In terms of the production of setting, the article concludes that the fiction freely rearranges the geography of the actual settlement to create a "landscape at once literal and symbolic" (93). In their acknowledgment of the deftness of Welty's style, Brookhart and Marrs point toward the ideological and representational approach that this study defines as surreal.

Although Russell noted the story's "certain shadowiness" (qtd. in Kreyling *Author* 92), this quality of the prose seems to generate the consistency of mood that he praises as one of the story's strengths. Such a mood reveals itself in the meticulously maintained dreaminess that pervades the narrative. For instance, when Jenny visits her mother's grave at the "dark shelf" (*Stories* 294) of a cemetery above town, she observes: "Everywhere there, the hanging moss and the upthrust stones were in that strange graveyard shade where, by the light they give, the moss seemed made of stone, and the stone of moss." In the uncanny light of the burial plots, flora appears petrified, and hardness yields to softness, as if Jenny's viewing of The Landing acts upon the items in sight, variously mollifying or stiffening their outlines. Like the girl of "A Memory," who also fails to distinguish between her internal reality and the external scene, Jenny shows little facility for differentiating herself from the corporeal universe, and Welty presents this inability as a potential vulnerability as much as a strength. When Jenny catches sight of Floyd, vigorously displaying his aggressive masculinity, she sees him as a god who makes her tremble in awe and prepare to undress. "At last she sighed," Welty observes, "and when she took up her skirt to go, as if she were dreaming she saw Floyd coming across the pasture toward her." Jenny accepts Floyd's initial advances because she has no reason to rebuff him; her motherless upbringing has perhaps shielded her from life so completely that she lacks the cynicism that might offer protection. If Jenny dreams of an ideal union with Floyd, Welty's choice of metaphors undercuts the speculation by describing them as a fixed pair of "mocking birds" (295), and as "black butterflies" that engage one another while remaining at an unbridgeable distance (296).

Troubled by the discovery of separateness between individuals and how it alters her worldview, Jenny carries out an act of self-examination that Welty couches in fantastic language. Jenny lies in grass that whispers in her ear, evoking a country she could travel to by descending into a nearby well. "She thought she could see herself," Welty records, "fleet as a mirror-image, rising up in a breath of astonished farewell and walking to the well of old Mag. It was built so that it has steps like a stile. She saw herself walk up them, stand on top, look about, and then go into the dark passage" (*Stories* 298–99). This moment witnesses Jenny's struggle to define herself as an adult against the chaos of threatening events, and against family conventions as embodied in her grandfather, whom she imagines "will call me back" (299). Wholly unprepared to handle life's brutal exigencies, Jenny imagines herself passing over the threshold into adulthood and meeting a watery death of the kind Clytie suffers. Her suicidal fantasy, mixed with thoughts of seduction, a grim foreshadowing of her fate, shows Welty pondering dangers that can follow the modest liberation some women of her generation enjoyed. A sheltered life could offer opportunity for daring and advancement, but it could also lead to exploitation and debasement.

Billy Floyd, of course, represents Jenny's greatest threat and greatest allurement. The potency of his desire creates high suspense and momentum in the story, as it moves toward the flooding brought by the river's return. Jenny's self-examination, however, reveals only her deep vulnerability to a predator like Floyd, whose rugged independence and worldliness supplies him with great power. Standing above Jenny "with his feet planted down," he surveys The Landing "spread out under his eyes." In contrast to Floyd's commanding position, Jenny lacks perspective from which to view the town, because she cannot imagine herself removed from it. Indeed, her suicidal dream buries her beneath the ground: "Not knowing the world around, she could not know how The Landing looked set down in it" (*Stories* 302). A traveler through and beyond The Landing, Floyd observes the environment spread out before him and clearly views the natural world as available for conquering. But Jenny's shocking naiveté prevents her from making a similar assumption. She lacks the knowledge of what lays beyond The Landing, so the town forms Jenny's whole world.

The narrative's suspense builds and plateaus around the midpoint of the story, when the flood inundates The Landing and Floyd rapes Jenny. Welty presents the onset of the rains ominously, her surreal language both evoking the town's duress and anticipating Jenny's distress. Every day of the storm, the "clouds were opening like great purple flowers and pouring out their dark thunder," and "[e]ach nightfall, the storm was laid down on their houses like a burden the day had carried." Biblical in its proportions, the river's floodwater at last reaches the town, coming "like a hand and an arm" and pushing "black trees before it." Jenny and the townspeople escape to the hills, besieged by the water "whirling and bobbing the young dead animals around on its roaring breast." The ceaseless rain extinguishes lanterns, and in the dark boat whistles "began crying as faint as baby cries in that rainy dark." This densely visualized scene of crisis and mayhem shows Welty merging description and intense feeling to produce moments of hallucinogenic vividness, operating at a deeply figurative level to enact Jenny's violation. The torn clouds and the pouring recess of the purple bloom—an obviously vaginal motif—predict the ensuing scene of violation. And when the flood comes, it takes Floyd's form. His hand and his arm push obstructions aside, and he breaks upon the land. As if to solidify her presentation of Floyd and flood, Welty has Floyd rescue Jenny in his boat, where she "looked in Floyd's shining eyes and saw how they held the whole flood, as the flood held its triumph in its whirlpools, and it was a vast and unsuspected thing" (*Stories* 303). Whereas Jenny cannot prevent nature's exploitation and can only submit, Floyd seems to have mastered and overcome nature's fury.

Although some commentators read Jenny's cruel and violent experiences as initiatory and ultimately somehow validating, Welty's decision to show her continued pursuit of Floyd undercuts these assumptions. Sex with men does not validate Jenny's self-possession; it merely confirms her own sense of vulnerability and helplessness. "The dream of love" (*Stories* 305) that leads her to Floyd, and her dream of his possible rehabilitation, which "held her spellbound, with the things possible that hung in the air like clouds over the world," founder when confronted by his brutality (304). These dreams serve her terribly. In fact, recovery from the rape intensifies her desire for Floyd and deepens her paranoid misreading of events. Welty reveals the soiling of Jenny's dreams through her description of the ravaged town after the floodwaters have receded. Mud and ashes stick to Jenny's body, as she descends from the hilltop scene of the rape and into the town "turned the color of river water." The trees nearby stand "in their shame of refuse rattled like yellow pebbles," and the houses "sank below them scuffed and small" (305). The flood has penetrated the houses of The Landing, shifting them on their foundations, "like people whose skirts are pulled," while the front of the Lockhart house has "been pulled away" and the furniture moved around inside. When Jenny arrives at her house, "It stood as before, except that in the yellow and windy light it seemed to draw its galleries to itself, to return to its cave of night and trees, crouched like a child going backwards to the womb." The town's battered and wounded state clearly reflects Jenny's harrowed and near broken condition, but she cannot undo time and return to the unfettered innocence of childhood.

Welty reflects Floyd's violence through her surreal description of the town and Jenny's home. The "muddy fingers" that seem to have written on Jenny's books remind her of Floyd's. In an attempt to purge the filth, she washes sheets and curtains, removes rust from knives, and wipes the "dark river from all the prisms" (*Stories* 306), yet pain and defilement excite her to pursue Floyd again. Overtaken by the intoxicant of his sexual violence, Jenny's dreams develop masochistically, and her predilection for pain hardens into a desire for further abuses: "She herself did not know what might lie ahead, she had never seen herself. She looked outward with the sense of rightful space and time within her, which must be traversed before she could be known at all. And what she would reveal in the end was not herself, but the way of the traveler" (307). Unlike Floyd, who contains space in his eyes and moves through space unimpeded, Jenny lacks the kind of self-knowledge that would allow her to predict and counter threats to her humanity.

The story concludes with Jenny's exit from The Landing. Compelled by a desire to "gain the next wisdom" of life through finding Floyd, she remains paralyzed in the hallucinatory grip of an enslaving fantasy, which Welty depicts in surreal rhetoric, creating a dreamland through which the young girl passes. Saturated by the thick moisture of July, the town "stretched and swooned," and two boys play as if "they seemed to tease a sleeper," sounding "like adventurers in a dream." As the sun drops, the "red eyes of altheas" close, and green "lily buds" hang "glittering" and "pendulant." In the last light of day, crape myrtle trees begin to "fill with light," which they drink every day, and "gave off their white and flame in the evening that filled with the throb of cicadas" (*Stories* 310). This scene of nearly impossible verdant richness enfolds an old mimosa tree, whose phallic mass imposingly bars the ravine. It is as if Jenny's grandfather has returned from the dead to oppose her desertion, like "the ancient fern, as old as life, the tree that shrank from the touch, grotesque in its tenderness. All nearness and darkness affected it, even clouds going by, but for Jenny that left it no tree ever gave such allurement of fragrance anywhere" (310–11). The magnificent surreal imagery composing this scene conveys the power of Jenny's hallucinatory state of mind. When she passes "under the trees," she casts a look backwards at her house, a symbol of lost innocence and beauty, and observes it magically transfigured: "As if it were made of shells and pearls and treasures from the sea, the house glinted in the sunset, tinted with drops of light that seemed to fall slowly through the vaguely stirring leaves. Tenderly as seaweed the long moss swayed. The chimney branched like coral in the upper blue."

The story reaches its end, then, as it began, traveling forward in the uncertainty of a dream, as if reader and character participate in the same act of somnambulism. "Green branches" close over Jenny, together with "big leaved vines" that make "pillars," "arches," and buttresses." Welty transforms the dense July foliage into strange architectural features, creating a kind of labyrinth for Jenny to wander before she reaches a fishing camp at the Mississippi's edge: "Veil behind veil of long drying nets hung on all sides, dropping softly and blue-colored in the low wind and the place was folded in by them. All things, river, sky, fire, and air, seemed the same color, the color that is seen behind the closed eyelids, the color of day when vision and despair are the same thing" (*Stories* 311). Jenny's sighting of these wide nets, potent images of entrapment and death, which fold river, sky, fire, and air into a single colored vision of despair expresses a moment of seemingly irrevocable blindness. Like her grandfather, whose somnambulism opens the story, Jenny walks in her sleep. Alive to the fishermen who abuse her, she appears dead and perhaps under the sway of a self-destructive dream. An "old bright-eyed woman" wonders: "Is she asleep? Is she in a spell? Or is she dead?" (312). While the old woman identifies these three conditions as mutually exclusive, "At the Landing" demonstrates their undeniable synchronicity.

The synthesizing of what appear oppositional categories of experience—such as the supposed gap between the past and present or waking and sleeping states—goes to the heart of surrealism's aims. Published in 1943, *The Wide Net* responded to surrealism's international call for artistic revolution, and Welty's opening sentence in the collection appears to sum up the zeitgeist: "Whatever happened, it happened in extraordinary times, in a season of dreams, and in Natchez it was the bitterest winter of them all" (*Stories* 185). Indeed, the late thirties and forties in the United States did represent the "season of dreams"—particularly in New York City, where a large assortment of surrealist innovators, including Breton and Dalí, found themselves exiled at the outbreak of war in Europe.[17] While obviously not a direct participant in the movement, Welty wrote letters to her agent at this time that show her engaged in a struggle to define an effective technique for synthesizing dreaming and waking realities. The initial draft of "First Love," the narrative that begins *The Wide Net*, perplexed both Welty and Russell, but the author felt it a good story. At the time, Russell himself had started work on an essay contemplating a "series of dreams" he had experienced and their relation to "exterior discipline and observation" (qtd. in Kreyling *Author* 57). Taking Russell's essay together with "First Love," Kreyling remarks that both writers, "writing about interior and exterior intelligences," reached a point of coincidence and that Russell "had mapped the creative terrain Welty was actually exploring in her new stories" (59).

Nonetheless, doubt over "First Love" persisted. In her letters, Welty enthuses over the story's technical strategy, which she suggests resolves interior and exterior juxtapositions. For example, she refers to the story's "extreme winter" setting and its "visual worth as a horizon & perspective" to reveal "inner intensity." Moreover, she claims this combining may cause problems with the fiction, because "everything (for me) carried the burden of being so many things at once." Rather enigmatically, she states that the story may succeed because "every word that is put down will be carrying along with it all these things that are floating around it" (qtd. in Kreyling *Author* 58). Despite the heavily abstracted and sometimes elliptical line of reasoning here, Welty seems to describe her technique as one that attempts to bring interior and exterior states into coincidence through language that does more than simply itemize objects perceived. The rhetoric of "First Love" shows this freighting of language or modified itemizing in action when the prose carries the wonder of the dream simultaneously along with the description of everyday scenes. Her approach in writing—which

Russell defined as "tightrope walking" (60)—closely parallels a Dalí's method in painting, both artists demanding a technique capable of resolving the contradictions of perception.

The opening descriptions of the Natchez Trace in "First Love" perform this surreal disarming through the presentation of setting, which at every moment seems concretely realistic but equally dreamlike. In this context, one cannot help but ask if the story's title reflects Welty's own seduction by art permeated by the force of fantasy:

> Whatever happened, it happened in extraordinary times, in a season of dreams, and in Natchez it was the bitterest winter of them all. The north wind struck one January night in 1807 with an insistent penetration, as if it followed the settlers down by their own course, screaming down the river bends to drive them further still. Afterwards there was the strange drugged fall of snow. When the sun rose the air broke into a thousand prisms as close as the flash-and-turn of gulls' wings. For a long time afterwards it was so clear that in the evening the little companion-star to Sirius could be seen plainly in the heavens by travelers who took their way by night, and Venus shone in the daytime in all its course through the new transparency of the sky. (*Stories* 185)

This astonishing paragraph opens *The Wide Net* and introduces readers to the heavily textured, surreal language that characterizes the entire collection. The softness and unpredictability of dreams attends each sentence in this largely visual description of Natchez in 1807. The prose has a smooth and even pace that belies the complexity operating below sentence level. The wind strikes, penetrates, and follows the besieged settlers, whom the rushing blast of air drives onwards under the force of its howling scream. The hypnotic snowfall, however, deadens the wind's piercing cry and confers tranquility on the scene. Against this calmer backdrop, the rising sun fragments space into a "thousand prisms," which glitter and turn, now prisms and then "gulls' wings." Subsequent paragraphs extend Welty's tightrope walking, such as when she records how the Mississippi lifts from its bed like a "somnambulist driven to go new places." Both river and dreamer, the Mississippi directs readers to "new places" and new knowledge derived from the blending of material and immaterial realities.

The writing demands its reader balance, along with Welty, on the tightrope between dreaming and waking states, imagining flatboats and rafts travelling downriver with "unsignalling passengers submissive and huddled, mere bundles of sticks," while "In the fastness of Natchez it began to seem then that the whole world, like itself, must be in a transfiguration" (*Stories* 185). In these examples particularly, Welty seems to contend that her language—like the depicted city itself—retains fastness in its presentation of material reality, while yielding that solidity to the transfiguring power of the sight. Thus, she infuses apparently externally perceived vistas with the hallucinogenic properties of dreams. "Bands of travelers moved closer together," she writes, "with intenser cautions, through the glassy tunnels of the Trace, for all proportion went away, and they followed one another like insects going at dawn through the heavy grass" (185–86). In Dalínian fashion—especially with regard to her use of anthropomorphized insects—Welty figures the Trace doubly as both paths and "glassy tunnels," and the settlers as travelers and "insects" picking through "heavy grass."

Such an introduction to a collection of short stories demolishes any expectation that the following narratives will draw a hard line of distinction between interior and exterior realities. Joel Mayes, the young deaf and dumb orphan—and the focal point of "First Love"—is another of Welty's innocents who possess great imaginative vitality. After his parents were lost in an Indian raid as their caravan traversed the "wild teeth" of the Trace, Joel works as a boot boy at a Natchez inn (*Stories* 187). Here, he observes the outlaw Aaron Burr, whom the federal government has charged with treason, negotiate with his collaborator, Harmon Blennerhassett. Haunted by the terror of the Trace, Joel represses the painful memory of his abandonment until the story's conclusion, when he collapses and weeps for his family after Burr departs. Welty seems to delay this moment in order to focus attention on Burr, who represents a distant father figure for the orphan. This charismatic man fascinates Joel, whose distressing memories combine with Burr's activities in Natchez. In fact, the surreality of Welty's presentation undermines any moment of certainty, leaving the whole experience equivocal.

Writing to Diarmuid Russell in July 1941, Welty said she longed to return home to "my dreamlike life in Mississippi where things are long ago or far ahead but never now" (qtd. in Kreyling *Author* 78). She had completed a revision of "First Love" earlier that month and, now, stuck in Saratoga, New York, she wanted home comforts. Her comment on her Mississippi mindset, which conjures dreams of the past or dreams of the future, points up the type of narrative technique identifiable in "First Love." She develops the "now" of the opening passages from a perspective gained over time. Historical facts, such as the migrating settlers and the cruel weather, acquire a unique tonality in Welty's delivery of them, but this production of fiction from historical facts reveals itself also in Joel's point of view, a perspective as charged and divided as the narrator's.[18] His tragic personal history freely mingles with the events contemporaneous to him, a surreal doubling of perception emblematized in a candle, the holder of which he keeps "carefully polished" and placed centrally on the table. Joel's totem possession looks forward to the nightlight that Welty introduces in *Delta Wedding* and develops into a symbol of her narrative technique in "Place in Fiction." Like the glowing china ornament, the candle reveals a dual reality when lit: Otherwise concealed by the light of day, Spanish "messages of love" stand out in "black relief" when the candle shines at night, whose obscurity and darkness Welty associates with Joel, the young boy (*Stories* 188). (A further and perhaps more tenuous elaboration of this symbol might suggest the presence of a certain Spanish surrealist, another devotee of the double image—but such a claim some may understandably deem altogether too fanciful.)

A child on the cusp of adolescence, Joel has not created a bulwark to isolate his conscious from his unconscious mind and to objectify what he sees in the world. Early in the narrative, Welty suggests the permeability of his mind and its openness to the irrational world of the dream, writing: "It might seem to him that the whole world was sleeping in the lightest of trances, which the least movement would surely wake; but he only walked softly, stepping around and over, and got back to his room" (*Stories* 188–89). Working as a boot boy, he toils at night, collecting boots from "sleeping men" who, on more than one occasion, have taken hold of and shaken Joel when they awake in a "sweat of suspicion or nightmare." Although nimble "as an animal," and so well equipped to evade the "frenzy" of these men's dreams, he cannot give his own nighttime imaginings the slip (188). They come to him vividly and in the form of two collaborators.

Joel seems remarkably unprepared to defend against the intrusions of Burr and Blennerhassett. Asleep, with his defenses lowered, he dreams the men who confront him in the room, which appears shining "like a brimming lake in the sun." These strangers to Natchez suddenly emerge sitting before him in the "strange multiplied light." He had "never been able to hear" their knocking at the door, and mysteriously "at some moment outside his knowledge or consent two men had seemingly fallen from the clouds and onto the two stools at his table." Feeling violated, Joel, like the young girl affronted by her dream in "A Memory," voyeuristically observes this scene "with the feasting the eyes do in secret" (*Stories* 189). He recognizes the men's activity as a "panorama in his own head," and as a second interior to the interior of the room. The dream's distortion affects Joel's vision of the men's hair, which seems strangely "light and floating" against the fire's flames. When he awakes at daylight, the men have vanished, but he immediately associates the "vision" with the mysterious Indians haunting the Trace and with ghosts. Nighttime apparitions and daytime memories merge for Joel, who contemplates the totality of his experience like a "deepening dream" (190).

The reverie-like atmosphere of the opening paragraphs and Joel's dreams makes dividing fact from fiction a practical impossibility. Surely, Joel does actually observe Burr and Blennerhassett in the flesh in Natchez, but Welty's prose creates ambiguity about what he views and what he imagines or dreams. The following extract shows just the kind of equivocation that characterizes the nightlight and the candle:

> There was an hour when the river was the color of smoke, as if it were more a thing of the woods than an element and a power in itself. It seemed to belong to the woods, to be gentle and watched over, a tethered and grazing pet of the forest, and then when the light spread higher and color stained the world, the river would leap suddenly out of the shining ice around, into its full-grown torrent of life, and its strength and its churning passage held Joel watching over it like a spell unfolding by night in his room. (*Stories* 193–94)

Again, Welty's stringently visual mode impresses the scene deeply and spectacularly on the mind's eye, yet subtle as well as more obvious textual details accrete to modify and ultimately to transfigure the vista completely. She shifts the smoky river out of its channel when she associates it with the woods that domesticate the Mississippi like a pet. Then, as the light alters with altitude, the river jumps beyond its icy apron and washes away in a torrent. The captivating spectacle mesmerizes Joel, who watches as if under a spell, because it reminds him of his room at night, another site of transfiguration. However, neither the stunning transformations of the river nor the equally marvelous nightly scenes furnish Joel with certain answers.

In Joel's last dream, though, Blennerhassett's wife joins the group to lead her husband home, and her emergence triggers for Joel a scene of *his* home—interior even to the dream—which in turn precipitates his delayed mourning for his parents. Blennerhassett's wife appears suddenly, and without speaking, husband and wife "stand looking at each other there in the firelight like creatures balancing together on a raft." She begins to play a fiddle that "she had simply picked up in the Inn parlor as she came through." Joel intently watches her "insect-like motions, the pensive antennae of her arms, her mask of a countenance," noticing that she never blinks, and that the curious slits of her eyes "were milky." Again, surreal insect imagery emerges, and the strange songs that she plays neither begin nor end, instead telling of another country, which Joel identifies with Virginia, his lost homeland and a "sight that he had nearly forgotten." In the context of the recollected sight, the fire in the room bizarrely reveals a "mimosa tree in flower," a tree Welty describes as "cloud-like," adding "[a]mong the trembling leaves the feathery puffs of sweet bloom filled the tree like thousands of paradisical birds all alighted at an instant" (*Stories* 197). The blooming tree gives off perfume and an illuminating radiance that lights the garden all around like the fairytale royal, Princess Labam, who lit her city from the roof at night. Joel's mother directs his gaze to the tree's upper reaches, where its fragrance sways "like the Asiatic princess moving up and down the pink steps of its branches" (198). This vision, which ministers to Joel's wounded psyche, soon dissipates, but he has gained new insight into his predicament and a reprieve from the memories that distress him. At the story's end, the western frontier beckons, and he follows the Liberty Road into its depths: "He did not see how he could ever go back and still be the boot-boy at the Inn" (203). Once a hazardous track designating danger and loss, the path into the wilderness now restores strength to Joel, who walks into his future on a surer footing.

The narrative tactic in "The Winds" recalls Welty's strategy in "First Love." In the latter story, her letters show, she intended the bitterness of the winter weather to form an illuminating context for the warm interior of Joel's room. And in *One Writer's Beginnings*, Welty advances a parallel argument for "The Winds," as her letters to Russell had for "First Love." Meditating on her father's caution and her mother's boldness in times of bad weather, she makes the following statement about "The Winds": "So I developed a strong meteorological sensibility. In years ahead when I wrote stories, atmosphere took its influential role from the start. Commotion in the weather and the inner feelings aroused by such a hovering disturbance emerged connected in dramatic form" (840). In the same way that the "commotion" of the Madrid earthquake and the bitingly cold winter setting foreshadow Joel's internal disturbances, the violent autumnal storm shaking the home in "The Winds" underscores the momentous changes affecting Josie, the pubescent girl upon whom the story focuses. In the dead of night, a storm bursts thunderously on the family home. Fearing for Josie's and her brother Will's safety, their parents evacuate them from the "sleeping porch" to ride out the storm in the calmer interior of the house (*Stories* 252). However, at a metaphorical level, "The Winds" emphasizes the futility of this protective act. The parents—but especially Josie's father, who seems most perturbed about the weather—cannot slow their daughter's development into a woman, any more then they can halt the storm that brings the winds of change blowing through this household.

The story's beginning, like the opening of "First Love" and "At the Landing," firmly locates experience at the uncertain juncture of dream and waking realities. Once again, Welty's language imposes a somnambulistic order on perception, prose that reveals the destabilizing pressure of a dream behind every supposedly concrete assertion. "When Josie first woke up in the night," Welty avers, "she thought the big girls of the town were having a hay-ride." Torn between the compelling sight of the hay-ride, which "she could see in her mind" going down the "Old Natchez Trace," and the sound and feel of her father's repudiating presence as he lifts her from her bed, Josie yields to the dream's allure, choosing the scratchy but soft nighttime ride reserved for the big girls. Close to dissipation, the dream's chorus of crying voices emits a siren's beseeching song, and Josie, who imagines the Trace—sometimes called "Lover's Lane"—situated at the "edge of town, an old dark place where the young people went" (*Stories* 252). A mysterious locale where "girls meet boys, confront love, and begin to deal emotionally with the physical change that Hazel confronted in 'The Wide Net'" (Kreyling *Eudora Welty* 25), the Trace's shadowy terrain, charged with the erotic energy, commands Josie's attention

The narrative that unfolds relates a series of memories and dreamy reminiscences that the story fashions into a contiguous whole, a body of knowledge for Josie to mine in order to answer the questions posed by her dilemma: how to manage the transition from girlhood to womanhood. The crashing storm, the voices of her parents speaking, and her brother talking in his sleep constitute the story's frame, but its edges fail to contain Josie's dreamt interior. In stories such as "Asphodel" and "The Purple Hat," narratives that Welty groups consecutively with "The Winds" in the middle of *The Wide Net*, the author demonstrates the permeability of boundaries between past and present events. Josie's father may remove his daughter bodily from the "sleeping porch" (*Stories* 252), but her mind remains thoroughly entranced by summer's adventures, which spill out into the fall. Both a victim of the storm and its creator, Josie occupies a surreal position, a location underlined by Welty's dispersal of dreamy similes bridging the chasm between past and present. Peter Schmidt points to this meeting of dreaming and waking realities as the story's foremost characteristic, remarking that the "texture of the story mixes the fantasia of Josie's dream-world with her waking perception of the comforting presence of her parents and the world she knows by daylight" (145). As Schmidt intimates, Welty's technique collapses the distinction between objects and events internally and externally perceived. For Josie, life merges with dream when she "seemed to have dreamed the sounds of all the windows closing, upstairs and down," and when she imagines being in "Lover's Lane" (*Stories* 252) on descending the stairs, where the steps "gave like a chain" and the clock's pendulum bizarrely shivers in its case.

In the living room, her sheet music has curiously "caved in" and "gleamed faintly like a shell in the shimmer and flow of the strange light" that illuminates the family, who wander "separately for a moment looking like strangers at the wicker chairs." Moreover, the scene reveals "cretonne pillows" transformed into "wet stones," near still curtains—which appear spectacularly metamorphosed into "poured cream" drapes—and seemingly crystalline flower petals that "shattered all at once from a bowl of roses" (*Stories* 253). The uncanny atmosphere and Dalínian rendering of the house's rigid but mollified interior clearly reflects the distortions and absurd juxtapositions of a dream. This point is acknowledged by Kreyling, who notes with regard to the "poured cream" curtains, "An author with such an informed knowledge of modern painting as Welty knew that her simile was Dali-esque, and directed the story's shifting register from to reality to dream by choosing it" ("History and Imagination" 595). The storm rattles the house "as if a big drum were being beaten down the street" (*Stories* 254), and "with the pulse of the lightning the wide front window was oftener light than dark, and the persistence of illumination seemed slowly to be waking something that slept longer than Josie had slept, for her trembling body turned under her mother's hand." Neither nighttime nor daytime, the conditions announce the awakening of Josie's sleeping desire. Subject to the overpowering force of the dream, the house "moved softly like a boat that has been stepped into" (255), taking young girl and reader into the past.

Periodically interrupted by outside commotion, Josie's dream contrasts a girl's sundry recollections of "lullabies, stories, playing songs, the chant of a man selling dairy products and vegetables from a cart, scraps of conversations with girlfriends, and her own private prayers to a fairytale queen and the moon and the tides" (Schmidt 145–46) with other less innocent thoughts centered on Cornella, who is "nearly grown," "transformed by age," and a "forbidden playmate" (*Stories* 257). This friend, who belongs to the rowdy family occupying the "double-house" over the street (254), recalls the alluring danger of the boy at school who fascinates the young girl in "A Memory." From Josie's point of view, Cornella and the anonymous boy promise the release of desire, but in both stories this freedom exacts a cost, the guilt associated with girls of upper-middle class backgrounds acknowledging their sexuality. In a story that pays homage to the American surrealist Joseph Cornell, Welty reveals her debt to the elder and perhaps more accomplished artist—as if "The Winds" enacts her assumption of Josie's position, while Cornell adopts Cornella's role. Whether the promise involves fulfillment bodily or artistically, some degree of consorting with forbidden playmates appears necessary. For a woman of Welty's somewhat genteel upbringing, that familiarity with Bohemia required daring indeed, the kind of strength that Josie shows. Josie's dream's interlacing of childhood play with the desire maturity brings permits Welty to illustrate her belief in the profound interrelatedness of memory and the present moment. In contrast to Josie's mother, who proclaims that "Summer is over" (254), Josie's reveries demonstrate summer's continuous and persisting influence.

In Suzanne Marrs's enlightening analysis of "The Winds," she places the story in the context of Welty's comments about the significance of daring internal adventures, which close *One Writer's Beginnings*. Quoting the memoir's last lines, Marrs notes the insights and the knowledge derived from memory when viewed through the lens of present circumstance. She claims that Welty, thirty-two years old when she wrote "The Winds," reflected upon her girlhood in the story and "certainly recognized the meaning implicit in her youthful experience and would live out its promise" (*One Writer's* 70). Marrs's assessment also seems to acknowledge the key statement that Welty makes in her autobiography about the concept of "*confluence*" (947), a term

One Writer's Beginnings builds toward and carefully reserves for use in the book's final pages. For Welty, the "greatest confluence of all is that which makes up the human memory" and "is the treasure most dearly regarded by me, in my life and in my work as a writer." Further, the determining force of confluence bends time, imparting life to otherwise dead recollections: "The memory is a living thing—it too is in transit. But during its moments, all that is remembered joins, and lives—the old and the young, the past and the present, the living and the dead" (948). In one way or another, all the stories of *The Wide Net* reach for the elaboration of confluence as Welty defines it. The meandering track of the Trace itself, winding through the nine narratives, serves as a motif for streaming these stories into the whole that forms the collection, a concept of unity defined with remarkable similarity by André Breton in his 1930 "Second manifesto of Surrealism":

> Everything tends to make us believe that there exists a certain point of the mind at which life and death, the real and the imagined, past and future, the communicable and the incommunicable, high and low, cease to be perceived as contradictions. Now, search as one may one will never find any other motivating force in the activities of the Surrealists than the hope of finding and fixing this point.(123–24)

For two writers who never met and almost certainly never read each other, the arresting theoretical coincidence evinced by these central formulations of their perspectives illustrates Breton's and Welty's shared set of philosophical values. The series of supposedly oppositional dualisms—old and young, past and present, living and dead, real and imagined, communicable and incommunicable, high and low—that both writers advance as bogus dichotomies dissolves when envisioned through a surrealist's lens. The stories in *The Wide Net* clearly share Breton's central aspiration for his movement to find and fix the point at which these dualisms disintegrate. In "The Winds," for instance, Josie's retrospective dreaming creates the conditions for the advancement of knowledge. The understanding gained at the story's close derives from her submission of the present to the authority of the past, to the thing "that slept longer than Josie had slept" (*Stories* 255). Welty shows her surrealist credentials most obviously in stories such as "The Winds," which fix points of intersection between ostensibly antithetical categories of experience.

The final discovery completing Josie's transformation in the story re-lates to her reminiscence about a family visit to the "Chautauqua tent," where an enchanting horn player captivates the young girl and presents her with a challenge. Perhaps remembered—but certainly presented as a kind of dream—the music heard in the tent begins "sparse and spare, like a worn hedge through which the hiders can be seen." One of the hiders, a beautiful cornetist who obviously suggests Cornella, soon moves forward, overwhelming Josie with her sound: "If morning-glories had come out of the horn instead of those sounds," Welty dreamily records, "Josie would not have felt a more astonished delight." This woman artist, another playful allusion to Joseph Cornell, assumes an enigmatic presence in the oddly lit tent, illuminated by a "flame-like glare that was somehow shadowy." She seems to have "come from far away" and, wreathed in white and blue folds of fabric, she looks "like a Queen" (or perhaps from Queens where Cornell lived) and stands "braced and looking upward like a figurehead on a Viking ship," while her "closed eyelids" appear "to whir" and "rest motionless, like the wings of a humming-bird, when she reached the high note." Her par-ents at a distance and distracted, Josie shares this deeply affecting moment of exhilaration with Cornella, who also sits enrapt, "not far away, with her face all wild" (*Stories* 265).[19] The dream reconstructs the waking event, yet records that Josie returns from the performance "tired, in a dream," so Welty presents one dream reproduced in another, further conflating wak-ing and dreaming states. Looking out over the town from a high porch, Josie sees only blackness, "except where beyond the farthest rim of trees the old cottonseed mill with its fiery smokestack and its lights forever seemed an inland boat that waited for the return of the sea" (266). Josie, too, waits for the sea's return, so she can bravely ride out on its swells like the Valkyrie, who boldly breasts the waves affixed to the Viking ship's bow.[20]

"Livvie" also adopts the theme of metamorphosis, girls transforming into women, and exposes the delights and dangers Welty associates with this "initiation story" (Manning "Hurston" 70). The eponymous protago-nist at sixteen marries Solomon, a man as old as his biblical namesake. However, he lacks the wisdom to acknowledge his marital oversight fully, and eventually—notwithstanding his fervent attempts to inoculate his young wife against temptation, including the attentions of younger men—Cash McCord, a field hand who "belonged to Solomon" (*Stories* 286) and is possibly a thief, almost makes the patriarch a cuckold. McCord seduces

Livvie, becoming the center of the young wife's dreams of escape, independence, glamour, and money. Like Jenny's grandfather, whose dreaming
creates the narrative context for "At the Landing," Solomon's moribund and
sleepy presence contributes greatly to the soporific atmosphere the story
establishes from its opening lines: "Solomon carried Livvie twenty-one
miles away from her home when he married her. He carried her away up
on the Old Natchez Trace into the deep country to live in his house" (276).
For nine years, Livvie assumes the surreal role of black plantation mistress
to black plantation owner, a servile and obedient adjunct and part of her
husband's dream, which he has spent his life acquiring. Ultimately, however,
Welty suggests that this dream may victimize and dispossess its creator,
who now lies dying, observed by Livvie and Cash:

> [T]hey could hear how, wrapped in his quilt, he sighed to himself com-
> fortably in his sleep, while in his dreams he might have been an ant, a bee-
> tle, a bird, an Egyptian, assembling and carrying on his back and building
> with his hands, or he might have been an old man of India or a swaddled
> baby, about to smile and brush all away. (288)

Although Livvie laments as much as she spurns Solomon and the symbols
of ownership and slavery that animate his reverie, the story's primary focus
rests with her and how at twenty five her emerging dreams begin to challenge and then displace her husband's.

Thoughts of disease and death contrast with vitality and life to impose
an insurmountable barrier between husband and wife, a set of distinctions
couched in language that has surrealistic overtones. For instance, Livvie
sees no way to connect with her spouse, admitting that "people never could
be sure of anything as long as one of them was asleep and the other awake"
(*Stories* 281). Evidently, Solomon's dream nears the long sleep of death,
while hers has not yet fully materialized, a tension Welty underlines when
she describes Livvie watching her husband sleep: "[S]he stood fanning the
flies away, and the light came in, his face was like new, so smooth and clear
that it was like a glass of jelly held to the window, and she could almost
look through his forehead and see what he thought." Here, she watches
as if she attended a corpse beset by flies, but the sense of her illumination
(perhaps a kind of mild epiphany) paired with Solomon's trivialization
and ridicule (his head is absurdly transformed into a jelly glass), probably

disarms most. The surreal style evident in the simile initiates a further series of transformations, as Livvie submits to the momentum of her growing
independence. Feeling the "stir of spring close to her," she looks from her
gilded cage out onto fields that Welty presents as a hypnotic and hallucinatory vision, half seen and half dreamt, "as if she dozed neglectfully in the
shade" (280). Women, men, and children fill the fecund scene in the fields,
a tempting carnival of increase and life at odds with Solomon's kingdom,
which is soon to pass into history, as foreshadowed by the burning sky:
"High above everything, the wheel of fields, house, and cabins, and the deep
road surrounding like a moat to keep them in, was the turning sky, blue
with long, far-flung white mare's-tail clouds, serene and still as high flames"
(281). The patriarch has done just about all humanly possible to monopo-
lize everyone's right to dream, but still, at his dream's edge, the "deep road"
of the Trace winds on.

Should it come as news that the right to dream symbolized by the Trace
extends only to the likes of Solomon, not Livvie? As his power wanes, she
ventures beyond the house's confines, "stealing away down the still, deep
Trace," and feeling "as if she waded a river when she went" (*Stories* 278).
Ultimately, she meets Cash on this highway of imagination—but only after
a visit from another traveler plying this route. Miss Baby Marie is a woman
whose cosmetics announce the arrival of modern femininity—even in a
place as remote as Solomon's farm, itself a metaphor for the South, bound-
ed by custom and safely sequestered from the modernity transforming
the rest of the nation. Despite the plantation's obvious isolation, Madame
Rubinstein and Miss Arden arrive on Livvie's doorstep in the guise of the
inimitable Baby Marie, and they brook no denial, countering the received
knowledge that "coloured cosmetics, particularly eye make-up, were the
province of actresses—and whores" (Woodhead 8). The moment that Livvie
accepts the "golden lipstick" proffered by the saleswoman, a dream of sex
transports the young wife, forecasting her yielding to Cash, from whose
pocket a "guinea pig" (*Stories* 285) suggestively pokes:

> Her hand took the lipstick, and in an instant she was carried away in the
> air through the spring, and looking down with a half-drowsy smile from
> a purple cloud she saw from above a chinaberry tree, dark and smooth
> and neatly leaved, neat as a guinea hen in the dooryard, and there was her
> home that she had left. On one side of the tree was her mama holding up

her heavy apron, and she could see it was loaded with ripe figs, and on the other side was her papa holding a fishing pole over the pond, and she could see it transparently, the little clear fishes swimming up to the brim. (283)

Guinea hens and pigs, so to speak, make for the dissolution of the world Solomon built, but Baby Marie's cosmetics, with their "secret ingredients," facilitate the liaison and play their part in rewriting the rules for modern women (283). The future for an independent Livvie seems beset with risks because her husband's death has released her into a world where glamour, sexuality, fidelity, and money mix dangerously. Consorting with Cash does signal a kind of autonomy, but the story ends equivocally, leaving readers to ponder whether Livvie's beauty, enhanced by makeup, has furnished liberty or landed her a gold digger.

When Welty first read Robert M. Coates's *The Outlaw Years: The History of the Land Pirates of the Natchez Trace, 1800–1835,* a historical account of lawlessness and banditry in the old Southwest, perhaps she expected a more experimental treatment of the Trace, especially given Coates's unimpeachable avant-garde credentials. He had spent several years in Paris during the twenties, one of many American expatriates who sought cultural leadership in exile, temporary or otherwise. In the early years of the decade, Coates shared the city with Sherwood Anderson, Malcolm Cowley, Man Ray, Djuna Barnes, Ernest Hemingway, Gertrude Stein, Fernand Léger, Pablo Picasso, Juan Gris, and Constantin Brancusi (Roza 28–30), among many other modernist innovators. There his fiction changed considerably: "While certain influences can be pinpointed in his work, it appears that Coates appropriated and experimented with many incarnations of modernism at once. He combined in pastiche fashion elements from symbolism, literary impressionism, expressionism, futurism, Dadaism, and surrealism" (43). On his permanent return to the United States in 1926 (66), he wrote for the *New York Times,* published "three prose sketches" in *transition* magazine, and began researching *The Outlaw Years,* which he published in 1930 (67). Marrs reports that at the instigation of Bill Hamilton, Welty and her friends read this book in 1934 as part of the "Night-Blooming Cereus Club" (*Eudora* 46), but Welty probably knew about and perhaps had even read it as early as the year that it appeared. Herschel Brickell, a Jackson native and host of "Jackson-in-New York" (28), consisting of Welty and her Columbia University comrades, glowingly reviewed the book for the *North American*

Review in the fall of 1930. Ten years later Welty would recommend Coates's study to her agent, Diarmuid Russell (66), and borrow from it for both *The Robber Bridegroom* and *The Wide Net*, testifying to the enduring influence that the characters and land had on her mind. More history than novel, *The Outlaw Years* appears to have left a gap that Welty's Natchez Trace stories occupied, appropriating the geography and history of the region as Coates conveyed them, but revising the presentation of the Trace in the context of surrealism, the avant-garde's most recent and final manifestation.

4

HYPNOTIZED LIKE SWAMP BUTTERFLIES IN *DELTA WEDDING*

Virginia Woolf's spirit permeates almost every page of *Delta Wedding*. Laboring to transform a long short story, "Delta Cousins," into her first full-length novel,[1] Welty drew technical and thematic inspiration from Woolf—particularly from *To the Lighthouse*, a novel Welty claimed "opened the door" and so astonished her when she first read it that she "couldn't sleep or eat" (Kuehl 75). Welty deeply venerated Woolf, a passion that John Crowe Ransom detected in his review of *Delta Wedding*, where he claimed that Welty "resembles Virginia Woolf more than does any other novelist of my acquaintance" (504). This assessment was later echoed by Ruth M. Vande Kieft in her inaugural book-length study of Welty (76). However, these passing remarks were not thoroughly elaborated until the nineteen-eighties and nineties, when Louise Westling's *Sacred Groves and Ravaged Gardens*, Michael Kreyling's *Author and Agent*, and Suzan Harrison's *Eudora Welty and Virginia Woolf* together developed a forceful case for *Delta Wedding*'s debt to the Bloomsbury writer. Westling's and Harrison's analyses supply cogent examinations premised on correspondences between plots, characters, themes, genres, and styles that demonstrate a clear line of influence, but neither commentator explicitly addresses Welty and Woolf's deployment of visually charged language, the primary means by which Welty creates and sustains her surreal literary effects.

Of the analyses cited, only Kreyling's includes a discussion of Welty's and Woolf's use of visual language. He advances the claim for inheritance by observing that Welty revised "Delta Cousins" into *Delta Wedding* in the context of her "rereading of Woolf in the Spring of 1944" (*Author* 108). Employed by the *New York Times Review of Books* in the summer of that year, Welty reviewed Woolf's posthumous publication, *A Haunted House and Other Stories*, noting what Kreyling defines as the "primarily visual" quality of Woolf's prose. Indeed, the review, entitled "Mirrors for Reality," teems with comparisons of writing and painting, anticipating Welty's statements documenting her own artistic philosophy in "Writing and Analyzing a Story" and "Place in Fiction." According to the review, Woolf's stories act like "spider webs" that collect "living morsels in the form of palpitating moments of time" to reveal "instantaneous perceptions" and "brief visions." Her prose transforms "[t]he scent, the gesture, the breath on the lips, the sound of the hour striking in the clock, the rippling texture of the surface in the moving air" into the "colored reflections of the abstract world of the spirit, the matter that mirrored the reality." Moreover, Welty concentrates on Woolf's technical decision to represent "palpitating life" through the device of the remove, formalizing materiality indirectly, as if "seen in a mirror." Welty cautions, "perhaps this treatment is given to a view of life which may well be too intense for us not to watch it through a remove of some kind." Woolf's frame, then, shows its subject remotely represented, with a level of obliquity that "gives its own dimensions to objects in view, and elongation, foreshortening, superimposition are all instruments of the complicated vision which wants to look at truth" (26). This focus upon obliquity—or the strategy of the remove—leads to Welty's consideration of Woolf's work in the context of impressionism: "And in the delineation of character and in detail she makes one think of painting. We are likely to see profile and full face and reflection and dream-image simultaneously" (27). Having zeroed in on one of the stories in the collection for closer consideration, she concludes by supplying a pellucid examination that anatomizes Woolf's sighting of her subject and the subjectivity of sight:

Here, like a technique of a technique, is the writer writing before her own eyes. Here are her word-pictures and word-sketches, mounting as if of themselves, in lists, parentheses, impatient naming of brief participants, all spaces filling with trees, colors, streets, furniture, seasons, objects on a table; choices of deed and character made, as they arise, before the eye; the helpless and magical building up and developing of a moment or scene along the way and its dissolving and ironical elimination which progress with the journey. A world complete with all its people and its objects the writer draws up about the twitching Minnie, as if compelled, desiring to see in this way a glimpse of her soul—only to watch all go to pieces as Minnie herself gets off the train and is, surprisingly, met. This relationship

made on a journey of unspecified purposes, in a moving vehicle with pan-
oramas flying and fading without, the changing and merging features of
persons, landscapes, character, color, motion in place and time, hope and
despair, seems to seek at the very source the attraction and the repulsion
in each moment of being. (28–29)

Welty's assessment, and the wide range of metaphors linking language
to the visual arts, impress on her readers the elder writer's debt to avant-
garde painting—particularly the post-impressionist cadre promoted by the
critic and impresario, Roger Fry, and Woolf's brother-in-law, Clive Bell, in
their landmark post-impressionist exhibitions in London.[2] Initially skepti-
cal of relations between the sister arts, Woolf's hard line softened by 1925,
when she publicly "reversed her opinion" (Reid 282) in an article entitled
"Pictures": "Now when she spoke of the 'dominion' of painting over literature, she meant that modern painting had shown writers how to transcend
appearances in order to present other, more essential realities" (282–83).
Matisse, Cézanne, Derain, and Picasso formed Woolf's touchstones in
her reassessment of relations between language and art, and in her latest
book, *Mrs. Dalloway*, "Virginia herself had written a painterly novel that
successfully captured—through the marriage of realistic referentiality and
formalist purity—the language of thought and the images of feeling, the
vision that she had sought for so long." Woolf's preoccupation with painting fundamentally shaped *To the Lighthouse*, her next novel and a "more
overtly painterly" (283) book that sent Welty into exaltation when she first
read it in 1930 (Kuehl *Conversations* 75).[3] Woolf, then, fully opened the door
to the house of fiction, but once inside the student quickly abandoned her
teacher's post-impressionist influences. Born a generation later than Woolf,
Welty inherited her icon's conviction that modern painting had taught
modern literature, but she rejected Woolf's selection of artists. If Woolf
wrote two of her major novels under the influence of post-impressionist
painting and Fry's aesthetic theories, Welty produced her first novel under
the sway of surrealism, which had by the late twenties begun to influence
visual media.

From its opening lines, *Delta Wedding* subverts the conventions of realistic representation through the importation of surrealist ideas and effects
drawn from the visual arts. The novel's presentation of life at Shellmound
reveals its surreality by upending a Newtonian worldview precisely in
those moments when language deforms time and space. Episodes reflect

the key metaphor of the china nightlight—a symbol of order and disorder co-mingling—that appears for the first time in this novel before it returns in "Place in Fiction." Further, the book expresses Welty's intention to underline subjectivity's role in human apprehension, such that objects framed by a viewer's gaze concede to the ordering power of the viewer's personality. In a 1930 essay, "The Rotting Donkey," which then appeared only in French, refined the ideas developed more elaborately in *The Conquest of the Irrational*. Dalí posits an artistic strategy strikingly parallel to Welty's, attempting to "systematize confusion and thereby contribute to a total discrediting of the world of reality." His paranoiac critical method empowers the artist to simulate delirium's trance in order to create hallucinogenic work that, like Welty's, combines abstracted forms with representational elements. For Dalí, "Paranoia makes use of the external world in order to set off its obsessive idea, with the disturbing characteristic of verifying the reality of this idea for others." He adds, "The reality of the external world serves as an illustration and proof, and is placed thus at the service of the reality of our mind" (223). Dalí's insistence upon integrating internal obsession and external reality into surreal visions neatly coincides with Welty's aims as a writer of fiction in *Delta Wedding*. The novel's opening pages show this tactic at work.

Delta Wedding's earliest moments transform traditional notions of time and space by introducing readers to the surreal perspective supplied by Laura McRaven, the nine-year-old girl who travels to the Mississippi Delta for the wedding of her cousin, Dabney Fairchild.[4] The choice of a young girl to frame the opening narration carries over from Welty's decision in *The Wide Net* to use childlike innocence as a strategy for undoing received ideas about the stability of time and the uniformity of space. When Welty claims that she devised the character of Laura, among other outsiders, as an observer who enters the "story on the train and everything was revealed to her," she foregrounds the revolutionary discovery of knowledge available to young, initiated minds (Yates 89). The description at the novel's beginning of Laura approaching the Delta shows a certain formality and builds a plausible world of surface appearances. Like Woolf's, Welty's prose sets detail alongside detail and object next to object in order to create a sense of verisimilitude through its provision of circumstantial facts and everyday observations. For example, the train, nicknamed the "Yellow Dog," carries the young girl to Shellmound on the "10th of September, 1923—afternoon." Her father has put her on the train at Yazoo City. She travels for a wedding, but her mother, a member of the Fairchild family of Shellmound, has recently died. Wind blows through open carriage windows, as do butterflies that race by outside. Mr. Terry Black, the conductor, looks out for Laura on her journey, moving through the cabin that itself moves through the Mississippi countryside from which the "long September cry rang from the thousand unseen locusts." A dog emerges to run beneath Laura's window (91). That Laura travels by rail should perhaps alert those mindful of Einstein's thought experiments involving trains to Welty's underlying suggestion: Objects viewed in time and space assume identities relative to the point of observation. "No physical law is entirely reliable," because the "observer's position will always affect the result" and make it "relative and contingent" (Childs 66). The early allusion to Einstein's theories of relativity paves the way for a narrative that makes a stylistic virtue out of erecting and then collapsing the solidity of its Delta world.

Laura's first experience of the Delta landscape shatters the brittle assemblage of facts, dates, and observations catalogued above that shape the novel's beginning: "And then, as if a hand reached along the green ridge and all of a sudden pulled down with a sweep, like a scoop in the bin, the hill and every tree in the world and left cotton fields, the Delta began." Welty's signature sentence highlights the vulnerability of the descriptions to language shaped by the modernizing influence of surrealism. An unexpected hand reaches like a scoop to shovel away greenery and undulations, replacing them with the flat whiteness of cotton, a crop synonymous with the Delta and a metaphor Welty explores later in the narrative. The surreality of the scene upends the representational conservatism of the opening descriptions, much like the plantation aristocracy wavers under the force of modernization the locomotive symbolizes. As the Delta begins, the drummer opposite Laura groans and sinks "into sleep" (92), and—seemingly together with him and the young girl—the reader feasts on the sights dreams convey, so that landscape and mindscape converge in a hallucinogenic singularity:

> Thoughts went out of her head and the landscape filled it. In the Delta, most of the world seemed sky. The clouds were large—larger than horses or houses, larger than boats or churches or gins, larger than anything except the fields the Fairchilds planted. Her nose in the banana skin as in the cup of a lily, she watched the Delta. The land was perfectly flat and level but it shimmered like the wing of a lighted dragonfly. It seemed

strummed, as though it were an instrument and something had touched it. Sometimes in the cotton were trees with one, two, or three arms—she could draw better trees than those were. Sometimes like a fuzzy caterpillar looking in the cotton was a winding line of thick green willows and cypresses, and when the train crossed this green, running on a loud iron bridge, down its center like a golden mark on the caterpillar's back would be a bayou. (92)

Laura has her head in the clouds. The uniformity of space and the orderly passage of time characteristic of the novel's opening sections dissolve irrevocably under the pressure of this paragraph's surreal narrative acrobatics. No longer a removed observer—like Audubon imagines himself to be in "A Still Moment"—Laura experiences the migration of the landscape into her mind. The separation between observed and observer collapses to produce a disorienting hallucinogenic vision of a surreal Mississippi landscape. A giant expanse of sky and enormous clouds dominating the vista, their massive proportions dwarfing the trivial affairs of humans. Property, business, and religion lose any significance when confronted with the natural environment. Only the fields equal the ether, as they stretch outward, flat and even, paradoxically in motion, shimmering and strummed. Welty signals the inwardness of Laura's sight by describing the girl's nose in her banana "as in the cup of a lily," a bloom that comes from the narcissus family. What Laura views outwardly assumes dimensions and shapes originating at least partially inwardly, so that "cotton trees" show human limbs, although nature has drawn the arms badly. Laura claims that she could draw them better, or at least more realistically. Further, the sinuous band of cypresses and willows marks the presence of bayou water, at the same time appearing like a furry caterpillar with a gold marking on its back. In the world of the Delta, both the band of trees and the caterpillar's body have equal claims to truth—and, from another perspective, the spectacle may look different again.

The deployment of these surreal descriptions mollifies the rigid sense of space and order that characterizes the traditionally realistic narration of *Delta Wedding's* opening, where objects remain at a distance, recognizable and stable. In the Delta, though, seeing does not produce clarity, and viewing from the carriage of a moving train leads to a destabilizing of the landscape's solidity. Time seems suspended in the Delta descriptions, too. The dreamy composition dilates the moment of Laura's apprehension.

While the clock does not stop, it seems to slow, allowing the narrative to unexpectedly spill and broaden in this widened and deepened increment of time. During this reverie-like interval, Laura witnesses the dying light as "rosy" and "diamond." Beams of light shoot out from the sinking sun, which descends "lopsided and wide as a rose on a stem in the west" that "was a milk-white edge, like the foam of the sea" (92). Before pulling into the station, the train runs over James's Bayou near the shadowy Yazoo River, two bodies of water that supply metaphors of transformation later in the action. The train also goes past a gin that at first looks "like a blue lake," and beside a platform where "cotton bales were so close they seemed to lean out to the train" (93). Here and throughout the opening section, Laura experiences moments when she seems to slip free of Newtonian limitations and enter the orbit of a world undergirded by the physics of Einstein, Planck, and Heisenberg.

The paradigm shifting discoveries of these three scientists, along with innovations in the fields of Zoology, medicine, sociology, and anthropology, created a modern worldview to which thousands of artists responded by probing the illusions of subjectivity. *Delta Wedding* forms a part of this investigation through its complex presentation of assorted narrative voices and tenors. In their evaluations of the novel, most critics adopt an elaborated version of Alfred Appel's early contention that Welty filters the "action through the separate consciousnesses of several characters" (201). Critical opinion has not strayed far from this general assessment, that *Delta Wedding* fragments point of view. With varying degrees of specificity and detail, Gail Mortimer (85), Louise Westling (*Sacred* 69–70; *Eudora* 90), Michael Kreyling (*Eudora* 61 & *Understanding* 83), and Suzan Harrison (35) all advance this position. The latter three in particular view Welty's splintering of the authorial voice as modeled after Woolf, with both novelists demonstrating that the "narrative's authority is thereby decentered in a way that challenges the patriarchal insistence on unity and identity" (Harrison 35). *Delta Wedding*'s narrative does indeed switch from consciousness to consciousness. More broadly, Laura's, Ellen's, Shelley's, Robby's, and Dabney's narratives serve as vehicles for the general expression of Welty's surreal context, often apparent in the "private thoughts" of the novel's women, "who are frequently conscious of, and dissatisfied with, their status as lesser Fairchilds" (Eichelberger 49). Welty's description of Laura's arrival in the Delta on the train supplies one example of how the narrative disrupts the realism of the book's earliest moments with the surrealism of the

Delta's emergence. *Delta Wedding* follows this pattern repeatedly, although different characters may provide the pivot for the swing toward the sur-real, which always seems to emerge most clearly when viewed against the largely unforgiving backdrop of Shellmound. In much the same way that the Delta assumes a surreal aspect that contrasts with the preceding evenly proportioned scenes, incidences of dreamy contemplation stand out con-spicuously when set against Shellmound's unchanging customs and rituals.

Welty makes one such tradition, marriage, key. But supposing it lies at the heart of *Delta Wedding* leads to disappointment. Welty tersely dis-patches with the union in one short sentence: "Mr. Rondo married Dabney and Troy" (303). Of little consequence in itself, the marriage augments the series of institutions designating tradition in the Delta. Although threats to convention line the Delta horizon, the story focuses on preparation for the wedding rather than on the exchange of vows. The novel's title, then, boldly suggests a climactic moment that Welty deflates, and this irony directs attention to the rituals Appel views as forming the book's major concern (201). These rituals mostly assume the shape of personal reflections and practical planning for Dabney Fairchild's marriage to Troy Flavin, the over-seer who works for Dabney's father, Battle, on the Fairchild plantation.

At the center of Battle's leisurely planter lifestyle stands Shellmound, the home of the Fairchild clan and the focal point for family life and the wedding arrangements. As Peggy Prenshaw has noted ("Woman's World" 48), unlike the Grove, the orderly yet arid home of the eccentric Fairchild aunts, both bastions of Fairchild history, Shellmound buzzes with life and pulses with the energy and playfulness of young lives. "It was hard to read at Shellmound," Laura complains at the beginning of chapter three, "There was so much going on in real life" (142). Ellen and Battle have a large fam-ily—nine children and a tenth on the way—and everyone's movements in and around the home, together with the arrival of wedding guests and the presence of house servants, combine to create a sense of activity and a pic-ture of white Delta plenty so profuse that "our attention may be devoured by this inexhaustible richness" (Vande Kieft 70). At the moment of Laura's arrival, for example, she recalls the "old blue water cooler" and "wooden ta-bles always piled with snap beans, turnip greens, and onions from the day's trip to Greenwood." She also reflects on the "joggling board, the neglected greenhouse, Aunt Ellen's guineas in the old buggy, the stable wall elbow-deep in a vine" (95). In the "parlor she knew was a clover-shaped foot stool covered with rose velvet where she would sit, and sliding doors to the music room that she could open and shut" (95–96). She remembers the "smell of girls' fudge cooking" and the "sound of the phone by roll-top desk going unanswered" (96). Such an evocation of life at Shellmound contributes to a picture of the household's business through a style of writing Victorian in its deference to elaborate patterning and general fussiness. Sentences pile image upon sound and taste upon touch, such that the planter's bounty forms a vision of Edenic plenty.

This sense of overwhelming abundance confronts Laura even more forcefully when Shelley takes her to the Fairchild store, a metaphor for the family's immense wealth and a place where any Fairchild could "walk behind the counter, reach in and take anything on earth, without having to pay or even specify exactly what he took. It was like the pantry at Shellmound. Anything was all right, since they were all kin." Fascinated by the store's astonishing array of items, Laura "went gazing her fill through the store" (225):

> Along the tops of the counters were square glass jars with gold-topped stoppers—they held the kernels and flakes of seed—and just as likely, crusted-over wine-balls, licorice sticks, or pink-covered gingerbread stage-planks. All around, at many levels, fishing boxes all packed, china pots with dusty little lids, cake stands with the weightiest of glass covers, buckets marked like a mackerel sky, dippers, churns, bins, hampers, baby baskets, popcorn poppers, cooky jars, butter molds, money safes, hair receivers, mouse traps, all these things held the purest enchantment for her. (226)

This excerpt from a series of passages exhaustively enumerating the store's contents, which stand "in the aisle as high as the waist," illustrates wealth—but it more subtly suggests the sense of claustrophobia endured by the family. Money can liberate, but an over-attachment can imprison and demean. The store's apparently endless inventory of goods crowds out space, threatening to drown Laura, who has to wade and twist "like a cat" so that the items do not to engulf her (226). Similarly, the material abundance and ceaseless activity at Shellmound itself diminish the already circumscribed space occupied by many of the novel's women. The plantation system, its rigidly enforced gender roles, its codes against racial equality, and its veneration of family history and expectation of loyalty all confront Laura, Ellen, Dabney, Shelley, and Robbie, supplying the apparently unbending social context that Welty subverts when the novel's language takes on sur-real dimensions.

In contrast to the tradition and order of Shellmound, *Delta Wedding* presents a collection of satellite locales, located beyond the family home's purview, where the narrative counteracts the emphasis on family consensus with moments of feminine self-discovery. Where these instances of textual disruption occur, Welty uses surrealistic techniques in order to show how knowledge can derive from embracing imagination and desire. Early in the novel, during Dabney's trip to the Grove, Welty deploys surreal imag-ery to convey the young girl's developing insight about her family and her impending marriage. Leaving the confines of Shellmound behind her, she dreamily starts out for the Grove, joined by her sister, India:

> On either side of their horses' feet the cotton twinkled like stars. Then a red-pop flew up from her nest in the cotton. Above in an unbroken cir-cle, all around the wheel of the level world, lay silvery-blue clouds whose edges melted and changed into the pink and blue of sky. Girls and horses lifted their heads like swimmers. Here and there and far away the cotton wagons, of hand-painted green, stood up to their wheel tops in the white and were loaded with white, like cloud wagons. (118)

Welty reserves this kind of surreal language for moments that deepen the psychological portraits of women throughout *Delta Wedding*. Traveling toward the Grove, a seat of family history and pride, Dabney rides on stars. The description subtly redirects the reader's eye from below to the flight of the red bird that forms a counterpoint to the dizzying "wheel of the level world," around which a circle of pink and blue clouds spreads and softens, seemingly into infinity.

At once concretely realized and plainly hallucinogenic, the language presents the Delta's materiality through the prism of a powerful shaping consciousness that adds depth and texture to the scene (in contrast to Welty's presentation of Shellmound that tends to emphasize surface and su-perficiality). The prose mixes actual with abstract so that cotton looks like stars, girls and horses appear like swimmers, and cotton wagons transform into "cloud wagons." Then Dabney encounters Troy, who menacingly waves "his arm like a gun against the sky" (118). While Troy's sinister gesture in-trudes upon the general optimism of her dream and perhaps augers badly for her marriage, Dabney continues on, sinking deeper into her daydream.

"The sedge was glowing," Welty reports, "the round meadow had a bloom like fruit, and the sweet gums were like a soft curtain beyond, fading into the pink of the near sky" (120). These altered circumstances establish the conditions for the secret upbraiding of her father's absurd traditionalism, the tender reminiscing of her mother's love, and the lusty anticipation of Troy's seduction. "He would," Welty intones, "—that dark shouting rider would throw back the skin of this very world, of this moment. . . . There would be a whole other world, with other cotton, even" (121). Here, Dabney seems to have Shellmound's replacement in mind. Fearing immurement within its suffocating walls, she desires the liberty that she hopes union with Troy (a kind of double for Floyd in "At the Landing") will deliver. Indeed, she naively stakes the reinvention of time and space on their marriage.

If life within Shellmound operates according to the conventions of an ebbing and increasingly obsolete Victorian world,[5] the environs beyond, like the path that Dabney takes to the Grove, undermine tradition, where "everything seemed to be happening strangely, some special way, now" (122). For example, her encounter with Man Son, a long-time field hand of the Fairchilds, triggers a dream that returns her to a childhood memory of horror and fascination, a scene she witnessed as young girl. Her venerated uncles, George and Denis, emerge naked after swimming in the bayou to find Man Son and his brother fighting with a knife. Denis ignores the confrontation and quickly disappears while George stays, gains possession of the knife, and pacifies the fighters before releasing them. Rather than quietly running away or staying hidden, Dabney screams loudly at the incident and runs at George, who catches her in a bloody embrace. "He hugged her tight against his chest," Welty writes, "where sweat and bayou water pressed her mouth, and tickled her a minute, and told her how sorry he was to have scared her like that." Frightened and fascinated by the excitement of the episode, Dabney acknowledges its significance only years later. The past, then, reaches powerfully into the present, supplying her with the knowledge that violating Fairchild codes of behavior does not automatically lead to ostracism. Unlike his brother, George intervened to defuse the dispute between two black servants. At the time, Dabney reviled George's compassion, "[b]ut all the Fairchild in her had screamed at his interfering—at his taking part—*caring* about anything in the world but them" (124). However, in retrospect it is clear that George demonstrated a level of independence, contravening family traditions in an act from which his niece now draws succor. Clearly, the waking dream's reconstitution of the incident on the bank of the bayou illustrates the narrative's fixing of a point where discontinuities of time resolve themselves into continuities, enabling the acquisition of knowledge. In *Delta Wedding*, time and space bend under the pressure of the novel's surrealistic language, which recovers the past and furnishes a fresh context for enlightening discoveries in the present.

Welty explores Dabney's psychology in *Delta Wedding*, and the dream of George at the bayou promises both an opportunity for a reassessment of Fairchild family values and an inquiry into her commitment to them. In her memory, George appears "like a man who had stepped outside" the limitation of Shellmound's rules, and now Dabney follows his lead (124). Her dream, which concludes chapter three, once again shows Welty's dispersing surreal imagery to enact revelation and reappraisal. Section six, which ends chapter three, begins on a note of uncertainty: "Much later, in her room, Dabney opened her eyes. Perhaps she had only just gone to sleep, but the silver night woke her—the night so deep-advanced toward day that she seemed to breathe in a well, drenched with the whiteness of an hour that astonished her." Both asleep and awake, Dabney, another of Welty's somnambulists, leaves her bed, pulled by the magnetism of the window that "invited her to see" a vision of breathtaking and tantalizing beauty. "She got out of bed (her filmy dress like a sleeping moth clung to the chair)," Welty writes, "and the whole leafy structure of the outside seemed agitated and rustled, the shadows darted like birds. The gigantic sky radiant as water ran over the earth and around it. The old moon in the west and the planets of morning streamed their light" (178).

Passages such as this dream sequence distort the realistic perspective that frequently reasserts itself in the narrative and that Welty's surreal literary effects critique. The vision that appears to Dabney here reveals a closely matched set of textual features to the Delta scene that meets Laura's gaze at the novel's opening. A hallucinogenic aura pervades the descriptions of both landscapes, imparting fluid, non-corporeal, disorienting, and mollifying elements to both compositions. Dabney's dress transforms into a "sleeping moth," and the world outside dissolves before her into a vibrating conglomeration of "leafy structures" with shadows swiftly jumping "like birds," while the unstill sky seems to have spread its watery glow over the entirety of the window's frame. Moreover, at a distance, she views the trees at the "bayou's edge," a location characterized by sex and passion that Welty sets in opposition to the discipline of Shellmound, with its crispness that extends to the "cotton like the rolling breath of sleep overflowed the fields"

(178). The reverie concludes with Dabney urging the vision to "draw me in—open the window like my window, I am still only looking in where it is dark," showing her yielding to the dream's portent of escape from Shellmound through the aperture opened by her imagination (179).

For Dabney, marriage to Troy Flavin,[6] someone who obviously ranks below her in the Delta's social hierarchy, represents an act of rebellion against family tradition. Attracted by his potent sexual energy,[7] she disobeys her "father's wishes" (121) in her unorthodox choice, intending to restore Marmion and with Troy "ultimately revitalise the outmoded 'aristocratic' world of Shellmound plantation" (Westling *Eudora* 95). Although Marmion has "lately come to horrify" Dabney, she feels the seductive pull of its mystery and makes another trip on horseback. But this time her destination is the Grove's antithesis, the house "out in the woods," a place charged with erotic energies where the Yazoo River, which links both properties, "always seemed swift" (210). Riding out from Shellmound "before any of them were awake," Dabney enters a still dreaming world, softened and magically transformed by the appearance of strange apparitions. It is as if she dreams the curious panorama. The "night cobwebs" remain unswept, yet she pushes on, "breaking the dewy net of spider webs" (208), where "morning-glories were turned like eyes on her pretty feet" (208–9), and the mysterious "bayou rustled within" while the "sky was softly blue all over, the last rim of sunrise cloud melting into it like foam on fresh milk" (209). Passing Troy's house with a defiant raising of her whip (a riposte to his earlier silhouetting of his gun against the sky), Dabney rides over Mound Field and Far Field and the Deadening to the Yazoo. She travels farther and farther to arrive at a point remote from Shellmound. When Welty first presents Shellmound through Laura's eyes, she describes a "tall, white, wide-framed house with a porch all around, its bayed tower on one side, its tinted windows open and its curtains stirring" (94), but when Dabney first views Marmion, Shellmound's double, she watches it "reflected in the Yazoo River—an undulant tower with white wings at each side, like a hypnotized swamp butterfly, spread and dreaming where it alights" (209). Welty's juxtaposition of two parallel representations of large planter residences focuses attention upon the economic, political, and social forces of modernization that are eroding the Fairchild way of life. Laura's fist sight of Shellmound's broad and imposing architecture takes in an image of Fairchild power as immovable as bedrock, but Welty suggests this impression's falsity by presenting Marmion, once a planter home as grand as its cousin and Shellmound's predecessor,[8] mirrored and wavering in the waters of the Yazoo, the river of death. The even and regular proportions of Shellmound stand in marked contrast to the uncertain and fragmented vista of Marmion, a surreally inspired image at once observed and dreamt.

Dabney has mixed feelings about Marmion. It both enrages her and gives her cause for optimism, for while she acknowledges the house's place in the context of the Fairchild mythology, she does not accept the values that inscribe that mythology or the continuation of the family legacy. A symbol of Fairchild honor and prestige, Marmion "had been empty since the same year it was completed, 1890" (209). Abandoned following a duel over cotton in which the owner, Dabney's grandfather, James Fairchild, died, the house stands as a testament to Fairchild honor maintained in the face of loss. Dabney, who "always resisted and pouted at the story when any of the boys told it" (210), opposes the narrative line of this history: "Fine glory! Dabney would not have done with it" (209). Like the "hypnotized swamp butterfly," an emblem of dreamy metamorphoses that Marmion resembles in the water's reflection, the house verges on transformation. This is an outcome suggested when Dabney witnesses the sun rising at the beginning of the new day, illuminating the building's façade: "[A]ll the tints of cypress began to shine on it, the brightness of age like newness. Her house!" (210). Welty clearly foreshadows Marmion's renovation, adding to *Delta Wedding*'s mythologizing of the house's "stylized grandeur" as the "romantic, fantastic Marmion" (Griffin 105). The abandoned home has this reputation in the novel, though, because Welty's evocation of Marmion gathers together a succession of erotic metaphors and images that create a cluster of surreal figurative expressions. Before departing Marmion, Dabney daringly inventories its attributes, which reveal a powerful series of secrets. Dabney's nascent sexuality and deep desire for Troy find affirmation in the house's suggestive architecture. Not merely large, white, and with a "wide frame" (94) like Shellmound, Marmion gives a magnificent "temple-like" and "castle-like" impression that Dabney struggles to articulate. Its phallic columns, like Asphodel's upthrust pillars, rise "naked from the ground." To this priapic display Welty adds a "lookout tower," a "freestanding stair," and a "chandelier, chaliced, golden in light, like the stamen in the lily down-hanging" (211). The architecture's egregiously sexual features and Welty's decision to present polymorphous sex organs multiplied, distorted, and arrayed in Marmion's dream-like design evince the influence of Dalínian art and theory. This influence also finds expression in Welty's decision to create surreal houses, such as Cornella's "double-house" in "The Winds" (*Stories* 254), Marmion, and the old MacLain house in *The Golden Apples*—all in the style of Dalí's "Dream of Venus" funhouse. His paranoia criticism targets the prevailing rationalization of reality by advocating that art should systematically simulate the delirious condition of perception, such that the surrealist method reveals the "hidden obsessive character of the object under consideration" (Finkelstein *Salvador Dalí* 189). In *Delta Wedding*'s presentation of Marmion, Dabney closely observes the mansion's appearance, which Welty renders as an externalized display of the young girl's welling desire. The flood of Welty's multiple images—like the hundreds of ambiguously shaped formations that characteristically spread over any number of Dalí canvasses—creates the fantastic Marmion, a house that seems both a temple and a castle, soft and hard, natural and artificial. All its metaphorically rendered features—the erect pillars, the tower, the stair, and the stamen—explicitly foreground Dabney's desire for Troy.

Nonetheless, *Delta Wedding* suggests that yielding to that desire carries a burden of anxiety and danger. Welty issues this warning through Dabney's contemplation of Marmion's whirlpool, which "was so creepy and scary" (211) that she almost never approached it. In her presentation of Dabney's encounter, Welty employs surrealist effects in order to deepen and complicate the conventional perspective that ordinarily characterizes the narrative when she directs its energies to recording what Carol Manning calls the "realism of everyday life," which she claims "is the world of most of Eudora Welty's fiction" (*With Ears* 13). At various sites distributed around Shellmound, Manning's realism yields to a deeper and more searching inquiry elucidated in Welty's surreal prose, which, from the beginning of her career, has persistently illuminated dreams as they penetrate the everyday. For example, when Dabney parts the "thronged vines of the wild grapes, thick as legs," she looks transfixed by the swirling eddy of the whirlpool: "She gazed feasting her fear on the dark, vaguely stirring water" (211). Simultaneously alluring and repulsive, the pool presents a startling mélange of sexual images engaged in a kind of orgiastic copulation. Peering between the grapevines, Dabney meets a multiplicity of eyes, perhaps "frog eyes" or "snake eyes," which seem both participant and voyeuristic. Snake bodies and heads twist and stick up through the water's surface intermittently, and vine and cypress roots lay entwined and thickly grown in the water where "some roots too moved and floated like hair." Drawn to the opposite bank of the whirlpool, Dabney spies a root on which a turtle sits with its mouth open and its tongue poking out, acting as an obscene commentator on the action.

The narrative technique employed here parallels the method Welty used to anthropomorphize Marmion's architectural details. For Dabney, the churning pool presents two compositions overlaid and compressed into one frame. Vines transform into meaty legs. The whirlpool appears to be a seething vaginal opening, mirrored in the circles of Dabney's and the creatures' eyes. Crisscrossing snake bodies and tangled vines and roots, swollen in the water, enact a roiling scene of unrestricted gratification. This episode, which presents an ingénue's dilemma shortly before her wedding day, leaves Dabney with a sense of vertigo. She ponders whether she should doubt all the old stories, "since childhood of people white and black who had been drowned there, people that were dared to swim in this place, and of the boats that would venture to the center of the pool and begin to go around and everybody fall out and go to the bottom" (212). As Noel Polk indicates, her "reactions to the whirlpool and the river seem clearly to reflect her own profound agitation here on the verge of her marriage, here on the edge of the leap into life's troubled and mysterious waters" ("Water" 97). Nonetheless, *Delta Wedding* leaves these agitating questions unanswered—even at the novel's conclusion, when the whirlpool has Dabney and Troy firmly in the grip of its maelstrom.

Dabney's mother, Ellen, on the other hand, feels the downward pull of the whirlpool from novel's opening. Between what Peggy Prenshaw calls the "cooking, sewing, gardening" and "nurturing" characterizing the swirl of life at Shellmound, Ellen has little time for the insights revealed to her daughter at Marmion ("Woman's World" 50). Despite the helter-skelter of her life (and like both her daughters, Shelley and Dabney, her sister-in-law, Robbie, and her niece, Laura), Ellen does gain understanding of her predicament. Welty deploys the same kind of surreal language in her depiction that she does for the others. Always "too busy when she was awake" to listen to her inner voice, Ellen takes direction in life from her dreams, which someone probably told her "were not real," but which she "always rather trusted" (153). On Shellmound's sleeping porch, reminiscent of the porch attached to Josie's house in "The Winds," Ellen lies with her child, Bluet, in a "big white-painted" bed that "was like a baby buggy that, too, would carry her away somewhere against her will" as the "summer day shimmered and rustled, and the porch seemed to flow with light and shadow that traveled outwards" (152). This moment of dreamy contemplation leads Ellen to search for a "garnet brooch, a present in courting days from her husband, that had been lying around the house for years and then disappeared" (153). She lulls Bluet to sleep by reciting a dream she had the night before that warned of the loss of this breast pin, which in her reverie she recovers under a "great big tree" near "James's Bayou" (152). The warning in Ellen's dream provokes her to leave Shellmound's clamor for the tranquility of the "bayou woods" (159), a location reached by treading the "old Marmion path" (156). But in the place of the lost lover's gift, Ellen discovers a "wild runaway girl" whose beauty, fearlessness, and bold sexuality impress the jaded housewife (167).

Led by her dreams, Ellen enters a magical wood that strongly contrasts with the genteel decorum and high activity of Shellmound. The realism that Manning identifies with Welty's fiction yields to a surreal episode, a dream-like forest encounter that develops Ellen's knowledge of herself in contrast to the rigid Fairchild family structure. As she travels deeper into the woods, an "ancient place" (157), fewer paths mark her way. Those that do peter out or crisscross over one another chaotically. Depth, shade, and distance from Shellmound also affect the forest's appearance, which has an otherworldly aura, at once seen and dreamt: "Moss from the cypresses hung deep overhead now, and by the water vines like pediments and arches reached from one tree to the next" (156–57). At the water's edge, she sees "cypress trunks four feet thick" that "stood opened like doors of tents in Biblical engravings," as well as cinders forming the banks of the bayou, where local lore "said it was where the Indians burned their pottery, at the very last." Perhaps Ellen secretly desires to destroy her pots and pans, instruments of her drudgery at Shellmound, which now seems to exist in universe separate from hers, one where the surface of the "cotton fields so solid to the sight" may at any moment fissure before her (157).

The solitude and quiet of the "dense wood" (157) makes it an appropriate location for the sudden appearance of a "shadowy girl" (158), a kind of alter ego and a figure that brings revelation. More dryad than actual person, the nymph refuses to identify herself, remaining untouchable outside the boundaries of family obligation and duty, and beyond the range of Ellen's admonitions. Appearing in a purportedly haunted locale (Battle believes a spirit inhabits the bayou), the beautiful girl at first frightens Ellen, who lectures her as she might one of her children. But the mysterious girl curtly interrupts Ellen's warnings about morals and men by telling her, "You couldn't stop me" (159). Ellen cannot and does not prevent the girl's passage to Memphis, the "old Delta synonym for pleasure, trouble and shame" (160), and later, when she reveals the episode to George, he claims to have had sex with the girl in an "old Argyle gin" (167). His braggadocio and vulgarity form part of the erotic byplay between George and Ellen scattered throughout *Delta Wedding*, but his boast gathers sinister overtones when the wedding photographer announces a girl's death on the railroad track leading to Memphis, George's hometown. Although George heroically saves his kin, Maureen, on the same track, he shows little sympathy for the "stranger" (160), whom he never again mentions. The episode in the woods and its corollary with George provide Ellen with moments of clarification about the threats that confront women who make their sexuality conspicuous, and about women who choose positions other than the maternal role she holds. With too much to lose, too many children dependent on her—and perhaps conditioned by the conventions of Fairchild propriety—Ellen confronts the same patriarchal force that her daughters, Shelley and Dabney, face. These younger women, however, are still free of the whirlpool's grip and react more defiantly and resist their ossification within Shellmound, a "permanent encapsulation of the values and ideas of the past, a corporate form which cannot adapt to change or to progress" (Griffin 105).

While Dabney plans a renovation of Fairchild family values through her marriage to an outsider and her recuperation of Marmion, Shelley reacts more dramatically to Shellmound's enervating set of expectations for women. A year older than her sister and incensed that her father deems her too "prissy" and "priggish" for marriage (173), she revolts by taking up the pen in order to challenge the limitations of her role in the family. Her appropriation of the pen, a conventionally male signifier, and her romantic poet's name suggest Shelley's rich imaginative life, which opens avenues for change through the surreal melding of daydreams with actuality in her diary entries. Only recently begun, the diary is a book with a "lock and key," an apt metaphor for desire's loosing through the act of writing. The number of probing questions and reasoned replies scattered through Shelley's six-page entry—which Welty inserts verbatim—shows her thoughtfully interrogating the limitations of her present life, analytically examining the behavior of her closest relatives, and propitiously speculating about her impending trip to Europe, "Aunt Tempe's graduation present" (172). Shelley imagines, for example, that the European experience may cause her to revise her opinion of Robbie Reid, George's wife. She wonders playfully: "Maybe Europe will change everything. When I see the leaning tower of

Pisa will I like Robbie any better? I doubt it. (Aunt T. will be with me all the time!)" (174). The allure of liberties of all kinds that Europe holds for Shelley, a young woman drawn to the high passion of F. Scott Fitzgerald's *The Beautiful and the Damned*, demonstrates how grossly Battle has misjudged his eldest child, whom he considers cold. Shelley wishes to overturn his conservatism, seeking to "push forward time in order to become the New Woman that she desires and deserves to be" (Crews 71). Shelley wishes to have her desires satisfied, but on terms other than the ones to which Dabney capitulates or which her mother endures. Perhaps removal to Italy could effect for Shelley the revolution of consciousness it provided for the satanic school of poets.

Shelley's diary daydreaming furnishes moments of quiet self-examination and discovery amid the perpetual hum of activity within Shellmound, where "it was hard for her to even see how to write"(172). The literary space of the diary, in which she fantasizes about subversion and escape, has an analogous literal space in the bayou, a site Welty repeatedly identifies with the women of Shellmound's intellectual growth. On an errand to retrieve Troy from his office, Shelley runs out of the house and into the blue air and grass that lead toward the bayou. She hears "falling waves of the locusts' song" as she views the "lightning bugs plainly even between flashes of their lights—flying nearly upright through the blueness, tails swinging, like mermaids playing beneath the sea." Shellmound seems a distant memory. She can hear "only faintly the sounds of the house" in proximity to the bayou, where the "startling towers of the yuccas" loom as if figments in a dream. In contrast to her house, where the "human voice was never still," the bayou "could seem like a lagoon in a foreign world, and a solitary person could walk beside it, with inward, uncomforted thoughts." While Shellmound "was charged with life," the bayou slakes Shelley's thirst for imaginative flight and for those moments when the apparently unyielding and closed world of the Fairchild mansion softens and liquefies under the mollifying effect of a dream. At this instant, the life of the house and the life of the "endlessly exploited" plantation fields surrender to the bayou calm, "filled with its summer trance or its winter trance of sleep, its uncaught fishes" (283).

In a passage that parallels the earlier identification of the Yazoo, the "River of Death" (283), with the demise of the archaic Fairchild ethic, Welty links the river to renewal born of deep contemplation. For Shelley, the river doesn't presage the "ultimate flow of doom," but the "more personal vision of the moment's chatter ceasing, the feelings of the day disencumbered, floating now into recognition, like a little boat come into sight." Welty couches this instance of profound personal reflection in surreal language that translates the elements of Shelley's material circumstance into the kaleidoscope of her dream, where feelings metamorphose into floating boats and the bayou appears transformed, going in and out of the Yazoo "like the curved arm of the sleeper, whose elbow was in their garden" (284).

As in so many pivotal moments of far-reaching awareness and surreal envisioning in *Delta Wedding*, the feeling crests and disintegrates when Shelley arrives at a place associated with the order of men. Here it is Troy's office, "one of the houses none of the girls paid any attention to" (284), where she sees Troy brutally enforce his power by opening fire on a group of insubordinate field hands. In a vulgar aside to Shelley he challenges her to stay while he picks buckshot from the backside of Big Baby with an ice pick. It is a powerful and complex scene, which draws together the intertwined themes of sexual violence, the preservation of white power, and homoerotic desire. Welty shows Shelley confronting the same threat of violence and sexual humiliation that Troy uses to manage his crew. Leaping angrily from the well-lit interior of the office, the young woman heads for the quiet darkness of the bayou, where she ponders the fragility of Troy's macho planter persona. This identity she views as inherited, passed from man to man: "Suppose a real Deltan only imitated another Deltan. Suppose the behavior of all *men* were actually no more that this—imitation of other men" (285–86).

Defiant, opinionated, and recalcitrant, Shelley endures what seems to her the interminably long fuss culminating in Dabney's marriage ceremony. "I wish now it would happen," she fumes in her diary, "and be past, I hate days, fateful days" (173). At midnight on the evening of the fateful day, at the wedding party, Shelley finds a quiet place for meditation shielded from the distracting hubbub. On the screened "back porch," moths and "hard beetles," attracted by the enclosure's light, futilely knock "upon the radius of light like an adamant door." Here, sequestered from the excitement of the party and swaying to the band's music as it fades from "Whispering" into "Linger Awhile," Shelley stops to reflect upon the day's preparations for the wedding, an event that reinforces her decision to go on the road (308). In this episode, Welty fixes a surreal point of synthesis at which the past—no longer an instant of time detached and inert—reaches forcefully into the present to generate a significant moment of personal insight and clarification. Shelley recalls arranging wedding flowers that day, when she

> had thought to herself, hypnotically, as though she read it in her diary, Why do you look out thinking nothing will happen any more? Why are you thinking your line of trees the indelible thing in the world? There's the long journey you're going on, with Aunt Tempe, leading out . . . and you can't see it now. Even closing your eyes, you see only the line of trees at Shellmound. Is it the world? If Shellmound were a little bigger, it would be the same as the world entirely. . . . Perhaps that was the real truth. (308-9)

In this passage, which parallels Jenny's speculation about her geographical context in "At the Landing," Shelley imagines the lay of the land beyond Shellmound's apparently implacable horizon, scolding herself for the narcissism that ultimately destroys her double. The typically visual metaphors, indicative of Shelley's anxiety about her ability to live beyond the Fairchild trees, accompany her probing of her interior world. The tension created by the wedding celebration, a time for reassertion of Fairchild customs and traditions, weakens Shelley's resolve, which strengthens when she recalls George, the man who stepped outside the family mythology and whom "she was much like." Now playing "Sleepy Time Gal" and fading back into "Whispering," the song that initiates Shelley's reverie, the band's seamless stream of music plays under Shelley's meandering line of thought, which ultimately results in her renunciation of *Delta Wedding*'s wedding. In contrast to Dabney, whose desire Shelley fears has led her sister into a marital mausoleum, Shelley dreams of her own desire dancing in "an opening wood" that has no obstacles (309).

Foreclosure on women's freedoms fundamentally shapes the code of feminine gentility that characterizes the Fairchild dynasty. Women of this clan must either submit to a sterile spinsterhood, like the Fairchild aunts, or concede their sexualities to expression within the protocols of family life, like Ellen. Both Dabney and Shelley stand at the whirlpool's edge, poised to immerse themselves in the waters of courtship and marriage. They feel its tug, stare at its depths, and prepare to take the plunge. Robbie Reid, however, jumped long ago, and, with her husband, George, swam at night in the whirlpool, feigning drowning by "sinking down with a hand up" (233). Congenitally at odds with the Fairchild sense of propriety, Robbie married into a higher social stratum, and, as her name suggests, stole the family silver. She comes from a non-planter family, the Reids, and has miraculously parted the "shiny curtain," of Fairchild prestige to win George, the family hero (238). Robbie and George left the Delta and live prosperously in Memphis, at the Delta's northern edge. But despite George's flight, he remains at the apex of Fairchild hero worship, a form of idolatry that Robbie cannot fathom. George's responsiveness to his family's persistent flattery enrages Robbie, who views her in-laws' saccharine doting as way of demeaning his marriage to an outsider from a lower class. When George risks his life to save his niece, Maureen, from a barreling train, Robbie interprets the act as a reckless demonstration of Fairchild loyalty. She believes he holds that loyalty above his marital commitment, and she promptly walks out on him. One of *Delta Wedding*'s most dramatic moments comes when Robbie angrily trudges in the midday heat from the Fairchild store to Shellmound, where she interrupts a family meal—a sacred event in this Delta home, where the "prestige of the family is gauged by the quantity and quality of the table it sets" (Prenshaw "Woman's World" 50). This tense episode begins a process of reconciliation between spouses, but not before Robbie has marched bravely to battle prepared for a fight.

The arduous trek to Shellmound shows Welty's use of surreal figurative language to portray Robbie's developing sense of opposition to Fairchild codes. "Robbie saw it would be a long hot walk in the boiling sun" (232), Welty begins section four of chapter five. The sun beats down mercilessly on the Fairchild fields, creating "an atmosphere of cruel and killing midday heat on a dusty road" that "is related to Robbie's sense of terrible exposure, hurt, ordeal, as she takes the long hot walk in the boiling sun" (Vande Kieft 80). In stark contrast to the cool, ministering vapors of the woods or the bayou in early morning, in the softened afternoon, or at nighttime—places that Ellen, Dabney, and Shelley visit at these times—the noon sun scorches the "Fairchild Deadening," the field the road traverses: "The white field in the heat darted light like a prism edge. She put a hand over her eyes, but the light came red through her fingers. She knew she was a small figure here, and went along with a little switch of elderberry under the straight-up sun" (233). A victim of the furnace's blaze, Robbie anticipates her incineration as the blood-red glow seeps through her parted fingers. She cuts a lonely figure stranded on the road to Shellmound, the metaphorical source of this vicious light and heat that does everything to blot her from the landscape. Despite the hellish torment, she manages to find refuge in the treeless wasteland. A "cotton shed" emerges just before "she dropped in the heat," and its shady interior supplies a shelter and a setting for Robbie's sleepy, perhaps delirious drift into the past (236).

Coming upon the shed, she discovers Pinchy, a young black girl in the process of "comin' through" (285), a rite of passage that Kreyling contends "is clearly an initiation in some form that transforms girls into women, women into mothers" (*Understanding* 107). Encountering Pinchy in a cotton shed that recalls the "old Argyle gin" (167) where George sleeps with the runaway girl, reasserts *Delta Wedding*'s recycling of themes of sex, race, and feminine desire. It seems as if Robbie may have interrupted Pinchy pleasuring herself—literally caught in a pinch. When Robbie enters the doorway, the young woman appears to be "panting," while sweat beads her forehead and cheeks "in pearly chains," her eyes "glassy."[9] Robbie's sudden interruption of the girl, who looks "like somebody startled in sleep" and whom she quickly orders outside, initiates an erotic sequence of daydreams for Robbie who, after eating, languorously stretches out like Venus: "It was nice in here. She felt as if she were in a shell, floating in that sea of light, looking out its mouth with good creature comfort" (236). No longer impugned by the unforgiving glare and heat of the noon light, she bobs on the light's surface, floating in swells of erotic reminiscences that gather strength when she envisions her lover, George, in the shape of Pinchy's darting figure:

> Across her vision the Negro clung and darted just outside, fitful as a black butterfly, perhaps crazy with the heat, and beyond her the light danced. Was this half-way? Her eyes fastened hypnotically on the black figure that seemed to dangle as if suspended in the light, as she would watch a little light that twinkled in the black, far out on the river at night, from her window, waiting. (237)

Here, Robbie watches Pinchy, both women transformed like the butterfly and throbbing with the heat and madness of desire. Viewing the flitting body hypnotically, Robbie slips into a trance that replays scenes of the "pure, animal way of love she longed for, when she watched, listened, came out, stretched, slept, content." George figures centrally in her fantasy, which transforms the gin into a site of erotic experimentation and freedom. She imagines him naked, rough upon her, and crying out while "she was outside herself as a cup those three drops fell in." Wailing elation, orgasm, and semen make George and Robbie intimate at a level deeper than Fairchild loyalty. "Any moon and stars there were could rise and set over his enfolding, unemanating length," Welty writes, "The sun could lean over his backside and wake her" (237). The overwhelming power of the dream so thoroughly transforms the torture of Robbie's material circumstances that the sun gently warms her face awake rather than assailing her every step.

Like Robbie Reid, the outsider who has penetrated to the core of the Fairchilds' closed circle of family loyalties, Laura McRaven also presents a force of change. Welty suggests this disjunction in the darkness of her name, McRaven, which clearly contrasts with the lightness of Fairchild. A McRaven and the only kin to the Fairchilds on her mother's side, Laura travels by train into the Delta at the novel's beginning, perhaps *Delta Wedding's* most conspicuous emblem of modernity's arrival. A nine-year-old girl who has recently lost her mother, Laura finds Shellmound's mayhem overwhelming at times, so when her cousin, Roy, asks, "Want to get out?" she gladly accepts (260). The ensuing trip to Marmion, the fantastic house that Welty always associates with dreams, fertility, and change, presents Laura with a set of clues that begin to explain where babies come from. Nine years old and on the verge of puberty, she senses the awakening of desire at Marmion, a surreal setting that Welty supplies as the stage for the young girl's acquisition of knowledge about womanly desire and the limitations imposed upon its expression. The narrowly defined notion of reality that prevails at Shellmound undergoes surreal enlargement and deepening at Marmion, where the oddities of the modern universe warp Newtonian physics.

Slipping loose of Shellmound's gravity, Laura and Roy run down to the "warm breath" of the bayou and step into a boat that ferries them to the time-ravaged house (261). Always in *Delta Wedding* the bayou provides a setting for the disruption of status-quo values, and for the opening of opportunity for reappraisal, progression, and growth. The boat, which Welty presents as "dark, unpainted" and the "color of water," transfers its passengers to an intensified reality that admits unconscious depths. The strange boat seems almost made of water itself, revealing a dark water line that "went like a snake along the bottom." Unstable dividing lines like these suggest the separation Welty imposes between the constant bustle of the Fairchild household and the scattered sites—often near water and always shady, tranquil, and visually rich—that supply the settings for surreal interpenetration of dreaming and waking realities. Here, on the bayou and in the "heavy shade" of cypress trees and vines, "leaves cut out like stars and the early red color of pomegranates lay all over the water, and imperceptibly they came out into the river. The water looked like the floor of the woods that could be walked on" (261). Approaching Marmion, water seems solid like earth and the earth, a "dark waterlogged landing," seems fluid like water—water that also forms Marmion's road. Stepping from the boat carrying Roy's pet turtle "like a hot covered dish," Laura enters a world transfigured by sprays of white clematis that festoon the "dark cedar trees," making them seem moonlit (262).

In this environment, part dream and part actuality, Roy and Laura encounter the inscrutable Aunt Studney, Marmion's sole inhabitant and an aunt who reveals secrets none of their other aunts acknowledge. In a moment parallel to Dabney's marveling at Marmion's imposing "down-hanging" (211) light, which penetrates the hall's towering enclosure, Laura witnesses the "chandelier with its flower-shaped head covered with clusters of soft and burned-down candles, as though a great thing had sometime happened here." Also like Dabney, Laura senses the exposure and danger that accompany romantic entanglements when she peers upward into the "depths of light" and experiences "a moment of dizziness . . . as if she looked into a well" (264). Just like her cousin, who suffers vertigo when gazing down into the whirlpool, Laura feels the disorienting and possibly lethal threat of the abyss. The "closed doors" in the walls all around, anticipating Shelley's anxieties about the foreclosure of her desire at the party's conclusion, subtly suggest that courtship and marriage may lead to the entombment of passion (265).

Laura's exposure to this knowledge occurs in a setting that has the mood of a dream. In a chase around Aunt Studney, Laura and Roy enact an adult convention of the kind immortalized on Keats's Grecian urn: maidenly chastity pursued by heated male suitors. In the excitement and trance of the circling chase, Laura wonders, "Is it still the Delta in here?" And when Roy climbs to the tower's summit, she presses a nearby piano's keys, which hardly give "at the pressure of her finger—as in dreams the easiest thing turns out to be the hard" (265). Suddenly bees, symbols of nature's prodigious fertility, fly out of the piano and out of Aunt Studney's sack: "Why, there were bees inside everything, inside the piano, inside the walls. The place was alive. She wanted to cry out herself. She heard a hum everywhere, in everything. She stood electrified—and indignant" (265-6).

Prenshaw rightly argues that Studney "appears, like an ancient goddess, to assure rebirth and renewal" ("Woman's World" 56), adding, "As if all the pains and pleasures of the world have escaped from Aunt Studney's sack,

Marmion suddenly comes to life. Bees fly out everywhere, startling Laura with a dizzying excitement" (57). Marmion's dream discloses a powerful set of secrets about the acts that create life and about the societal pressures that shape expressions of desire differently for different genders. Welty presents these truths in the highly visual and dreamt interior of this playhouse, a surreal site where unconscious desires feed into the conscious mind (266). The boaters' return trip to Shellmound reflects their gentle awakening from Marmion's spell. Roy "seemed almost to be falling asleep rowing" (267) and, after he tips Laura overboard into the Yazoo's baptismal waters, the two sit trancelike, "transfixed in their two ends of the boat" (268). When the boat nudges the shore, the dream promptly dissipates, and its hold evaporates as they jump onto land and part company, running.

Written under the influence of Virginia Woolf's literary spell, *Delta Wedding* displays a Woolfian sensibility for a new generation of readers, an audience attuned and receptive to art expressing a surrealist worldview. As part of the larger modernist enterprise, this movement helped sweep away the crumbling Victorian confidence in representational art as a meaningful approach to exploring the realities of twentieth-century life, and *Delta Wedding* takes its place alongside the thousands of works devoted to carrying this project to completion. In the fossilized world of nineteenth-century plantation society, Welty found a familiar Mississippi stage on which to enact this drama of rebellion and obsolescence, a production that in many ways mirrors her own artistic evolution as she dared to redefine archetypal Southern scenes, settings, and characters in the context of learning acquired in New York.

5

VISIONS OF PEOPLE AS THEY WERE NOT
IN *THE GOLDEN APPLES*

The 1949 publication of *The Golden Apples* established a new standard of literary excellence for Eudora Welty, although *The Wide Net* and *Delta Wedding* had already greatly enhanced her reputation, nationally and internationally.[1] A painter, photographer, journalist, critic, short story writer, and novelist, Welty leveraged the collective energies of these diverse talents, directing them toward creating a book like none of her others. Not a collection of short stories, a novella, or a novel, *The Golden Apples* presents an organic grouping of seven "inter-related, but not inter-dependent" (qtd. in Kreyling *Author* 136) stories that eludes easy classification—although one of her earliest critical champions, Ruth M. Vande Kieft, characterizes the work as a "short story cycle" in the tradition of Sherwood Anderson's *Winesburg, Ohio* and Faulkner's *The Unvanquished* (87). Arranged in approximate chronological order and covering roughly four decades, all the stories except one return their readers to the Mississippi Delta and to the town of Morgana, a name Welty has associated with the "conception of *Fata Morgana*—the illusory shape, the mirage that comes over the sea" (Kuehl 88).[2] Some thirteen years later, in another interview, she reprised this analysis, but with a more searching elaboration. "I saw it was right," she maintains, "because all the characters, as you know, were living under dreams or illusions or even obsessions" (Yates 94). When Eugene MacLain, one of the volume's several obsessive personalities, utters "*The forties. Psychology*" as the context for marital breakdown (Welty *Stories* 476), Welty conspicuously asserts a Freudian perspective, the worldview without which surrealism has no progenitor. Dalí critic Paul Moorhouse reveals this debt in an observation that might equally apply to many surrealist artists, whose work reflected the intellectual climate of the era. Dalí's art, Moorhead states, offers a "journey through a reality dominated by fantastic and irrational forces."

In "Dali's universe, desire, phobia and obsession are the terrorists of truth" (6). Without exaggeration, one could claim a parallel vision of truth for the world projected through the kaleidoscopic *The Golden Apples*, a cycle of stories frequently depicting people and places ostensibly "as they were not" (Welty *Stories* 491).

Although Welty's publisher, Harcourt, at first seemed inclined to market *The Golden Apples* as a novel, the author soon intervened to prevent the book from being publicized as a contribution to that genre.[3] In fact, an examination of the intriguing compositional history of *The Golden Apples* shows an author unawakened from the dreams that had overtaken the production of *The Wide Net* and *Delta Wedding*, an author struggling with the question of how best to express her surreal sensibility in the form the stories would take. More adamant than ever about the vital importance of the short story form, Welty wrote *The Golden Apples* from this resolute perspective, a position that letters between her and her agent, Diarmuid Russell, demonstrate she assumed while struggling to develop a new fictional strategy minimizing the demands imposed upon her by the heavy plot requirements of novel writing. Michael Kreyling's *Author and Agent*, a key study that lucidly contextualizes more than three decades of letters that passed between Welty and Russell, supplies an illuminating account of the approximately two-and-a-half year period during which she composed the stories that ultimately developed into the "jigsaw puzzle" of *The Golden Apples* (Jones 332).

Like one of Morgana's wandering protagonists, Welty traveled widely between 1946 and 1950, and although Jackson remained the center of gravity for her writing life, she "made two extended visits to San Francisco, one long vacation to New York City, the usual weekend trips, and capped the decade of the 1940s with plans for her first trip to Europe" (Kreyling *Author* 117). Even though she traveled outside the state, dwelling at some distance from its familiar sights and ways, she wrote almost exclusively about the Delta, as if *Delta Wedding*'s completion, publication, and healthy sales had not released her from its soporific hold. She remained firmly under the spell of the novel's surreal uncertainty and more defiant than before in her belief that, as Kreyling remarks, "ambiguity might be the proper mode for certain experiences," and that "obscurity might be more powerful than clarity in the right circumstances" (*Author* 118).

By September 1946, Kreyling reports, Welty had "The Whole World Knows" and "Golden Apples" (later titled "June Recital" in *The Golden*

Apples) underway "simultaneously" (*Author* 118). On her first excursion to visit her lover and the dedicatee of *Delta Wedding*, John Robinson, in San Francisco, Welty wrote the story that ultimately carried the title "Music from Spain" (123). Next came "Moon Lake," a story she had had in development since her return from California (125), and, by May 1947, she began suggesting to Russell that "Golden Apples," "Music from Spain," and "Moon Lake" should form a book (127). However, Welty's acceptance of an invitation to participate in the Northwest Pacific Writers' Conference in August that year postponed sustained work on the stories of *The Golden Apples*. While the speech that the conference required of her tested her prowess as a critic and severely strained her patience, the paper, heavily influenced by her most admired literary commentator, E. M. Forster, concentrated on the virtues of the short story, and precipitated what Kreyling calls her "summit treaty with plot" (*Author* 138). Although the essay's preparation and revision for eventual publication turned into an ordeal, its writing galvanized Welty's preference for thoroughgoing characterization over the limitations of plot into a deep-seated conviction, seemingly a tacit acknowledgement that any writing attuned to the ambiguities of dreams must prioritize character.

Immediately after giving the presentation, she went south for a second stay with Robinson in San Francisco, where she wrote another letter to Russell, dated August 22, 1947, in which she first imagines the broad outline of *The Golden Apples*. "Do you understand," Welty questions her then most significant critic, "for I think the stories in it are all of a certain kind, or of a long, ruminative, etc. turn of thought—and it would be nice to have one or two other kinds in a book—do you agree?" (qtd. in Kreyling *Author* 132). Over the next few months, the idea of the extant narratives' interrelations began to suggest itself more forcefully to Welty, as she edged toward the book's final synthesis of seven stories. A month later, in September, 1947, she speculated that the stories "might really be a novel," but by October 6, her position against the novel had hardened into solid opposition (134). "I now think that the novel isn't necessary," she wrote to Russell, "—that would be, at this point anyway, an artificial way for me to go ahead with the material. So why not just go my own way, writing the stories as short stories, the way they occur to me, but letting them go on and be inter-related, but not interdependent, just as they actually are in my head" (136). The lightening-fast composition of "Shower of Gold"—the fifth in order of creation and written and in only one day—shortly before the drafting of this letter, marks Welty's decision to draw the stories into a conglomeration that would "[n]ot have plots and strings tied to them except for the short stories' sakes," and "yet wouldn't have the burden of the novel, with all that tying up of threads and preparing for this, that and the other" (137). In the months to follow and between trips to New York City, "Sir Rabbit" appeared, and, in July 1948, she wrote "The Hummingbirds," a story later renamed "The Wanderers," which rounds out *The Golden Apples* collection.

Beset by anxieties focused on the genre of the evolving work, Welty first seemed to have thought of the book as a collection of short stories, and then as a novel, only at the final moment turning against the novel form. Writing to Russell on March 28, 1949, on the eve of the book's publication, she suggested, "Maybe we could call it something like 'Variations on a Portfolio' or something from the other arts where such groupings are more common?" (qtd. in Kreyling *Author* 146). Her interdisciplinary suggestion for *The Golden Apples* indicates the visual orientation of her thinking about the succession and arrangement of the narratives at this time, having what Kreyling calls a "suite or portfolio of related stories" (*Author* 136). The previous year, in June, 1948, she had made a similar, although more indirect, overture, using a common set of visual analogies when she wrote to Russell of her new story, "The Hummingbirds": "You might when you see this make a little composition of them all in your head and see how it looks, I mean an over-all picture" (qtd. in Kreyling *Author* 143). The long, ruminative stories mostly characterizing *The Golden Apples* clearly show Welty ordering their integration in terms of visual metaphors. Her remarks in interviews regarding the obsessive lives of Morgana's inhabitants and the work's detailed compositional account, supported by the letters exchanged between author and agent, foreground Welty's drift toward fictionalizing the deep recesses of character over the shallow conveyance of plot. Along with E. M. Forster, she considered the revelation of character as a central plank in her artistic platform, an aesthetic philosophy that exalts the "vastness of our secret life, which is endlessly explorable," and diminishes plot, which "no matter how strenuous or intriguing, is without escape superficial" (138). The sequence of the stories' production in *The Golden Apples* shows an author so deeply probing the shifting permutations of the unconscious and the best way to convey them that she almost neglects to supply even the barest elements of plot. However, this shift toward greater characterization at the expense of plot illuminates Welty's surreal perspective. The surreal emerges most conspicuously at those points in the narrative where the author most completely suppresses the superficial concerns of plot and focuses on psychology.

In production by 1946, "The Whole World Knows" vividly exposes the wretchedly claustrophobic atmosphere of a paranoiac's demented personality, verging upon disintegration. Written first, along with "Golden Apples," it marks the book's point of origin and the beginning of its circuitous path's. Its title boldly evokes the paranoiac's delusional conviction that the entire world conspires to create and intensify his anguish. Ran MacLain—son of King MacLain, Morgana's almost endlessly wandering lothario, and Snowdie MacLain, King's snow-white bride—narrates this fifth segment of *The Golden Apples*, which picks up the story in the 1930s. Around thirty years old at the time of the events, Ran has left his wife, Jinny Love, because of her affair with Ran's colleague at work, Woody Spights. Furious but titillated by his wife's infidelity, Ran has taken a room in the house that he "grew up in" in the town, which swelters in the burning August heat (*Stories* 458). His fractured and disordered first-person narrative is reminiscent of Quentin Compson's highly-introverted journey toward suicide in Faulkner's *The Sound and the Fury*—but Welty directs her protagonist's focus to the mother, Snowdie, in her dramatization of Ran's troubled psychology.[4] The morbidly plaintive, gently accusatory—and always intrusive—maternal voice opens the story and returns intermittently, posing antagonizing questions, making unsolicited suggestions, and incessantly urging Ran's restoration to her in MacLain. It is as if his abandonment of Morgana would lift the stain of his wife's unfaithfulness. At one point, he imagines his mother's voice reminding him, "*The whole world knows what she did to you. It's different from when it's the man*" (469). Unable to command his spouse's loyalty, Ran feels the vindictive stab of his mother's remark, which condones and entrenches the double standard. In the delirious trance that pervades the whole chapter, he responds to the situation by seducing a naive "*country* girl" (458), Maideen Sumrall, whom he initially uses against his estranged wife and ultimately debases in a cheap Mississippi dive. Soon after, Maideen "hurt herself" (472) in what probably was a successful suicide attempt.

To create the extended trance of "The Whole World Knows," Welty had merely to re-engage and perhaps intensify the surreal sensibility that had guided the production of her fiction from the start. In fact, examining the parallels between her text and Dalí's paranoia-criticism is one way of revealing surrealism's general effect on her work. *The Conquest of the*

Irrational, Dalí's definitive 1935 statement propounding the theory, claims that the "precise apparatus" (263) of paranoia-criticism could synthesize the "world of imagination and concrete irrationality" to generate in the resulting cultural product an "objective clearness, of the same consistency, of the same durability, of the same persuasive, cognoscitive and communicable thickness as that of the external world of phenomenal reality" (265). Thus, the theory predicted that the artistic object created using the paranoia-critical method would display a synthetic texture, at once representational and abstract. Paranoia-critical activity, then, "intervenes uniquely as a liquid developer of images, associations, coherences, and *finesses,* which are systematic, weighty and already in existence at the moment in which the delirious instantaneity occurs" (267), so Dalí claims irrationality's conquest in his art by carefully simulating the systematic logic of a paranoid's apprehension. His artwork of the thirties and forties largely shows him following through on the promises made in his method's foundational texts, such that paranoia-criticism spurred the production of hundreds of sketches, paintings, and surrealist objects that demanded a radical reappraisal of bourgeois values (Finkelstein *Salvador* 189). Considering Welty's "The Whole World Knows," a text that deploys a parallel set of artistic strategies and criticisms of middle-class superficialities, and *The Golden Apples* generally reveals both artists engaged in the same struggle—to encourage their audiences to acknowledge the shaping force of dreams, mirages, and obsessions in people's lives.

The experience of reading Ran MacLain's hallucinogenic narration compares favorably with the act of viewing a Dalí from the thirties or forties, the sort of dream paintings in which phobias, compulsions, and obsessions are writ large. Moreover, when Welty began drafting "The Whole World Knows," the Spaniard had only just finished collaborating with Alfred Hitchcock on the revolutionary dream sequences featured in the 1945 movie *Spellbound,* five years into the eight-year exile he and his wife, Gala, spent in the United States while they sat out the war. Unlike the elitist Breton, who scorned the grubby products of popular culture, Dalí "saw the aims of Surrealism and the American film industry as practically identical in the way they answered the public's hunger for the life of the imagination" (Radford 198).

And it seems that Welty shared Dalí's enthusiasm for the significance of mass culture in a democracy. A "constant moviegoer" (Ferris 169) all her life and a devotee of Hitchcock in particular, she admits to seeing a "relationship between film and short-stories" (168), especially concerning the "use of flashbacks and memory" and "dream sequence." In the same interviews (from 1975 and 1976), she also suggests that from film she "must have absorbed some of the lessons which have come in handy." In her published interviews, Welty never mentions any of the films she saw during the early years of her career, although she proclaims their importance to her writing, especially in terms of transferable cinematic techniques. She maintains, "We never missed one. And part of my life in New York was spent running out to the Thalia and all those places, every little foreign film place in New York, seeing all those films" (169).[5]

While avant-garde surrealist films, such as Luis Buñuel and Salvador Dalí's collaborative ventures, *Un Chien Andalou* and *L'Âge d'Or*, did reach New York in the early thirties, the audience for them remained small. As president of the short-lived Film Society of New York, Julien Levy organized several private and public screenings of *Un Chien Andalou* in 1932 and *L'Âge d'Or* in 1933 (Schaffner "Alchemy" 36). Following the American premier of the latter film, Levy wrote to a friend that the "film is still the only topic for dinner conversation all about New York" (qtd. in Schaffner "Alchemy" 37), and in his memoirs, written decades later, he notes that his showings of *Un Chien Andalou* "more than anything else established Dalí's reputation in this country" (150). Although in her interviews with William Ferris Welty does not share what films she saw on her visits to New York, she does admit a preference for the lyric film that

> teaches you more than the adventure film or anything like that. The mood films show you what is focused upon and how atmosphere is used. The French always do it better than anyone. They've got so many people who were trained in a world of art—like Jean Renoir. How could he have escaped a great knowledge of the making of a film from the painter's household he grew up in? (170)

Even if Welty did not view surrealist films in the early thirties, she must have felt the buzz they created—especially given her comments above, which illustrate her preference for mood movies more influenced by painting than by the narrative structure of the realistic novel.

Nothing proves that Welty saw *Spellbound* or earlier surrealist classics like *Un Chien Andalou* or *L'Âge d'Or*, but her liking for Hitchcock and admission of "running out" to "every little foreign film place in New York"

Luis Buñuel (director) and Salvador Dalí's film, *Un Chien Andalou* (1929). Video Yesteryear/ Photofest © Video Yesteryear.

(Ferris 169) certainly does tempt one to imagine her slipping into one of Julien Levy's Film Society of New York meetings. (Frank Lyell had alerted her to the gallery and its artistic preferences as early as 1933.) In any case, by the forties, the scene of a razor slitting a woman's eyeball in *Un Chien Andalou* had assumed legendary status: "Any viewer with a passing knowledge of cinema or of Surrealism would have recognized the reference to the shocking scene of the razor slicing through a woman's eye in Dalí's previous collaboration with Buñuel" (Cochran 178). The reprised ocular imagery in *Spellbound*—a film in which persecutory dream sequences conspicuously deploy conglomerations of observing eyeballs that watch and condemn as well as suffer dissection—serve as key motifs. They articulate a fundamental surrealist principle, that dreams and the unconscious distort the experiences of watching and recording, and that the "lacerated eye" symbolizes a "comment on, and denial of, the visual and the rational" (Gale 83). Perhaps Welty's viewing of Hitchcock's *Spellbound* reinforced this view apropos of a movie that "was the first Hollywood film to take psycho-analysis seriously as its subject," deploying dream imagery in order to reveal the source of the lead character's infantile neurosis (he accidentally caused the death of his brother) (Ades 203). According to Sara Cochran, the concept of repression

Alfred Hitchcock's *Spellbound* (1945) featured dream sequences by Salvador Dalí. United Artists/ Photofest © United Artists.

and its role in creating neurosis, as outlined in the movie, now seems "dated," but "it was then considered an ambitious exploration of Freudian analysis and was nominated for the 'Best Picture' Academy Award" (176). Several shades darker than Hitchcock's film—which was released at about the same time that Welty had her story about brothers underway—"The Whole World Knows" also presents a male protagonist spellbound by infantile neurosis and a conclusion that features a suicide by handgun.

In surrealist stories, films, and art, paranoia and confusion pervade life, rendering suspect claims to rationality. "The Whole World Knows" makes ample and productive sense when read in this context. Rebecca Mark, for example, points out that readers err in blithely accepting things as they appear in the story. She questions whether Ran and Maideen's sexual encounter at the Sunset Oaks motel can "be read as a literal rape" (*Dragon's Blood* 145), and asserts that in this story Welty "creates a mixing of the real and the imagined, which informs the rest of the collection" (146). Another commentator, Peter Schmidt, in his searching analysis of the story, supplies a psychoanalytic account of both Ran's and his brother Eugene's mental

breakdowns, cautioning that Ran's assault on Woody "is difficult to deci-
pher, for Ran's point of view has trouble distinguishing between his own
hallucinations and what actually happens" (67). However, neither Schmidt
nor Mark extends his or her observations to an accounting of the whole
fabric of the story that reveals Ran's hallucinatory state of mind at every
turn. From the desperate urgency of the chapter's opening line, "Father, I
wish I could talk to you, wherever you are right now" (*Stories* 451), Welty's
language creates a suffocating mood of enclosure and confinement, forcing readers, pressed tightly into Ran's confessional box, to gasp for air and
struggle for escape from an episode "that is half confession, half supplication, as though spoken to a priest or even to God" (Vande Kieft 104). Try
as Ran may, he cannot free himself from the cell of his own persecutory
condition, a narcissistic state of mind that Welty variously describes as inescapable and hellish.

Working as a clerk at the Morgana bank, Ran cannot run from the vault
of his anguished and frustrated desire, but can only watch as outsiders,
such as the busybody, Miss Perdita Mayo, leave him paralyzed in a state
of chronic paranoia. She "backs away leaving her hands out, pulling-like
at the air, like I'm floating on my ear suspended, hypnotized, and she can
leave." With varying degrees of sincerity, Miss Perdita Mayo, Mr. Drewsie
Carmichael, and Miss Jefferson Moody all suggest solutions to Ran's problem, but none can release him from the "cage" that imprisons him at the
bank (*Stories* 458). Introverted and deep in the grip of his narcissistic compulsions, he lives a tortured existence, trapped in the boarding house, which
once housed his mother's "wedding dress" (459), and where the "roasting"
(453) August sun threatens to scorch him to death in that "little hot upstairs room with a western exposure" (458). Another emblem of alienation
and torment, the room in the "burning building" evinces Welty's surreal
melding of material and metaphysical dimensions to create a space at once
internal and external: both Ran's mother's room, where he speaks to her on
the phone, and the inside of his head (460). Like the hallucinatory vision of
the backwoods cabin in "Death of a Traveling Salesman," and the deluding
heat and light that Robbie experiences on the road to Shellmound in *Delta
Wedding*, the furnace of Ran's apartment supplies a fitting metaphor for his
tortured interior state. Even—or perhaps especially—his mother, Snowdie,
cannot stop him from "*walking around in a dream*" (457). Everyone in
Morgana has his or her own neurosis to nurse, but Ran's somnambulism
seems to have reached a terminal point.

The paranoia verging on psychosis that Ran experiences in "The Whole World Knows" affects his sight, which Welty shows as compromised by distortions and mirages. One should skeptically acknowledge what Ran says he views and when he views it. That his hallucinations often get the better of him foregrounds in an obvious way Welty's integration of surrealist ideas about the simulation of delirious states in artistic productions, the sort of duplicity intrinsic to seeing what a sliced or multiplied eyeball symbolizes. For example, the opening passages of the chapter show Ran turning his back upon the bank: "I rolled down my sleeves and stood for some time looking out at the cotton field behind Mr. Wiley Bowles' across the street, until it nearly put me to sleep and then woke me up like a light turned on in my face" (*Stories* 451). In a futile attempt to protect himself from exposure, the paranoiac turns his sleeves down, but his covering up fails to shield his eyes from the blinding light of the cotton field that mesmerizes him, putting him into a somnambulistic trance. Then, having stopped to give Maideen a ride home, he makes conversation with her, conceding that he cannot rely on his vision: "I told her my eyes had gone bad" (452). The next time he picks her up, he takes her to the Starks' house in an effort to provoke Jenny. "Maideen was at my side," Ran explains, "We walked across the Starks' baked yard to the front porch, passing under the heavy heads of those crape myrtles, the too bright blooms that hang down like fruits that might drop." The testicular flowers hang immaturely, their heads not having fallen, drooping precariously before the "steel crochet hook" that Jinny's mother, Miss Lizzie Morgan, raps on the "window sill." Strangely elated by this threat of castration, Ran feels "curiously light-hearted." Like Laura, who smothers her nose in a lily before entering the trance of the Delta in *Delta Wedding*, he inhales the scent of blooming lilies, taking a "full breath of their ether smell: consciousness could go or not. I pulled open the screen door" (454). In a direct allusion to the opening line of T. S. Eliot's "The Love Song of J. Alfred Prufrock," Welty initiates a dreamlike sequence that unfolds from Ran's narcotized perspective and ends with Snowdie's aggravating accusation that he lives in a perpetual daydream.

Entering the Starks' house, Ran still has castration on his mind. He views his unfaithful wife "with her legs apart," and sees her wielding a pair of "stork-shaped scissors" in an act of disfigurement, as she cuts clumps of her hair impulsively in the "hall mirror" (*Stories* 454). Indeed, Welty presents Ran's world as if refracted through a whole hall of mirrors, which reflect a world distorted and deformed by the overpowering force of his obsessions and phobias. Clearly, he has slipped out of full consciousness here, disclosing in his daydreaming his fear of impotency, the wreck of his marriage, and the pain of Jinny, who appears transfigured into Medusa ("I looked at Jinny's head with the ragged points all over it"). Walking through the house toward the back porch, Ran seems almost drunk on his wife's act of self-mutilation, for he experiences an intoxicating lightness that recalls the hypnotized, floating head at the bank. "That lightness came right back," Ran admits: "Just to step on the matting, that billows a little anyway, and with Jinny's hair scattered like feathers on it, I could have floated, risen and floated." On the porch, they sit in rockers, but not everyone rocks to sleep like Ran, whose eyes fail him again: "The outside—a sheet of white light—was in my eyes. The ferns close around us were hushing on their stands, they had just been watered. I could listen to women and hear pieces of the story, of what happened to us, of course—but I listened to the ferns." An analgesic alternative to the women talking and the implacable expanse of sheeting light, the anthropomorphic ferns hush him into a light reverie, during which he hears "town words" rushing like fern water (455), and imagines local gossips creating a heroic myth for him that can rival his father's.[6] For example, he dreams that the gossips fear his possible retaliatory violence against Jinny and Woody, fear that maybe he might "kill them all" (456).

But later Welty plainly shows that Ran's gun sticks. Thoughts of impotency and disease waft in the "slow breeze" from the porch fan, whose "old white blades frosted like a cake, with flies riding on it" lifts the women's hair "like one passing hand." The fly-infested blade—a motif that may echo any number of self-obsessed Dalí paintings in which ants swarm hungrily over decaying formations—suggests Ran's impotence, his mental disease, and his powerlessness in his frozen marriage to Jinny. Their wedding cake putrefies, and distance has hardened their emotions. But Maideen, who features prominently in Ran's erotic daydream, makes "intervals in the quiet, like the ferns dripping," and so promises a thawing of the frost and relief from the parching heat (*Stories* 456). A young employee at Morgana's Seed and Feed, Maideen Sumrall symbolizes purity, fertility, and optimism, yet Ran ultimately makes her an "innocent victim" of his debilitating neurosis (Kreyling *Understanding* 135).

Although a broad seam of paranoid hallucinations winds through the fabric of "The Whole World Knows," two instances in particular stress the overpowering intensity of Ran's narcissistic desperation: his imagining a violent assault upon Jinny's lover, Woody Spights, and his equally ferocious fantasy of shooting his wife. These imaginary acts of violence prefigure the unknown violence done to Maideen at the denouement, but Ran's incoherent, faltering narration toward the close forever obscures precisely what happens at Sunset Oaks. Welty couches all Ran's tantrums and subsequent acts of aggression—whether real or imaginary—in surreal language that transfigures the realism of the moment, charging it with paranoiac overtones and infusing it with the overdetermined quality of a dream. After work one afternoon, Ran goes over to Jinny's, where the men play croquet in inescapable heat that "held on." In the evening swelter and "still quiet" of Ran's mind, insulated from the distracting noise that reminds him of the world outside his consciousness, a young girl's innocent remark about the game reaches him, triggering a violent fantasy in which he viciously beats Woody with a croquet mallet.[7] "But I brought Woody Spights down with it," Ran brags, "He toppled and shook the ground. I felt the air rush up. Then I beat on him. I went over his whole length, and cracked his head apart with that soft girl's hair and all the ideas, beat on him without stopping till every bone, all the way down to the numerous little bones in the foot, was cracked in two." Satisfying himself that a human body "could be finished up pretty fast" with "one good blow after another" (*Stories* 459), he contemplates doing the same violence to Jinny.

Regardless of his vaunting misogyny, homoerotic desire, and profound self-loathing, Ran's assault has not injured Woody, whose name obscenely ridicules Ran, and whose blue eyes appear "unharmed," "impervious," still reflecting the world like "unbroken" bubbles (*Stories* 459). In fact, he speaks without pain, astonishing the nearly unhinged Ran with his ability to open his mouth. "He was dead on the ruined grass," Ran hallucinates, "But he had risen up." When confronted at such close range by overwhelming evidence of his powerlessness to resolve his Oedipal struggle by killing Woody, his father's double, and in the disavowing his mother, Ran screams out inwardly, "All is disgrace!" He visualizes the surreal August grass "like the floor of the sea, and we walk on it slowly playing, and the sky turns green before dark, Father, as you know. The sweat ran over my back and down my arms and legs, branching, like an upside-down tree." Here, crucified by failure and driven to a new low, he courts death by drowning in green seas, suggested by the running trickles of salt water that spread out over his back.[8] Then, as if in a dream, he abandons the Starks' "bright porch," which he views "like a boat on the river," and so ignores the "excursion boat I wasn't going on" (460). Turning from the riverboat trip with Jinny, he suggests one to Maideen. They go to Vicksburg and a paralyzed floating barge, the setting for the story's bleak finale.

The trip to Vicksburg occupies the final third of the narrative and shifts even more confusingly between time frames, and between what Ran dreams and what he actually observes. The language's hallucinogenic imagery reveals an addled mind on the verge of breakdown. Ran confronts his mother, Snowdie, in the figure of Maideen, who reads a magazine, flipping its pages on the nineteen-mile car ride by "moistening her finger first, like my mother" (*Stories* 465). The Civil War battleground supplies a fitting locale for Ran's internecine struggle with Snowdie, the pale ghost who haunts her son's memory. As Louise Westling indicates, "To return to his mother would mean a return to childhood dependency" and a disastrous capitulation to his phobias and compulsions, bluntly expressed in the cold death written into Snowdie's name (*Eudora* 147). The totality of the action in this last segment of the story occurs in an almost narcotic haze Welty creates by repeatedly recycling allusions to sleep, developing hallucinogenic descriptions of the landscape and people, and generally establishing a dangerous atmosphere of confusion, disarray, and panic. For example, while driving to Vicksburg, Ran iterates to himself how Maideen "would get stupefied for sleep" and "would be simply dead for sleep" when he drove her home from card parties at the Starks (*Stories* 465). And later, after leaving drunk from the barge floating on the Mississippi, Maideen slouches in the car only half conscious and dreams that they lose their way, while Ran drives as if in sexual frenzy, turning the car "up the steep hills" and following the river before going off along a dark "deep rutted path" and "circling and rushing down" to a fetid dead end (468). Back on the road, Ran thinks: "Maideen was awake because I heard her sighing faintly." But only a few lines later, as he guides her into the grubby recess of the Sunset Oaks motel, he admits his mistake, recognizing, "She had been asleep after all." Inside the motel room, a double of Ran's boarding house apartment in Morgana, both fall "dead asleep" instantly. Maideen gets up to cut the light off and goes back to sleep, only for Ran to awaken as the "never dark enough" night falls around him "like a bucket let down a well," leaving him alone, trapped and alienated (470).

The tension created by Welty's surreal blending of night and day, blindness and sight, drunkenness and sobriety, and dreams and actuality precludes an easy literal, interpretation of events. For instance, Ran's depleted sexual energy revives upon his exit from his hometown. "And suddenly all sensation returned" (*Stories* 465), he announces. But Morgana, at which he "had looked too long," travels with him in his mind's eye, the street appearing like a "pencil mark on the sky that jumped with the shaking of the gin," strangely in motion like a "little toy train" with its "indelible red-false-fronts joined one to the other." Vibrating, liquid, half dreamt and half seen, Morgana appears as a mirage in Ran's memory, and this abiding sense of fraudulency extends to the unreality of Vicksburg, whose rigidity also softens and risks dissolving as he views it. "It was sunset," Welty writes, "The island was very near across the water—a waste of willows, yellow and green strands loosely woven together, like a basket that let the light spill out uncontrollably" (466).

Tipsy on the alcohol, some of which Ran has forced Maideen to drink, they speed along the river's edge, turning into down a cul-de-sac where the car, seemingly metamorphosed into an insect, hangs precariously "on the wall of the bluff" before Ran backs up, reversing the car "like a bee pulling out of a flower cup" (*Stories* 469). In a crescendo building toward violence, Welty disperses this series of heavily sexualized metaphors, prefiguring Ran's attempted seduction of Maideen. Taking the sleep-prone Maideen on long meandering drives and plying her heavily with alcohol, Ran perhaps hopes to rape her while she sleeps so that he can simulate sex with a corpse or a ghost, suggested by the "coon, white as a ghost" that haunts Sunset Oaks motel, the final scene of confrontation with the wraithlike Snowdie. However, Maideen frustrates Ran's necrophilia. She stays awake and undresses before him, sending him into a violent fit: "I propped myself up against the rods of the bed with my back pressing them. I was sighing— deep sigh after deep sigh. I heard myself. When she turned back to the bed, I said, 'Don't come close to me'" (470). Here, Welty surreally compresses two scenes into one to reveal the genesis of Ran's phobic response: He sees the Vicksburg motel room and the Morgana boarding house room superimposed on one another. Maideen's dress, spread out tenderly on the bedroom chair, finds its psychological counterpart in Snowdie's wedding dress, which the Morgana apartment once housed.

Although Ran brandishes his father's pistol in an attempt to drive Maideen off, she reacts calmly, coming "into the space before my eyes, plain in the lighted night. She held her bare arms. She was disarrayed. There was blood on her, blood and disgrace. Or perhaps there wasn't. For a minute I saw her double. But I pointed the gun at her the best I could" (*Stories* 471).

Ran sees Maiden multiply, as if he watches through an eye made double by a razor or endlessly reproduced. Perhaps she has blood on her, but perhaps Ran hallucinates the marks—signs of menstrual flow, fertility, and murder—associating them with the disgust he feels toward women. Perhaps he literally sees Maideen double up to avoid a bullet, or she is doubled because his sight has blurred. But perhaps he sees her double in Morgana, maybe Jinny but more likely Snowdie, the source of his complex, advancing toward him seductively. As a last resort, he directs the gun on himself, sucking on the muzzle before he fires.[9] The pistol jams, and Maideen retrieves the weapon while echoing Snowdie's aggravating questions about why he carries that "*old pistol of you father's in your nice coat pocket*" (460). While Ran sees Maideen, he hears his mother's patronizing voice as the girl coyly observes, "Now you see. It didn't go off. Give me that. Give that old thing to me, I'll take care of it." Disarmed, vulnerable, cornered, and stirred erotically by Maideen's inadvertent mothering, Ran claims, "And I had her so quick"—but he takes her, perhaps against her will, when the mood had obviously turned frigid. Returning to the bed after folding the gun away in her dress, Maideen tries to comfort Ran, putting her hand out "differently, and laid it cold on my shoulder" (471). Fixated on his mother and excited by the gentle snow-like touch of his lover, Ran interprets these gestures as sexual cues. Afterward—humiliated, dirtied, and weepy beside Ran's implacable and sleeping body—Maideen apparently attempts or succeeds in suicide.

Peter Schmidt's *The Heart of the Story* rightly groups the insanity of "The Whole World Knows" with Welty's other stories about madness in *The Golden Apples*, "Music from Spain" and "June Recital." He further contends that unlike the first two stories, which focus, respectively, on Ran's and Eugene's spiraling descents into chaos, "June Recital" "is not written from the point of view of its principal character," Miss Eckhart, and, therefore, distances "us from her inner life" (102). While Welty movingly presents the cruel twists of fortune that characterize this piano teacher's life in Morgana, Schmidt's assumption that she represents the narrative's principal focus minimizes the distorting effects created by the mediating presence of the narrators, Loch and Cassie Morrison. The Morrisons alone convey Miss Eckhart's myth, and subjectivity suffuses their accounts just as deeply as the paranoia of Ran's self-obsessions runs through "The Whole World Knows."

Furthermore, Welty's discarded title for "June Recital," "Golden Apples," suggests a writer preoccupied with the eroticism circulating in W. B. Yeats's "The Song of the Wandering Aengus," a poem that restages desire's obsessive pursuit of gratification as enacted on Keats's Grecian urn. As Patricia S. Yaeger observes, Welty appropriates Keats's and Yeats's theme of desire's inexhaustibility, so that if "at times Welty's female characters resemble the passive, mysterious figure of the glimmering girl whom Yeats portrays as the object of man's desire, in other moments they resemble the ostensible subject of Yeats's poem, the Aengus, in their imagination and their desires" (152). "June Recital," then, revises Yeats's hierarchy through its presentation of both men *and* women compelled by the fire that burns inside them. Loch Morrison, a young boy on the verge of puberty, and his sister, Cassie, a teenage girl on the verge of college, must resolve a puzzle whose rarely satisfying solution discloses society's protocols governing desire. Although the narration smoothly switches between these two young observers, Welty's control of their perspectives on Miss Eckhart's life teaching in the old MacLain house, next door to the Morrisons', shows a writer once again employing a rhetoric derived from surrealism.

Suffering a high malarial fever, Loch Morrison opens the renamed "June Recital." Danièle Pitavy-Souques's article, "Watchers and Watching: Points of View in Eudora Welty's 'June Recital,'" insightfully ponders the subtle shift in emphasis effected by this title change, which accents "seeing and being seen" in contrast to the "search." Thus, Pitavy-Souques focuses on Loch's narration of the "show" that the MacLain house puts on, as he watches—first through the screen of his bedroom window and, then from the alternately upside-down and right-side-up vantage point of a tree (503). In addition to these connotations, the new title directs attention to the problematic nature of information derived from visual observation. Optical illusions of the kind prized by surrealists or mirages that roll in over Morgana's cotton fields can play cruel tricks on observers. "June Recital," rather like the eye bisected in *Un Chien Andalou*, plays upon the eye's fallibility as a sensing organ owing to its perpetual viewing and reviewing of phenomena over time and through the prism of memory, experience, and prejudice. Only a few years later, Welty would go on to elaborate the intrinsically surreal phenomenon of double vision when she remarked on the novelist's facility for "always seeing double, two pictures at once in his frame, his and the world's" ("Place in Fiction" 789). This concept of double vision finds expression in "June Recital" when Loch views and recounts Miss Eckhart's June return to her studio in the MacLain house, which she attempts to burn down. He acts as a mediating entity, seeing while re-seeing, sighting while re-sighting, observing in order to record, and viewing in order to recite.

Welty's title stresses the illusions of the observing eye here—at least for story's first movement. Indeed, Loch's name suggests the firm hold he has upon what readers see when they read. Through his recitation of events, Welty reveals a surreally inflected perspective at once dreamt and actual. When the story begins, "Loch was in a tempest with his mother" (*Stories* 333), immediately evoking the maritime mirage of the fata morgana, the controlling metaphor unifying all seven of *The Golden Apple*'s stories, through the allusion to Shakespeare's stormy romance. The substitute title, the first line of the narrative, and the action described in the first paragraph—Loch's reluctant swallowing of a medicinal potion—forecloses any expectation of realism, rendering suspect critical evaluations that assume otherwise. Instead, an expanded reality or surreality predominates in "June Recital," a story that prominently displays Welty's intoxicating language, creating a mood irreducibly dreamt and literal.

Like Ran, Loch suffers from a sickness of the blood: Both of their mothers are endlessly antagonizing, domineering, and unwanted presences in their lives. In the echo chamber of his mind, Ran endures Snowdie's reverberating accusations. Loch, newly alerted to the stirrings of desire, has only just begun to experience his mother as intrusive. She keeps him confined to his bed, and she wields the hated "brimming spoon" of medicine. For Loch, maternal care comes across as maternal persecution. Rather than "kissing him" when she leaves for a nap, she wobbles his "pompadour cap" (*Stories* 333) as if to aggravate and not comfort, roughly pushing and pulling him "as she put cool pillow cases on the pillows and pushed him back straight" (338). However, in "June Recital," Loch enjoys a hiatus between moments of maternal oppression: His mother has gone to Miss Nell Carlisle's card party, leaving him unmolested and free to watch the X-rated show put on at the MacLain house. Virgie Rainey, Miss Eckhart's most talented piano student, enters the ramshackle house accompanied by a sailor, with whom she has sex in an upstairs bedroom.[10] Below, Miss Eckhart returns to her one-time studio, now abandoned, and makes a fire inside the piano's shell—only to suffer humiliation when two guards extinguish the fire, escort her from the house, and make plans to have her institutionalized. Old Man Holifield, the night watchman who supposedly supervises the MacLain house for its new owner, sleeps through all the activity, but by way of explanation, Welty points out that he "was having a dream" (334). Such a defense might seem ludicrous if *The Golden Apples* did not repeatedly expose the way that dreams permeate waking life and inform the conduct of Morgana's inhabitants. Moreover, dreams reflect the obsessions by which these people live; in "June Recital" Loch also represents a dreaming night watchman, spellbound by the dream's delusion.

Loch views and reviews scenes watched through various distorting fil-ters: the optic of his malarial eye, the screen of his window, and the lens of his telescope. He observes both clearly and unclearly, both concretely and abstractly, and both surely and as if hallucinating. Readers see events through the haze of his fever, which creates a mood of surreal delirium and paranoia that Welty's prose simulates by mapping his dream's desires onto the house he views. The first person narrator running a high tem-perature cannot be trusted, because, like the abandoned MacLain house, he has "wrapped" his recitation "with the summer's love." Viewing the house, his eyes "rest or go flickering along it, as over something very well known indeed. Its left-alone contour, its careless stretching away into that deep backyard he knew by heart. The house's side was like a person's, if a person or giant would lie sleeping there, always sleeping" (*Stories* 333). Loch's eyes alternately pause and flicker along the house and backyard, forms that as-sume insubstantiality within the frame of the boy's vision. Yet the scene threatens to dissolve, wavering when his eye runs over familiar shapes, and he defers to imagination and memory when he reaches the limits of his view. Does he see movement or stasis, something familiar or foreign? A backyard, a house or a giant? Something asleep or awake, himself or some-one else?

Looking from his window into the MacLain house's upstairs window, he spies another bed that "faced his." Like Narcissus, he gazes into a re-flective surface, as Welty suggests with her description of the front room window, which "was dazzling in the afternoon," and with a picture hang-ing on the wall that sometimes "reflected the light outdoors" (*Stories* 334). Adding to the surreal and disorienting atmosphere of the episode, Welty writes of Loch's sight: "Even under his shut eyelids, that light and shade stayed divided from each other, but reversed," and "Some whole days at a time, often in his dreams day and night, he would seem to be living next door, wild as a cowboy, absolutely by himself, without his mother or father coming in to feel his skin, or run a finger under his cap." Released from the prohibiting presence of his parents and spellbound by his desirous dream, Loch hauls his telescope from under the bed. Mr. Morrison's instrument, the "telescope had been gripped in his father's hand like a big stick." Now Loch, the heir, holds it, shooting its end out the window and sweeping the "glass lovingly toward the house" to enjoy a "sweet self-indulgence" that "could visit him in his bed" (335).[11] In the ensuing action, Welty likens Loch to Argus, the mythological sentry with a thousand eyes. It is a comparison reminiscent of scenes from Hitchcock's *Spellbound*, and, because his malarial delirium—also a metaphor for the hormonal surges of puberty—a reflection of Yeats's flame of desire, which burns in his head and distorts his perception. When he observes Virgie and the sailor cavorting on the bed, Loch squints through the camera-like lens of the telescope with one eye open and the other shut, another reference to the bisected eyeball.

The surreal scene seems a show he has watched before, because he "was waiting for the day when the sailor took the figs" from Virgie. Ancient fertility symbols that suggest ripeness, reproduction, and renewal, the figs split open tantalizingly, transformed by the telescope's system of lenses and mirrors into symbols of the female body. "They were rusty old fig trees," Loch notes, "but the figs were the little sweet blue. When they cracked open their pink and golden flesh would show, their inside flowers, and golden bubbles of juice would hang, to touch your tongue to first" (*Stories* 336). Fighting against the fever and sleep, Loch daydreams of the sensual MacLain house, from which emanates an approaching "stillness" that he senses "coming nearer" and "coming very close to him" like an orgasm. "Sometimes," Welty observes, "he threw his arm across his eyes and counted without moving his lips, imagining that when he got to a certain amount he might give a yell, like 'Coming, ready or not!' and go down by the hackberry limb" (338). This moment of simulated masturbation and climax is interrupted when his mother's changes his bed linen. Nonetheless, when he moves the telescope's eye over Virgie and her lover, no adult interferes with his fantasy, imagining the mattress on which they have sex as "where he would love, himself, to lie on a slant and naked, to let the little cottony tufts annoy him and to feel the mattress like billows bouncing beneath, to eat pickles lying on his back." Here, Welty reprises the language of rough softness that is attractive to Josie when she dreams of the big girls' hayride in "The Winds." Loch does not precisely understand what he sees in the bedroom, but he embraces the throb of its energy. "Sometimes they lay just alike," he records of the couple, "their legs in an M and their hands joined between them, exactly like the paper dolls his sister used to cut out of folded newspaper and unfold to let him see." The initial created out of Virgie's and the sailor's joined legs perhaps indicates that Loch has the prohibitory figure of his mother on his mind, as well as his father, the bearer of the Morrison name—and his sister, too, perhaps because her newspaper illusion creates the metaphor operating in the young boy's mind. The shape of a cutout newspaper doll initially appears unbroken to the eye, then the doll splits to reveal the string of imagoes composed in its likeness. Similarly, Welty has Loch creating a set of similitudes by associating the coupling lovers with his mother and father, and with his sister, who shares Virgie's age. Leaning back like a spent lover, he closes the telescope's "little eye" (341), the aperture through which he discovers the world and through which his desires shape its subject.

If Loch's sighting by telescope surreally blends the compulsions of desire with the materially apprehended, Cassie's narration effects a similar, if more subtle conjoining of the dreamt and undreamt. Obviously, she does not display Ran's mania, nor quite share her brother's malarial suffering, yet Cassie has a fire in her head, too. The swelling currents of desire surge so strongly that she yields to their promise, intoxicated and unable to resist. The opening bars of Virgie's signature piano piece, Beethoven's *Für Elise*, issuing from the MacLain house trigger a series of erotic daydreams. They inundate Cassie's consciousness and constitute the long second section of "June Recital," with episodes that surreally suture the past to the present through her recitation of the events of Miss Eckhart's life and her re-sighting of these events in the context of the present. If the burning fever of Loch's malarial infection supplies a fitting metaphor for the desire welling in the young boy, the siren song of *Für Elise*, mysteriously sounding from the house next door, provides a countervailing metaphor for Cassie's drift "like a dreamer dreaming with reservations" (*Stories* 358). While Loch responds to the seductive pull of the MacLain house's "dark magnet" and precariously crawls from his bedroom window out onto the limb of the hackberry tree to get a better view, Cassie experiences frustration and disappointment because of a failure of sight. "She could not see herself do an unknown thing," Welty writes plaintively, "She was not Loch, she was not Virgie Rainey; she was not her mother. She was Cassie in her room, seeing the knowledge and torment beyond her reach, standing at her window singing—in a voice soft, rather full today, and halfway thinking it was pretty" (382). This image of the caged bird, paralleling Miss Eckhart's canary, concludes Cassie's musical reverie, a daydream that idealizes the heroic figure of the pianist.

Welty initiates Cassie's extended daydream in "June Recital" with the beginning phrases of Beethoven's *Für Elise*. The sound of the "gentle opening" mesmerizes Cassie, who almost immediately drops "what she was doing." Having fallen under the piano's spell, she reflexively responds to it by dutifully repeating Miss Eckhart's praise: "Virgie Rainey, *danke schoen*" (*Stories* 345). She looks through her window for the source of the music, but only observes the unguarded and absurd Argus, Mr. Booney Holifield, the MacLain's house superego, who has fallen asleep at his post. With the night watchman—perhaps a double of her father—asleep, Cassie observes the house next door, which uncannily forms an optical illusion, "something you saw without seeing it" (345–46). Clearly in the grip of a powerful daydream, she remarks upon the home's "unpainted side," which changes

> passively with the day and the season, the way a natural place like the river bank changed. In cooler weather its windows would turn like sweetgum leaves, maroon when the late sun came up, and in winter it was bare and glinty, more exposed and more lonesome even than now. In summer it was an overgrown place. Leaves and their shadows pressed up to it, arc-light sharp and still as noon all day. (346)

Cassie perceives the MacLain house as if through a lens that softens and bends the structure, almost imparting a liquid aspect to its appearance. Windows smoothly metamorphose into deeply colored leaves, hard and shiny surfaces, and screens against which the dark shadows of foliage create stark and clean silhouettes. In her June reviewing of the scene spread outside, she depicts the town stiffly and without movement, depth, or vitality: "That rainless, windless June the bright air and the town of Morgana, life itself, sunlit and moonlit, were composed and still and china-like."

In contrast to the brittle rendering of Morgana, the MacLain house stirs with a "restless current that seemed to flow dark and free around it (there would be some sound or motion to startle the birds), a life quicker than the Morrisons' life, more driven probably, thought Cassie uneasily." Like her brother, she feels the magnetic pull of the house, from which Beethoven's passionate music issues. Suddenly, lines from Yeats's "The Song of Wandering Aengus" begin flowing through her mind like water through a long dry channel. But almost immediately the flow halts, and she returns to her "tie-and-dye" scarves that she may wear to woo boys on the hayride she will go on that night (*Stories* 346). The colorful scarves suggest a lethal potential, however; once tied around the neck, there "had never been one yet that didn't take the breath away" (347). Death by suicide, a demise her mother suffers, hovers over Cassie's room, whose door displays the "skull and crossbones" (346). But Welty organizes this set of bleak metaphors in opposition to those she uses to create the subsequent surreal reverie that promises resistance and the assertion of life. Cassie's third hearing of the tune unstops a flood of surreal imagery. She sees herself "without even facing the mirror," and appears "staring-clear inside her mind." Standing frightened in her paint-stained petticoat at the window, her "pale hair was covered and burdened with twisty papers, like a hat too big for her." This young incarnation of Medusa, a monster like Jinny whom she may develop into, holds a "spoon like a mean switch in her right hand," and "seemed to be favored and happy and she stood there pathetic—homeless-looking— horrible." But this moment of profound loneliness and self-loathing yields to a memory of the "gathering past," evoked by the resurgent music and invoked by the poetry that flows unimpeded "all around her, pellucid and lifting from side to side." Desperate, suffering, and still trying to resist the incoming tide of memories, she ultimately concedes to the anaesthetizing wash of the dream: "Then the wave moved up, towered, and came drowning down over her stuck-up head" (348). Cassie experiences the uniformity of the Newtonian universe disintegrating under the force of an inundating artistic revolution, where memories and dreams converge to create a hallucinogenic present.

Although Cassie's dream of the past reveals memory's intersection with the paranoid present, Welty presents little of Miss Eckhart's and Virgie's "inner life" in "June Recital" so as to concentrate attention upon the inner lives of Loch and Cassie (Schmidt 102). For both young people, Miss Eckhart's studio—and the pianist figure more generally—symbolize the potential triumph and the potential tragedy of desire's and imagination's contravention of social expectations. Welty shows her rebels drawing strength from the piano itself. If *Delta Wedding's* Shelley wields the artist's pen, and Cassie tentatively grasps the artist's brush in her paint-splashed smock, then Miss Eckhart and Virgie assume their artists' poses by sitting between the legs of the piano, caressing its keys. For Cassie, however, the sweet riches accrued by pianists always remain at a distance, because she daydreams "with reservations" (*Stories* 358). Prohibiting qualifications, the set of middle-class proprieties observed by girls of Cassie's age in Morgana, tinge the otherwise passionate and erotic reverie. For instance, her dreamy description of the interior of Miss Eckhart's studio reflects the tempting sensuousness that Welty associates with the passionate music venerated there. Forbidden golden chairs, used only for recitals, seem surreally "set the way pulled candy was," while the beads forming the curtained access to the studio "were faintly sweet-smelling, and made you think of long strings of wine-balls and tiny candy bottles filled with violet liquid, and licorice sticks." Although Cassie feels attracted by the studio's magnetism, she resists, remembering that her mother, a disfigured Medusa, likens Miss Eckhart to the witch inhabiting the "house in *Hansel and Gretel*" (349).

Later, Welty reprises this assessment of the studio as the focal point for temptation and desire when she describes it as being "like the inside of a candy box," decorated for the recital night, an occasion in June celebrating school's letting out. For the recital, an annual event (excluding the Morgana men, except for Fate Rainey), Miss Eckhart elaborately prepares the room, a fitting stage for Virgie's graduation to womanhood. "Streamers of white ribbons" crisscross the room, along with "nosegays of pink and white Maman Cochet roses and the last MacLain sweet peas dividing and re-dividing the room." She bans "electric fans" from the studio—which burns in the June heat "hot as fire"—so the music sounds clearly (*Stories* 377). On the piano's top, the metronome sits "like a vase," and within its concealed interior, the erect ticker sounds involuntarily, adding to the combination of "agitation and decoration" that could turn a child "pale with a kind of ultimate dizziness." Disorientation follows, with Welty's echoing Marmion's rapturous architecture, noting that those looking upward "for surcease would be floundered within a paper design stemming out of the chandelier, as complicated and as unavailing as a cut-out paper snowflake." Miss Eckhart positions herself under this chandelier like Venus in her satin dress, "as rich and hot and deep-looking as furskin" (378). Miss Eckhart's adornment of her studio creates a temple for the worship of music and for the celebration of feminine sexuality on this "first night of June." It is an evening for the exaltation of Venus, Virgie's archetype, as suggested by the allusion to Botticelli's *The Birth of Venus* in the fabric "scalloping the mantel shelf" (377).[12]

That a surrealist writer like Welty should have been influenced by Botticelli and Venus in the mid-forties should not greatly startle us. Dalí famously appropriated Botticelli's *The Birth of Venus* as a centerpiece for his *Dream of Venus* installation at the New York World's Fair in 1939. This egregiously sensual exhibition—which Welty may have seen when she visited the fair in 1940 and which the press eagerly publicized—featured a rectangular surrealist pavilion that "took on a plaster-cast biomorphic appearance, covered with protruding hands and organic appendages."[13] Two gartered legs created the entrance, and above the "entryway was a large photomural of Botticelli's *Venus* and on the side was another mural of the *Mona Lisa*, beneath which was inscribed 'Dream of Venus.'" Inside, two "large tanks, one filled with water, the other dry" greeted patrons (Tashjian 61). In the first, mermaids swam through an underwater scene that recycled iconography "borrowed from Dalí's paintings" (62). Included were what *Vogue* described as a "writhing woman chained to a piano, with the piano keys carved out of her rubberoid stomach" ("Dalí's Surrealist" 56). And *Life* reported that in the second tank, Venus spread out on a "36-ft. bed, covered with white and red satin, flowers and leaves. Scattered about the bed are lobsters frying on beds of hot coals and bottles of champagne" ("*Life* Goes" 67). Whether Welty saw the sensational installation in person or in the pages of national periodicals, it probably would have appealed to her sense of the bizarre and to her fascination with the world of the carnival, a logical setting for all things surreal. Dickran Tashjian records that the *Dream of Venus* presented a surreal "fun-house" (58), which occupied a "120-foot frontage in the amusement section" of the fairground, and which nestled "among a variety of girlie shows" (60). Moreover, he claims that the "setting was certainly appropriate" because the "fair itself had surreal overtones, providing a playground for the marvelous, for those moments when dream and waking reality were magically united" (56). Welty instinctively understood the surreal potential of the carnival atmosphere as well as Dalí or any other surrealist. Her stories from the thirties—most conspicuously "Petrified Man" and "Keela, the Outcast Indian Maiden"—and her photography documenting the freak shows and sex shows of traveling carnivals and Mardi Gras parades demonstrate a conviction like that held by the surrealists. Such events have significance because they subvert traditional categories of experience, propriety, and decorum. At the carnival or at any number of Welty's funhouses, the spectator could encounter Venus's allure at close quarters.

At Miss Eckhart's June recital, a kind of carnival for the timid, Cassie witnesses a reenactment of Venus's birth. Virgie's transition to womanhood appropriates the theme of Botticelli's *The Birth of Venus*, but under the influence of surrealism, modernizes its presentation. "But recital night was Virgie's night, whatever else it was" she observes. In the crucible of Miss Eckhart's studio, the summer's heat oppressively smothers the crowd, as Virgie takes to the stage wearing a "Christmas-red satin band in her hair" and a "red sash drawn around under the arms of a starched white swiss dress." Here, Welty not only enacts the summer flowering of youth, but she

Eric Schaal's interior photograph of Salvador Dalí's *Dream of Venus* pavilion at the New York World's Fair (1939). Eric Schaal © Fundació Gala-Salvador Dalí, Figueres, 2011.

re-creates a Dalínian Venus, who also appeared draped in white and red fabric. At the end of the performance, Virgie gets up from the piano and presents herself before the audience like Botticelli's Venus, rising from the shell of a sea scallop, resplendent and naked. Virgie's red sash has bled over the white "front of her waist," and she stands proudly on display, like a dripping Venus emerging from the ocean, "wet and stained" with a "delirious and enviable sweat" glazing her "forehead and cheeks." Spellbound by the spectacle, Cassie looks on as Venus rises before her in a simple white dress stained red. The dress seems a double of Wallace Simpson's white dress with a red band, which was inspired by Dalí, but designed by Schiaparelli. While Botticelli paints Venus blown to land by wind gods, who shower her with roses as attending nymphs present her with a red robe, Welty portrays Virgie in her reddened dress, "waved and beckoned" with fans while flowers "were lifted high, shown off, thrown, given, and pulled to giddy pieces by fingers freed for the summer" (*Stories* 379). The surreal revision concludes with the author's comically simulating Zephyr and Chloris's breeze in the "two fans" that send recital programs into the air and decorations fluttering (380).

This surreal envisioning of recital night also draws attention to Welty's preoccupation with the liberating power of music and feminine fertility.

Cassie's dream of Venus collapses Botticelli's scallop shell, antiquity's metaphor for the vaginal opening, with the "dark squarish piano" (*Stories* 349),
whose front opens like a shell to reveal its stringed interior, an anthropomorphic image at once musical and anatomic. Welty seems to confirms
this analogy when she describes Miss Eckhart's insane attempt to sterilize
the piano's insides. Hanging upside-down like a "folded bat" (345), Loch
assumes a surreal perspective, observing Miss Eckhart busily constructing
a pyre ("a kind of nest") on the exposed piano wires that. This is a uter-
ine metaphor that Welty twice deploys in "June Recital," recycling it from
Delta Wedding, where Laura disturbs a hive of bees nesting in Marmion's
piano (383). In addition, Loch's and Cassie's dreams of Miss Eckhart's surreal funhouse, where Mr. Voight might suddenly leap out, exposing himself
"like an old turkey gobbler," and the threat of rape by a black man hovers,
shows Welty imbuing the metronome, a pianist's indispensable tool, with
clitoral associations (356).[14] A possession "Miss Eckhart worshiped" and her
"most precious secret" (354), the metronome puzzles the neurotic Cassie,
who cannot understand why her teacher keeps the instrument housed in
a safe. Someone has probably told Cassie that it "was the very opposite of
a jewel." She appears to have inherited the cynical and self-loathing view
of her prudish mother, who thinks the metronome an "infernal machine"
(355). Its perpetual clicking, ticking, and threatening to explode like "dy-
namite" set within its closed doors suggest a kind of feminine pleasure.
Loch examines the device curiously, describing it as a "ticking stick" that
"went like a tail, a tongue, a wand" and beat like a "pendulum that instead
of hanging down stuck upwards" (391). Loch, who cannot precisely identify
what he inspects, is not the only one of Morgana's male inhabitants who
fails to understand female sexuality. For instance, when Cassie hears the
piano played in a "labored, foolish way," she wonders whether a man plays
it "using one finger," because the town men have an aversion to music and
have not the first idea about how to create it—no more than they know how
to make their lovers sing (366). Furthermore, Mr. Fatty Bowles and Old
Man Moody, who together prevent Miss Eckhart from razing the MacLain
house, appear repulsed by the piano and the metronome. Trying to extinguish Miss Eckhart's fire, they nearly destroy the piano by beating it,
"fighting over it hard, banging and twanging the strings" (387). And when
Mr. Fatty Bowles picks up the metronome, he sets "it down again quickly"
(389), before slyly wresting it from Miss Eckhart and viciously throwing "it
with all his might out the open window" (390).[15]

Welty's selection of the piano motif, used as a means of subverting Morgana's parochial social codes, certainly owes something to Beethoven's enduring position in the public mind as an icon of Romantic heroism.[16] In addition, her decision may also owe something to Dalí's preoccupation with the instrument as an emblem of bourgeois hypocrisy and crisis. The surrealist painter first appropriated this symbol of middle-class refinement in his 1928 cinematic collaboration with Luis Buñuel, *Un Chien Andalou*. When Dalí presents two grand pianos skidding across the screen and sandwiching two decomposing donkey corpses, he directs a salvo against what he considers the diseased condition of bourgeois civilization. In his paintings of the thirties and in his *Dream of Venus* installation, Dalí re-cycled many images of pianos—which he thought "female in gender"—in order to shock and scandalize his audience (Descharnes & Néret 51). For example, the first of his paintings in a sequence that depicts the William Tell legend, displays a piano in flight with a donkey corpse spread across its top. Painted in 1930, *William Tell* also shows a seated pianist with a lion's head (a Dalínian symbol of desire) emanating from his own, and a stallion shooting "out of the piano, its genitalia shown explicitly" (Moorhouse 53). Moreover, in paintings such as *Atmospheric Skull Sodomizing a Grand Piano* and *Skull with Its Lyric Appendage Leaning on a Night Table Which Should Have the Exact Temperature of a Cardinal Bird's Nest*, also from 1930, Dalí presents pianos in states of surreal metamorphoses, whereby the "animate is transposed into the inanimate, and vice versa" (Lubar 93). In both pictures, Dalí uses his theory of hard and soft matter in order to represent the pianos in anthropomorphic transition. Skulls reveal piano keys, piano keys show teeth, teeth create phallic shapes, and phallic shapes penetrate the pianos' oddly softened shells. Perhaps following his surrealist lead, Welty scandalously sexualizes this venerated motif of feminine respect-ability in order to outrage and shock the guardians of middle-class values. In antebellum America, the piano developed into the "leading symbol of middle-class domestic life" (Burns 165), the kind inherited, preserved, and widely on display in Morgana. Welty, a onetime piano student, finds in the piano a perfect vehicle for the expression of her surrealist critique of the status quo.

By 1946, Welty had begun "The Whole World Knows" and the story that developed into "June Recital" on separate but parallel tracks. Only lat-terly integrated as two movements in the seven that comprise *The Golden Apples*, both stories demonstrate what Welty called that "long, ruminative" mood that predominates in the collection (qtd. in Kreyling *Author* 132). As each new story emerged, lines of correspondence began to grow between initially discrete narratives. Writer and agent shared in the steady and wondrous revelation that together, the ensemble of stories, gradually produced over a two-and-a-half year period, showed a deep network of interrelations, associations, and identifications which imparted a strength to the whole that no one story in itself possessed. Welty's determination not to write a conventional novel and, therefore, to avoid the limitations intrinsic to plot, must have posed significant difficulties in drawing the separate narratives into coincidence. She had set out to contravene the conventions of received novelistic logic by offering what she described as seven "inter-related, but not inter-dependent" stories (136). Although ordered in a particular, approximately chronological sequence, the several narratives survive dismemberment or reading out of order, and the final arrangement does not at all reflect the order of composition.[17] By August, 1947, Welty had written versions of "The Whole World Knows," "June Recital," and "Music from Spain," and had started "Moon Lake." During the autumn of that year, she seems to have decided to pursue the novelistic potential of the project and produced one of the two shortest works in the suite, "Shower of Gold" (Kreyling *Author* 136). This story, which she ultimately placed first in the volume, orients Morgana according to the more conventional expectations of realistic fiction. Together with "The Wanderers," the story that concludes the chronicle, this narrative includes some of Welty's most traditional writing in the collection, providing a standard against which to measure the avant-gardism of the other stories in *The Golden Apples*.

"Shower of Gold" toys with expectations about the veracity of narrative perspective that modernist fiction generally problematizes. The story opens on that most clichéd of modernist conventions, the unreliable first-person narrator. The garrulous Katie Rainey has sole possession of the facts, so, the argument goes, readers should question her observations skeptically. To an extent, Welty agrees with this assumption. Of all the narrators in the collection, Katie participates most heavily in the elevation of King MacLain to the position of a deity in Morgana. Ironically titled "Shower of Gold," the episode anticipates King's mythical status in the community as one who showers Morgana with life. His seed impregnates his wife, Snowdie, "like a shower of something" (*Stories* 322) and has populated the county orphanage. Yet the remaining six stories together dismantle Katie's establishment of King's heroic reputation, irrevocably tarnishing his glamour. Despite her delusional assessment of King—who has obviously seduced and perhaps made her pregnant with Virgie, who inherits King's sensuality—Katie remains a seemingly reliable source of Morgana history. No evidence in the succeeding pages greatly undermines her general observations about the way life goes on in Morgana, a small Delta town where the rumor mills grind day and night. In section one, she recounts King's marrying Snowdie and his siring of twin boys, Lucius Randall and Eugene Hudson. King wanders far and wide, and ambiguous reports about his heroic exploits in Jackson or California trickle back to town. Katie knows more than she should about "Morgan's Woods" and the shady spot by the "oak tree," where she imagines "King MacLain leaning his length against that tree" (320). She casually demeans her husband, mentions her baby, Virgie, and establishes Miss Lizzie Stark as the "real important" figure in town (324). In section two, she narrates King's recent fleeting return to Morgana and his sighting by an old man, Plez. Confronted by his boisterous children, King absconds once again, making for the Big Black River. Perhaps Katie's most sincere moment comes right at the beginning, when she disparagingly declares, "That was Miss Snowdie MacLain. She comes after her butter, won't let me run over with it from just across the road" (319). Although "Shower of Gold" does much to organize Snowdie's sympathetic, pure, and angelic persona, Katie calls her "whiter than your dreams" (321). These opening lines anticipate the antagonistic, hostile, and confrontational Snowdie, who possesses Ran in "The Whole World Knows," a story wherein she assumes the whiteness of a haunting ghost.

Neither entirely reliable nor entirely honest, Katie serves as an entertaining, though often tiresome vehicle for the conveyance of town history, information about family relationships, and more general plot strands. Beginning in medias res, "Shower of Gold" nonetheless creates a point of origin for the subsequent narratives, which revise Katie's distortions regarding King, but little else. The near absence of surreally inflected language in this story derives from Welty's predominating interest, establishing a framework with novelistic potential. The incessant noise of Katie's gossiping voice prevails upon the reader. "Time goes like a dream no matter how hard you run," she admits. Yet her monologue contradicts her caution by running hard against time, as if the continuous sound of her voice may succeed in arresting time's progression, and thus repressing the dreams that she dare not publicly concede (*Stories* 324). Nonetheless, Welty's sure and satiric pen reveals Katie's transparency through her numerous Freudian slips of the tongue.

If the white noise of Katie Rainey's voice insulates her from acknowledging the obsessions that swell beneath the surface of her language, these desires achieve full voice in "Sir Rabbit," another late addition to the collection. This story directly critiques Katie's worship of superficiality and her mythologizing of King MacLain in the opening story. If "Shower of Gold" presents a hagiography of King, "Sir Rabbit" delivers a robust correction from the pen of an outlaw biographer, Mattie Will Sojourner, one of King's most vocal critics. The latter story seems to juxtapose two separate incidents removed in time. Some commentators, such as Carol S. Manning (100–104) and Louise Westling (*Eudora* 131–33), analyze the tale along these lines. However, reading the events depicted through the prism of surrealism shows Welty synthesizing the episodes in order to create a single sustained moment of contemplation, rather than presenting discrete frames of action juxtaposed and divided in time. The first reverie focuses on a fifteen-year-old Mattie Will, wrestling in the woods with the MacLain twins, also fifteen, in a kind of rough-and-tumble sex-play. The second describes Mattie's seduction by King in the same forest, and her discovery that his legendary performance does not correlate with her disappointing experience. Although Welty presents the second dream as if it occurs a "few years later" (Manning 100), she collapses both events into a single surreal moment that—through its splicing of past and present events—offers Mattie a profound insight about illusions reinforcing the inequitable distribution of power in Morgana.

Significantly, the first memory comes to Mattie while she "churns" butter, a term that suggests the recuperating operation that this story performs—and a fact that Welty withholds until around a quarter of the way into the text. As Mattie stirs the butter, she mentally folds the past into the present, soon drifting into an abstracted state of mind. At first, she imagines that King assails her in the forest, that he chases her around a tree (King's known trysting spot), and that he has "two eyes here and two eyes there, two little Adam's apples, and all those little brown hands." However, Mattie misconstrues, and through her character's misapprehension, Welty suggests vision's deceptiveness, a refrain that reverberates throughout her canon and a concept central to all surrealist art. King's sons pursue Mattie, not their father. And she freely submits to their roughhousing "in the soft downy light under the dark tree" (*Stories* 400). They seem to her harmless and quite comic, "like a pony pair" who trot in "time to the music in the Ringling Brothers'" circus. Here, in the world of make-believe, the boys roughly drop Mattie to the ground, pinning her while she returns their violence by threatening to bite, setting "her teeth in a small pointed ear that had the fuzz of a peach." Like Virgie and the sailor, who languidly gorge on figs at the MacLain house, Mattie and the boys ate "as many sticks of candy as they felt like eating" while dreamlike "playing" light washes over them "like a fountain" (401). Mattie returns to these scenes of aggressive and erotic play as she churns the butter, a metaphor for the masturbatory quality of the reminiscence, which subverts the misogynistic regime operating in Morgana—symbolized here by Junior Holifield, Mattie's husband. A relation of Old Man Holifield, the MacLains' bumbling night watchman and metaphoric superego, Junior, "would have given her a licking for, just for making such a story up, supposing, after she married Junior, she had put anything in words" (402). The sex and violence implicit in the dream spill over into the anxious present. Should Mattie indulge her sexuality by expressing her desire, her husband threatens a violent retaliation, but Mattie mounts a symbolic insurrection by merging "the act and the telling, joining sexuality and voice" (Mark *Dragon's Blood* 104). Despite her husband's threats of violence, she pities and belittles Junior's chest beating. "Poor Junior!" she cries—and swiftly imagines a second and equally illicit woodland encounter (*Stories* 402).

If Mattie's violent episode with the MacLains leaves her feeling betrayed by an illusion, the second memory reverses this scenario, because it concludes with King's dethroning. Patricia S. Yaeger, for example, observes that Mattie daydreams her encounter with King, and that her "dreams are inspired by the very taboos that deny them" (147). Thus her surreal blending of the dream and the actual subverts the moral order imposed by the likes of the Holifields, and dispels the mythological illusion that maintains King's sovereignty. Mattie's ensuing dream puts into words a flagrant violation of gender conventions by depicting King insubstantially, as a "white glimmer" (*Stories* 403), and by identifying him with the "glimmering girl" who haunts Yeats's "The Song of the Wandering Aengus." Welty has, however, rewritten Yeats's poem, so that Mattie wanders after the glimmering man, a dreamy and even puny presence who "was moving waywardly along, and sometimes got as completely hidden by even a skinny little wild cherry as if he'd melted into it" (404). He appears to the hunting party—Mattie, Junior, and their servant—"immediately from the waist up" (405). Later, Welty presents him like a rabbit, going "bobbing on to another tree while he was cajoling, bright as a lantern that swayed in the wind" (406).[18] Although Junior attempts to ward MacLain off, King easily foils him by shooting buckshot through Holifield's hat, causing him to faint. Mattie's dream, however, transforms the shooting into Junior's murder, when blood shows in the shape of a "Big red hand spread out on his shirt" (407). In this reenactment of Leda's rape by the swan, Zeus ravishes Mattie as his sons had earlier, but she reacts disappointedly, remarking "No pleasure in that!" (409), and soon creeps up on the witless King, who sleeps ingloriously, slouched against a tree, ignominiously snoring. Inspecting him at close range, she sees the man and not the myth. "With her almost motherly sway of the head and arms to help her," Welty surreally observes,

> she gazed at the sounding-off, sleeping head, and the neck like a little porch column in town, at the one hand, the other hand, the bent leg and the straight, all those parts looking no more driven than her man's now, or of any more use than a heap of cane thrown up by the mill and left in the pit to dry. (410)

Like a discarded bundle of sugarless cane stalks, he lies spent, pathetic, and comically reduced.

Read alongside one another, "Shower of Gold" and "Sir Rabbit" illustrate Welty's satiric exaltation of King MacLain through Katie Rainey's narrative, and his deflation and discarding through Mattie Will's, which provides a necessary correction. These stories present Morgana's king as a comic and absurd poltroon, whom even the young and inexperienced Mattie Will succeeds in deriding. Vande Kieft maintains that Welty makes "little attempt at complexity of characterization" (91) in King's case, and Manning concurs that throughout the cycle he "is a flat, comic character," in contrast to the authentic heroes of *The Golden Apples*. Stories like "Moon Lake" show "hero-making-in-progress," rather than the dull presence of King, a ludicrous and lampooned antihero (107). A large part of Welty's aim in these two stories resides in ironically undermining the beliefs that maintain King's power. She deploys little surreally inflected language, apparently because King has no depths to plumb. Instead, Welty draws only an outline of a man whose hollowness forms a counterpoint to the depth and substance created by the surreal language used to depict heroes like

Miss Eckhart, Virgie, and their analog in "Moon Lake," Easter, another rebellious and Romantic female figure who harkens to the music of a new kind of femininity.

"Moon Lake" provides an account of a girls' camp at the local lake, a "strange place" only "three miles from Morgana, Mississippi" (*Stories* 415). At the camp, "county orphans" and other town girls share the attraction to the water, a key metaphor in Welty's fiction, frequently identified with dreaming, desire, danger, and the potential for transformation (412). The story identifies the lake's possibly hazardous waters with Mrs. Gruenwald, a camp supervisor "from the North" (413). Mrs. Gruenwald, a proponent of the girls' morning dip, is an expert swimmer and a believer "in evolution" (416). The young hero, Loch Morrison, supplies the only male presence (with the exception of the hunter Ran MacLain), and he reluctantly acts as lifeguard to the girls. "He was hating every day of the seven," Welty writes. "He had been roped into this by his mother" (412). In what Mark deems the "pivotal story" (*Dragon's Blood* 109) in *The Golden Apples*, Welty tells the story of the parentless and precocious Easter, a girl who "was dominant among the orphans," and whom Welty develops into a camp hero (*Stories* 417). A hallucinatory aura prevails when Easter appears. Of all the girls, she has matured most. "She had started her breasts," Welty notes. "Moon Lake" presents Easter as a counterpoint to Nina Carmichael and Jinny Love Starks, two upper-middle-class Morgana girls, who are also on the verge of puberty, but who react more distractedly when they sense their awakening desire (418).

Early in the narrative, Jinny suggests that she and Nina abscond from "basket weaving," that most traditional of womanly chores. Instead, they set out to investigate the swamp edging Moon Lake, an occasion Welty uses to open a door on a dreamland the girls pass into by going "out the back end of the tent, barefooted." As they go out the wrong way, they spy Miss Moody slouched lazily in a hammock, and a Dalínian cat strangely jumping "like something poured out of a bottle" (*Stories* 423). Nina and Jinny trek through a surreal landscape, past Loch's tent, a site later associated with sexual discovery, and toward the swamp: "They were eye to eye with finger-shaped leaves of the castor bean plants, put out like those gypsy hands that part the curtains at the back of rolling wagons, and wrinkled and coated over like the fortune-teller's face" (424). Welty creates a richly textured dreamscape onto which she projects the girls' desires and anxieties, inter-secting and finding metaphoric expression in the setting. They are attacked by mosquitoes carrying the malarial fever that ravaged Loch's pubescent body in "June Recital," and their Sweet Dreams Mosquito Oil, undoubtedly supplied by their parents, has failed to halt the march of their biological clocks (422). The densely layered and tiered vegetation creates a series of thick walls and imposing barriers, like a maze over which "Buzzards floated" and alighted "shouldering one another on the solitary limb of a moon-white sycamore" (424).

Choosing to take the "serpentined" path leading from the tent's forbidden exit leads them to the swamp, whose noise sounds "nearer to the dreaming mind," and where they discover Easter indulging herself, walking "unconcernedly on, her dress stained green" (*Stories* 424) and "her lips stained with blackberries" (425). In the company of this siren and emboldened by her boyish confidence, Nina and Jinny crawl under the fences encircling the lake and discover a mysterious "old gray boat" (426), much like the one that ferries Laura and Roy to Marmion in *Delta Wedding* (261). "The water was quiet," Welty observes, "the color of pewter, marked with purple stobs, although where the sun shone right on the lake seemed to be in violent agitation, almost boiling. Surely a little chip would turn around and around in it." In this half-dreamed world, which seems "struck by moonlight," Welty presents an image recycled from *Delta Wedding*: the Scylla of desire or churning whirlpool that forecasts entry into the stormy waters of adulthood. Lying in the boat at Moon Lake's edge, Easter slips into a reverie, her eyes "rolled back" (*Stories* 427) and her drooping head surreally "pale and featureless as a pear." Nina, mesmerized by the orphan's abandon, also dreams of escape from Morgana's inhibiting restrictions. As she pushes the boat free, Nina imagines pears, luxurious fruits like the split figs in "June Recital," that suggest fertility, ripeness, and pleasure. "Again she thought of the pear," Welty writes, "not the everyday gritty kind that hung on the tree in the backyard, but the fine kind sold on trains and at high prices, each pear with a paper cone wrapping it alone—beautiful, symmetrical, clean pears with thin skins, with snow-white flesh so juicy and tender that to eat one baptized the whole face" (428). Nina's hedonistic daydream, as materialistic as it sounds, dissipates when she discovers the "old mean chain!" that manacles the boat to the shore, leaving it grounded (429). Nonetheless, she has learned from following Easter and from conceding to her desire's pull. Welty shows through these surreal scenes that all the girls—even the recalcitrant Jinny, who insists on building and then trapping her foot in sandcastles—have the potential to resist the chains that tie them to convention.

Although the tug of the binding chain and the din of Loch's bugle calling them back to camp limit these acts of self-examination, nighttime provides a tranquil window of opportunity for desire's reassertion. The outsider, Mrs. Gruenwald, leads the girls on a trail through the "wild moonlit woods" (*Stories* 434), where the "presence of night was beside them—a beast in gossamer, with no shine or outline, only of ornament—rings, earrings. . . ." (432). Darkness envelops the file of walkers in its shadowy grasp that shows Moon Lake "like a flood below the ridge," where Miss Moody takes her dates on boat trips (433). Indeed, for Welty the boat assumes a surreal significance because it designates a still and dreaming point on the turning surface of the world. "And in the boat," Welty writes, "it was not so much that they drifted, as that in the presence of a boat the world drifted, forgot. The dreamed-about changed places with the dreamer" (433–34). Following the woodland walk around the lake, and feeling the drawing force of the water's gravity and its liquid presence, the girls "wormed into the tents" (434), while outside the lake "streamed out in the night" luminously and by "moonlight sometimes it seemed to run like a river." Deep in the dark recess of the tent, Nina "still lay dreamily, or she had waked in the night," and so assumes the somnambulist's curious double vision, at once waking and sleeping. Gertrude Bowles gasps "in a dream" and Etoile snores, but Nina contemplates her metamorphoses, entertaining forbidden thoughts about whether she may "slip into them all—to change. To change for a moment into Gertrude, into Mrs. Gruenwald, into Twosie—into a boy. To *have been* an orphan" (435). When Nina dreams of herself as another girl, an adult, as black, as a boy, and—most illicit of all, as an orphan with her family dead—she grossly contravenes Morgana's rigid moral system, which renders a woman like the unmarried and childless Miss Eckhart a perversion of the natural order.

In her instant of profound identification with Easter, the Venus of Moon Lake, Nina feels the pulse of her awakening desire, inviting the "pale dark roaring night with its secret step, the Indian night." Welty's prose-poetry duplicates the sense of distraction and disorientation that characterizes Nina's dream, intentionally obfuscating what occurs inside the tent. Yet the moment recalls the delirium associated with Robbie and Pinchy, the two women who find the abandoned shed on the road to Shellmound in *Delta*

Wedding. Both the shed and tent supply the darkness of a cool and ministering interior that forms a backdrop for the action in each scene. Here, Nina admits the rude "pondering night" inside the "opening fold" where "it, him—had risen up inside" (*Stories* 435), and she beckons its/his worship of her, her hand thrust forward and opened like Easter's, the "only part of her now which was not asleep." Offering the open cup of her palm to the night and presenting her "fingers' bursting weight and stillness," Nina discovers her desire's "single ecstasy, a single longing" before her hand and fingers rest. She then dreams frighteningly that her hand, the instrument of her pleasure, "was helpless to the tearing teeth of wild beasts" (436).

The guilt and punishment associated with the pleasure Nina experiences have many parallels in Dalí's art. He famously enacted his phobias—particularly about masturbation—in the anguished forms he stretched over his canvases. Welty may well have felt the influence of his iconography in the construction of such scenes as that in the tent. Oversized hands feature prominently in Dalí's art of the twenties and early thirties, but one example suggests itself as a useful reference point for Nina's beckoning of the night. His 1930 *The Hand, Remorse* displays a giant masturbatory hand offered open-palmed and in supplication to a vast moonlit sky. Dalí critic Moorhouse argues that this "painting is one of Dalí's last works on the theme of masturbation," inscribing his "adolescent discovery of onanism." Above the figure, whose arm reaches out, a bearded leonine face stares out boldly at the spectator, a ferocious emblem both of desire's intensity and the intensity of its prohibition. This theme in also reinforced by the Medusa, a key figure for Welty, one whose streaming hair threatens to turn the dreaming masturbator into stone. Moreover, the hand, "grossly enlarged, appears to be flesh, suggesting that all life is concentrated in that part of the body which serves its obsessive auto-erotic activity" (46). There is no evidence that Welty saw this painting, but her presentation of what is probably Nina's first experience of her sexuality puts Dalí's visually presented themes into circulation in "Moon Lake." Like Dalí's agonized seated figure, stretching out his hand in remorse, Nina invites the night, yet in both painting and fiction wild beasts stand sentry, glaring at the spectator and threatening castration.

The high visibility of Dalí in the forties, when he lived in the United States for eight years, may also have influenced the construction of other scenes in "Moon Lake." For example, at the story's close, Nina and Jinny spy on the Boy Scout, Loch Morrison, and Welty's depiction of his display appropriates the legend of William Tell, a figure from European folklore also favored by Dalí. In "Moon Lake," Nina and Jinny wander into the woods one evening and run across the "Boy Scout's tent" (*Stories* 449), where they see "[o]n the other side of the tent wall the slats of the Boy Scout's legs shuttered open and shut like a fan when he moved back and forth. He had a lantern in there, or perhaps only a candle" (449–50). They watch as he violently undresses and studies his sunburn in a mirror, naked "with his little tickling thing hung on him like the last drop on the pitcher's lip." But this sighting of Loch puzzles the girls, because he loiters so aimlessly. Initially, it seems as if they caught him masturbating, even though they do not understand what they saw. "Hadn't he surely," they question, "just before they caught him, been pounding his chest with his fists? Bragging on himself? It seemed to them they could still hear in the beating air of night the wild tattoo of pride he must have struck off" (450). Loch's beating spectacle, behind the screen of the tent in the woods, seems an allusion to the legend of William Tell, the mythological woodsman and heroic hunter. This association is reinforced when Welty reports the arrival of the only other man at camp, Ran MacLain, who appears with his hunting dogs and with his "gun under his arm" (445). Ran and Loch together in "Moon Lake" represent the ideal of conventional masculine heroism explored by Dalí. He, too, borrowed from the famous Swiss legend in his 1931 *The Old Age of William Tell*, in which he shows the bowman frenetically "engaged in some undisclosed sexual act" concealed behind a tent of shadowed material (Moorhouse 20). The tent only partially obscures his body and the naked "hermaphroditic bodies of the players, behind the sheet that was put up for puppet show theatre performances" (Radford 151). In the performance that Dalí paints, William Tell's arms reach down beneath the level of the concealing tent and toward his genitals, while his head arches upwards and to the side, as if in passion or pain. The artist's perennial symbol of desire and desire's prohibition by castration, the lion, parades across the tent's front in the shape of a shadowy form, both leonine and phallic. By contrast, Welty's rendering of Loch and his shadow play minimizes Dalí's phallocentrism, comically substituting the lion's head found in *The Old Age of William Tell* with the boy's limp "tickling thing" (*Stories* 450).

In addition to the themes expressed in Dalí's paintings of the early thirties, "Moon Lake" may echo a more recent surrealist composition, Dalí's 1944 *Dream Caused by the Flight of a Bee around a Pomegranate, a Second before Waking Up*, a painting dated a year before *Spellbound* and one that shares the film's focus on traumatic dreams of violence and sexuality. Although no evidence indicates that Welty knew about or had seen this painting, it too depicts a moon lake, vindicating Mrs. Gruenwald's contention that "Moon Lakes are all over the world" (*Stories* 449), and prominently recycles some of Welty favorite subjects: bees, pomegranates, water, dreams, sleeping women, and dangerous men. Indeed, the painting's dramatic iconography almost predicts the climactic scene in Welty's story: Easter's near-drowning and brutal resuscitation by the lifesaver, Loch Morrison. The paradigm of psychoanalysis deeply influenced Dalí, along with many thousands of intellectuals, throughout the twentieth century. He declared that this painting in particular demonstrated Freudian dream-work theory by showing that a chance event waking a dreamer could spur the production of a dream that would integrate the event into its narrative. In this way, the "buzzing of the bee in the painting prompts the bayonet prick that wakens Gala," and the "burst pomegranate gives birth to the entirety of creation" (qtd. in Descharnes & Néret 141). The work displays a flat blue expanse of motionless water, over which a faintly drawn and weeping moon presides. In the foreground, a reclining nude, an incarnation of his wife and muse, Gala, lies naked in a dream state, hovering above a flat stone tablet. A circling bee and floating pomegranate, both of which Welty's fiction identifies with fertility, represent the seed of Gala's dream. Dalí theatrically presents this dream emerging above her in all its terrifying fury. Exploding from the ripped skin of a second, larger pomegranate, its seeds scattering below, a large fish attempts to eat a viciously roaring tiger, which in turn disgorges a twin with its eyes fixed ferociously upon Gala's vulnerable form. Wild beasts leap through the air toward the exposed woman's body, while in the background an elephant with an erect trunk and giant spindly legs marches by, carrying an obelisk on its back. On the underside of Gala's upraised arms, which are thrown over her head, a rifle's bayonet lightly pricks, its blade extending from the gun suspended between the tiger's hungry claws. The golden-hued Gala also figures here as Venus emerging from the waters of Dalí's Moon Lake, and as Leda, another of Welty's key mythological figures, attacked by a rapacious assailant. With one leg folded and her head turned backward, away from the spectator—who cannot quite tell whether she sleeps or not—her arms flung over her head, Venus reclines, her back arched in pleasure and her wet hair cascading in tendrils. Gala appears on the edge of consciousness, just before the blade's spike rouses her and terminates this masochistic dream of self-sacrifice on a stony priapic altar.

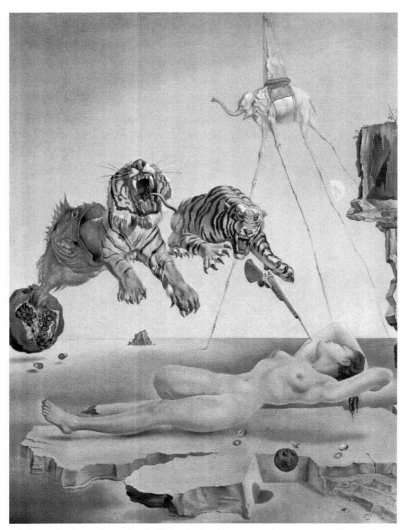

Dali, Salvador. *Dream Caused by the Flight of a Bumblebee around a Pomegranate a Second Before Awakening.* 1944. Oil on board, 51 x 41 cm. Museo Thyssen-Bornemisza, Madrid, Spain. © Salvador Dalí, Fundació Gala-Salvador Dalí/Artists Rights Society (ARS), New York 2011.

The knotted collection of classical myths and Freudian symbols that inscribe this painting would have stimulated the curiosity of a cultural polymath like Welty. But perhaps the painting's reproduction of tigers from the "posters of the Ringling Bros. and Barnum & Bailey Circus " would have aroused her interest, too (Pitxot, Aguer, & Otero 6), especially given her attraction to popular culture, especially carnivals of all types, represented in *The Golden Apples* by the MacLain twins, described as dancing ponies in the "Ringling Brothers'" (401). Little comedy, though, attends Dalí's astonishing image of Venus on the verge of violent sexual assault. If the picture reproduces Western culture's narrative of idealized sacrificial women, Welty's presentation of Easter's revival supplies a reappraisal. Balanced high above the water, Easter falls when, like Achilles, her heel is injured. She cannot swim, so the lifeguard, Loch Morrison, springs into action. Like William Wallace in "The Wide Net," he takes a "frog dive" into the lake, where he "swam destructively into the water, cut through the girls, and began to hunt Easter where all the fingers began to point" (*Stories* 438). Quickly finding her, he drags her clumsily ashore and dumps her heavily upon a wooden "camp table" on which the girls eat. "He stood over her," Welty writes, "put his hands on her, and rolled her over; they heard the distant-like knock of her forehead on the solid table, and the knocking of her hip and knee" (440). He lifts and drops her again, scoops lake mud from her mouth, and begins to resuscitate her by falling upon her back, groaning as he "drove up and down upon her, into her, gouging the heels of his hands into her ribs again and again." Neither alive nor dead, neither awake nor asleep, Easter endures Loch's "lifesaving" as she if she lies dreaming like Venus ravaged by wild screaming beasts. Easter's "eyes were neither open nor altogether shut but as if her ears heard a great noise, back from the time she fell" (441). A fallen woman spread out unconscious across a wooden tablet, she endures Loch's assault as if suffering the penalty Morgana exacts for contraventions of its paternalistic laws.

Like a chorus amplifying Easter's pain and disgrace, Exum howls, while his mother beats him for tipping Easter into the lake, violently cursing her son as a "little black son-a-bitch!" (*Stories* 440). Even the arrival of Miss Lizzie Stark, the town's most prominent woman and the "Camp Mother," cannot prevent Loch's mutilation of Easter's body. Lizzie clamors for cessation but seems to tolerate the attack. Welty claims that "she could have stopped everything," yet perversely "she hadn't stopped it" (443). Like everyone else, she stands observing the spectacle as if transfixed and under the spell of a dream herself, powerless to intervene and content to watch the orphan's debasement. Drawn by the commotion, Ran MacLain appears with his hunting dogs, his gun carried under his arm, moving "under the tree" where the action on the table occurs. There he sets his "seasoned gaze" upon the simulated sex Loch performs with the girl's lifeless body (445).

Ran's frisking dogs and hunting rifle and Loch's animality curiously re-cycle the features of Dalí's dream painting. In the picture, two vicious tigers and a rifle's sharp point threaten the sleeping Venus, just as Welty's two male figures and their phallic emblems prevail upon Easter, the Venus who rises drenched from the depths of "Moon Lake." In both texts, one visual and one verbal, the women dream their victimizations, carried out by animals and guns upon sacrificial tablets. But Welty replaces the symbol of Gala's desire, a pomegranate's fleshy interior, with "two watermelons" that Marvin, Miss Lizzie's servant, unloads on the table (443). Despite the similarities, Welty revises Dalí's account by bringing Loch's necrophilic attack to an end, and by staging Easter's miraculous resurrection, when she aggressively repulses her assailant, kicking the Boy Scout, who "tumbled backwards off the table" (447). By contrast, Dalí's flying tigers show no sign of retreat, and their exposed claws forever stretch agonizingly close to Gala's delicate flesh. If *Dream Caused by the Flight of a Bee around a Pomegranate, a Second before Waking Up* visualizes a scene of feminine sacrifice upon the altar of male glory, Welty's "Moon Lake" revamps this account by displaying the spectacle of Easter's battered but resurgent body.

Easter's rebirth in the waters of Moon Lake augments the collection of episodes, dispersed through Welty's fiction, that thematically links immersion in water with dreams, desires, and the liquidation of Newtonian principles. The final story that rounds out *The Golden Apples*, "The Wanderers," also contributes to the maintenance of this thematic pattern. Repeatedly, dreams create an expanded range of possibilities for any number of female protagonists, who sense that their individuality is compromised by powerful social expectations enforcing what many in Morgana regard as the natural order. Welty satirizes these conservative and self-perpetuating codes of conduct in "The Wanderers," archly critiquing the elaborate machinery of social custom and ritual that Katie Rainey's death sets to motion. This final story caps the collection with a definitive silencing of the voice that knew no quiet in "Shower of Gold."

Welty expends much effort in "The Wanderers" creating a noxious mood of intolerable claustrophobia for Virgie, now in her forties, as she attends to her mother's funeral arrangements. The story opens with the flinty Miss Lizzie Stark observing the proprieties of local convention. She meanly scolds her black servant, dispatching her to the Raineys to help with the preparations. By "mid afternoon" on the Sunday of Katie's death, the "house was filling with callers and helpers" (*Stories* 521). Far from a comforting presence, the voices of well-wishers merge with the shouts of the children, whose "[s]creams surrounded the house," rendering Virgie's experience hellish (533). Welty uses the opportunity afforded by the congregation of townspeople to tie up some loose ends. Novels traditionally require such neatening, and even though she views *The Golden Apples* as a loosely pack-aged suite of narratives and not as a conventional novel, Welty performs that task with "The Wanderers." "As an epilogue," Vande Kieft observes of the story, "it provides the denouement of several careers, lends perspective to the meaning and interrelations of these life histories, and gives a sense of mutability." "The Wanderers" carries out all of these operations, in addition to showing Morgana "engaged in a major tribal ritual" that serves as a re-minder of the suffocating atmosphere at Shellmound, another home in the Delta and another stage for Welty's exploration of of community traditions (112). Moreover, like Laura, Dabney, Shelley, and Ellen, Virgie periodically flees her domestic prison in order to maintain her sanity amidst an army of invading relatives—not least the unimpeachable Snowdie MacLain, who has taken up residence for the duration and who is in charge of preparing the body.

It seems Welty could not resist the delicious irony of a ghost readying another dead body for interment. This collocation of Snowdie and death reinforces one last time an association expressed in her name and born out in "The Whole World Knows." Perhaps Juba, Miss Lizzie's servant, has Snowdie in mind when she claims, "I seen more ghosts than live peoples round here" (*Stories* 549). King MacLain is another ghost from the past, emerging appropriately from behind a "big boxwood" (528) tree, suggest-ing a coffin, and outfitted in the "stiffest-starched white suit" (535). Here, King appears a lamentable senex, a frail old man with white hair and a shaky grip. Even his wife, who until now has preserved King's mystique by swallowing her outrage, openly scorns him. "But I'll never forgive myself for tracing after him," she concedes to Virgie, as if she regrets duplicat-ing King's likeness by giving birth to his two sons (541). Welty presents the funeral gathering as a collection of the living dead, ghosts who parade around "like people waked by night, in the shimmering afternoon" (540). Ran MacLain, Jinny Love, Cassie Morrison, Nina Carmichael, and Perdito Mayo either say nothing or offer platitudes and vacuous advice to Virgie, who endures an orgy of unwanted and sometimes lewd solicitousness and officious pandering. Despite the almost endless round of pawing, push-ing, and tugging she undergoes at the hands of the prurient townsfolk, she shows that "her inner life radiates authority" (Schmidt 173), and that she retains her dignity in a sea of posturing.

In marked contrast to the tightly controlled and wonderfully satiric language Welty deploys to create the asphyxiating confinement of the funeral reception, the prose depicting Virgie's late evening swim adopts a deeply surreal and meditative quality, replacing the clichéd language of superficiality and death with the poetry of dreams. In this scene, Welty returns to the surreal prose-poetry deployed in "Moon Lake," for Virgie now swims in a Moon Lake of her own. Reached by a route that leads "through the old MacLain place," Venus's surreal funhouse, the Big Black beckons Virgie, who "took off her clothes and let herself into the river," an open stretch of water that appears strangely bathed in the bright "mid-afternoon" light, although she swims at sunset (*Stories* 530). Commonsense notions of time and space falter and collapse when Virgie enters the purifying river "like walking into sky." Unlike Loch Morrison, who swims "destructively" (438) through Moon Lake, as if it needed conquering, Virgie gently pushes through the water "as she would wish for gentleness to her body." Entering this liquid medium dissolves the distinction between her material essence and her metaphysical life, for what appeared rigid and unforgiving now yields and mollifies. She closes her eyes and dreams the river's total permeation of her body to its last molecule, until "[a]ll was one warmth, air, water, and her own body. All seemed one weight, one matter." The sensitivity of her breasts heightens, and they register a sensation like the "tips of wings must feel to birds, or the antennae to insects" (530). Below her in the river's channel, she feels "minute shells of old seas." Touching and leaving mud and grass, which threaten to manacle and drown her, she senses the loosing of "some bondage" and "moved but like a cloud in skies, aware but only of the nebulous edges of her feeling and the vanishing opacity of her will." Welty's provision of this scene and other similar episodes and surreally inflected passages relieves the tension of the funeral scenes, showing Virgie's discovery of an expanded reality— a surreality that promises redemption and reprieve from the stultifying demands imposed by the conventions that enforce conduct in Morgana. This swim in the river enacts a heroic divesting of social expectations. She baths naked, she revels in her sensuality, she washes away the deathly touch of Morgana's ghosts. And she rises wet like Venus from the river, before disappearing godlike into the woods, as two boys who "did not move or speak" watch spellbound (531).

Hands, palms, and fingers assume an array of erotic associations in Welty's depictions of female heroes in *The Golden Apples*. Virgie, Miss Eckhart, and all the Morgana girls strike and stroke piano keys with varying degrees of success in "June Recital," the story that recounts Miss Eckhart's decline and final fall. In the end, the law forces her from her studio with her hands raised in surrender over her head, making her hold a "scorched black cloth" (*Stories* 390), a tragic emblem of her shame. In "Moon Lake," Easter's and Nina's hands draw names in the dirt, throw knives in the ground when playing mumblety-peg, pull frustratingly at the old chain that tethers the boat, light and smoke vines in the forest, and pleasure the body inside the fold of the tent at night. In contrast, Nina's hands also build prisons in the sandcastles that she creates. Unlike her companions, her arms need bandaging because, returning from the woods, she "was the only one that came back with poison ivy" (447). In "The Wanderers," too, hands and fingers denote pleasure's acceptance or pleasure's denial. Virgie's fingers have "set half-closed" because of her typing routine and her milking of her mother's cows. Nina's and Easter's hands, in contrast, stay young and supple. "And if," Welty writes of Virgie, "as she dreamed one winter night, a new piano she touched had turned, after one pristine moment, into a calling cow, it was by her own desire" (546). This eminently surreal image, combining piano and cow into a single arresting symbol of desire and fertility, illustrates Welty's identification of fingers that milk and play music with the frisson of passion.[19] Such energy begins returning to Virgie when she bathes in the Big Black River, where a cloud runs "fingerlike over the sun" (531. And the energy continues to gather strength when she sits on the stile at the story's close, as raindrops shower her, running down her arm "like a cool finger" (555). The pattern of metaphors linking hands, fingers, palms, pianos, keys, and cows with sexual pleasure does not apply to Morgana's men. Cassie, for example, blames clumsy piano playing on a man's finger. No men come to the June recital except for Fate Rainey. And Loch can only spit a din through his bugle at Moon Lake.[20]

Welty develops this male insensitivity to music and perhaps to women generally, too, in "Music from Spain," a central contribution to the collection owing to its presentation of the virtuoso performer. "Music from Spain" takes place sometime in the forties, and it recounts a day in the life of Eugene MacLain, who now lives in San Francisco. Welty has placed his story next to his brother's in the collection, and the malignant misogyny that permeates the entirety of "The Whole World Knows" instantly reasserts itself in "Music from Spain" when Eugene reaches over the breakfast table and slaps his wife's face. He does this in the morning as he "was opening his paper" (*Stories* 473), suggesting that he has habitualized his hate, making it as routine as breakfast or reading the daily news. Readers should expect the threat of violence to women to loom over the pages that convey Eugene's story as it does over Ran's. Despite the impulse to flee suggested by his name, Ran can't run from his psychological crisis. Neither can Eugene escape, even allowing for his nickname, "Scooter," given to him because "he had been noted for his running when he was a boy back home" (483). Although he has scooted all the way to the waters of the Pacific Ocean, he has not outrun the chronic sense of paralysis and intense paranoia that characterize the lives of the brothers. Both live and work in cages—Ran at the bank and Eugene at the repair shop—and both fantasize about escape from burning buildings. They cannot free themselves from Snowdie's ghostlike presence, any more than they can remove the self-loathing that their father's abandonment has created.

During Eugene's daylong sojourn in the streets and on the coastline of San Francisco, he encounters an enigmatic Spanish guitarist who doesn't speak English, and whom Eugene had watched perform the previous evening at the "Aeolian Hall" (*Stories* 482). This venue, from which the winds blow, promises a change in direction and a lifting of the fog that obscures Eugene's sight. Welty claims that she wrote "Music from Spain" as a kind of homage to San Francisco, what she describes as her "response to the place, an act of love at first sight." But considering the sustained mood of psychological malaise, entrapment, and crisis that the narration evokes, one feels surprised by the cruelty of this joke and by the cool irony with which she delivers it, demolishing the stereotype of southern gentility that colors her reputation and that, outside Welty criticism, still has widespread currency (Kuehl 88). She may have responded to love at first sight, but her story supplies a devastating critique of love that exposes perversions, and a twisted logic of the sort dramatized in T. S. Eliot's "The Love Song of J. Alfred Prufrock."[21] Indeed, "Music from Spain" underscores Eugene's alienation from love, from others, and from himself. Time and circumstances have deadened his senses. He hears the music of the Spaniard's guitar, but "his failure to respect music" prevents him from submitting to its healing rhythm, so he joins he host of deaf men Welty features in *The Golden Apples* (*Stories* 482).

Reading Welty's account of Eugene's wanderings through the busy San Francisco streets and the less-peopled beach areas of Land's End, provides a rich portrait of west coast life in the mid-to-late forties, when she composed this story. However, she laces every line of prose—which so assuredly reproduces the city's serried visual spectacle—with caustic reminders of Eugene's hallucinatory paranoia. San Francisco's famous fog does not lift for the whole day. He steps outside into a "foggy morning" (*Stories* 474), and "wet fog" (511), rolling off the sea like the mirages Welty describes rolling in "over the cotton fields," chases him home in the evening (Kuehl 88). Like his delirious brother, Ran, and the malarial Loch Morrison—both of them purblind and visually challenged—Eugene can't shake the fogginess that hampers his clear picturing of reality, a reality shaped by the raft of obsessions and phobias generating the surreal atmosphere of "Music from Spain."

Welty leaves the artist anonymous for most of the story in order to facilitate his assumption of an array of identities relative to Eugene's multifaceted paranoia. Meditating on an embrace between the two men, Kreyling contends that Eugene confuses the "Spaniard with his father" (*Eudora* 98), while earlier he argues that the artist may allude to Virgie or Easter (96). The Spaniard's "big floppy black" (*Stories* 488) hat certainly recalls King's hat, left "on the banks of the Big Black River" (319). And the guitar player's hair resembles that of the "old senator from back home," another of King's doubles (484). In addition to Virgie and Easter, Welty also pairs the artist with Miss Eckhart and other women. When Eugene rushes to save the Spaniard from colliding with a car, the artist proves "light on his feet, like a big woman who turns graceful once she's on the dance floor" (483). Welty repeatedly feminizes the man. She makes him a musician in a book where only women perform this role. She reveals his fingernails as "painted bright red" (485). She describes him as "muscular, but in a story-like way womanly" (491). She depicts him in the "lumpy pose of a woman, a 'nude reclining'" (505). She associates him with the "sirens" (508). And she shows him ridiculed derisively by Mrs. Herring, Emma's best friend, for his long womanly locks that "needed a haircut" (513). In Eugene's addled mind, the anonymous guitar player (whom Welty based on Andrés Segovia, a musician she had seen play [Marrs *Eudora* 152]) assumes a kaleidoscopic identity at once male and female, paternal and maternal, lover and enemy, young and old, threatening and alluring, dreamt and seen. He appears as King MacLain, the old senator, Easter, Virgie Rainey, and Miss Eckhart, as well as an incarnation of Eugene's wife. Just as he may have treated Emma to a day in the city and a stroll down lover's lane, Eugene accompanies the

Spaniard, in a gentlemanly way paying for their meals and refreshments. In addition, Eugene walks him out to "Land's End" (*Stories* 503), a romantic spot above the beach on the cliffs where "sweethearts" (510) roam, and where he had once picnicked with his wife. She and Eugene got drunk on red wine and went to sleep "in the hot sun on the rocks, lying on their backs, knees up, heads tipped together" (503).

This happy moment, now consigned to history, presents only a brief interlude in a story which otherwise viciously denigrates and demeans women, all of whom double Emma and Eugene's ma, Snowdie. For example, Eugene saves the Spaniard from colliding with a car, but he cannot save Emma's double, a "dumpy little woman" the streetcar hits and kills outright (*Stories* 493). Dead, disfigured, and mutilated women proliferate in Eugene's dream. He cruelly demeans a young woman reported dead in the paper by renaming her "*Miss Dimdummie Dumwiddie*," and he takes the Spaniard to a seedy side-show, whose poster advertises the spectacle inside with the grotesquely distorted face of a woman—who not incidentally shares his wife's name (476). "An enlarged photograph showed the side-show Emma," Welty declares, "—enormously fat, blown, her small features bunched like a paper of violets in the center of her face. But in the crushed, pushed-together countenance there was a look; it was accusation, of course." Emma's accusatory grimace obviously incorporates Eugene's wife's facial expression, crushed and embittered by the death of their daughter, Fan, whose name suggests a dissipating of the cloud that fogs her father's mind. Emma too suggests Snowdie because Eugene identifies the wounded glance as "like a mother's."

The Emmas promise a fantasy of sexual gratification in the "lace panties" that the side-show woman wears in her photograph, but opposite the picture Welty supplies a powerful image that undercuts the titillation: A "real pair of panties—faded red with no lace—was exhibited hung up by clothespins, vast and sagging, limp with dust and travel." Confronted with Emma's underwear in the advertisement, Eugene acknowledges the picture's falsity in the dirty, depleted, and maternal sexuality he sees symbolized by the real panties. In fact, this moment returns him explicitly to Morgana, where as a boy he probably saw his mother's underwear hung out on a clothesline just the way he sees Emma's here. He recalls sinning when he used his "Sunday School collection money" to pay to see another sideshow, the optical illusion Thelma, another double of Emma, whose decapitated head sat "on top of a stepladder" (*Stories* 487).

In such scenes, Welty re-creates the surreal world of Mississippi carnivals, New Orleans Mardi Gras, and Jackson parades that she photographed in the thirties, together with the amusement section of the 1939 New York World's Fair. Later, Welty reprises the circus imagery when Eugene and the Spaniard find themselves on a carnival midway, where a "carousel went around, with no child riding," and where the "excited and unrelieved sound of laughter" issues maniacally from a "shouting mechanical dummy of a woman, larger than life, dressed up and with a feather in her hat . . . beckoning on the upper gallery of the House of Mirth and producing a wound-up laughter" (*Stories* 502). Here Welty perhaps evokes a distorted version of Dalí's surrealist funhouse, above whose entrance an oversized Venus presided. On a platform at her feet, "real women wearing late-1930s bathing suits and beach jackets make ballyhoo by waving bamboo fishing rods. Catching your attention, they reel you toward their grotto" (Schaffner *Salvador* 10). The mechanical laughter issuing from "The House of Mirth" also recalls the "continuous laughter" that comes from the mouth of the grotesque woman bather in "A Memory" (*Stories* 95), another taunting image. And on the midway Eugene feels the female dummy's jeer, which excites his misogyny. At any moment, one expects Doctor Caligari, whom Eugene identifies as one of the Spaniard's many personas and whom he imagines "ringing his bell on the side-show platform" (500), to open his cabinet and release his caged somnambulistic murderer, represented here by Eugene, another man who lives in a box, the "cage in the repair department" at work (478).

Eugene's hallucinatory experience of San Francisco reflects Welty's surreal sensibility. The spectacle of the city and the bay assumes a kind of multiplicity that Welty simulates by creating a surreal dreamscape in which a clear view of any object or event remains beyond reach, unknown, and suspect. Eugene's viewing exposes forms that appear visually congruent yet are logically incongruent. For example, he closely watches the Spaniard but fails to determine the man's identity with any certainty. The fog of his paranoia precludes clear sight, so at various points Eugene identifies various members of a group of individuals with the artist. Like Cassie's cutout newspaper doll, which unfolds to reveal a string of identically-shaped sibling dolls attached at the hands, the Spaniard's identity appears both singular and multiple, sometimes Miss Eckhart, sometimes Doctor Caligari— and perhaps sometimes even Dalí, the artist from Spain who—if not the most famous Spaniard in the United States, at least by 1948—"was the most

talked-about painter in America" (Gibson 499). Perhaps following the example of T. S. Eliot, whose "Little Gidding" section of *Four Quartets* dra-
matizes a meeting between the poet's persona and the ghosts of Stéphane
Mallarmé and W. B Yeats, Welty imagines a meeting between a tone-deaf
Southerner and the Spanish surrealist on the stage of America's west coast.
In the summer of 1941, Dalí and is wife lived in California at Pebble Beach,
which "over the following years was to become their American Port Lligat,
an illusion suggested by the vague similarity of the Pacific coastline to the
Costa Brava, and by the Spanish placenames in which the area abounds:
Monterey, Carmel, Buena Vista, Santa Rita" (467–68). One might add to
that list the place Welty stayed in 1946 and 1947 with John Robinson, San
Francisco, the nearest large city, only a few miles to the north of Pebble
Beach (Marrs *Eudora* 150–60).[22]

Not only does "Music from Spain" associate Dalí with San Francisco, but
it also likens the artist to the bullfighter, an enduring emblem of Spain's
national identity. The story depicts the Spaniard satanically, associating him on two occasions with France and in particular with Paris, the
mecca of surrealism Dalí had conquered in the early thirties. When Welty
describes the Spaniard "dancing in a red smoky place," wearing "horns on
his head," and breathing "fire from his nostrils" (*Stories* 491), she perhaps
parodies Man Ray's devilish photograph of the surrealist on the cover of
Time in 1936. Like the guitarist, who appears as a "black clad-figure" (483),
and who sports "thick black hair" combed back over his head, in the photo
Dalí wears a dark suit and has his hair similarly pulled backwards (484).
He stands and stares out eerily under prominent arched eyebrows, which
recall the musician's "black brows," and light from a source below the waist
throws shadows over his face, creating a sinister effect, as if this devil augers the arrival of surrealism on American shores (488). Above all, Welty's
linking the Spaniard to France perhaps constitutes the best evidence for
Dalí serving as one of the guitarist's alter egos. When ordering food at a
restaurant, Eugene imagines him talking to the waiter "probably in French"
(489) rather than in Spanish, and later Eugene daydreams that "he might
have been over in Paris, looking at the Seine!" (501). Does Welty intend
for her readers to miss the identity of a French-speaking Spanish artist in
America during the forties? (Dalí learned his French during the thirties in
Paris, a city to which Welty would soon travel.)

Naming the town that provides the setting for most of the action in *The
Golden Apples* after fata morgana puts the unlimited chicanery of "dreams,"

"illusions," and "obsessions" at center stage (Yates 94). The name Morgana fits thematically because it furnishes a context for the visitation of all sorts of hilarious and not so hilarious ironies, mistakes, and misapprehensions. Collectively such episodes form a cosmic perspective, a position underwritten by the idiomatic tendency of surrealism toward replacing complacency and orthodoxy with uncertainty and liberation. How does Welty perform these substitutions in *The Golden Apples*? She returns again and again to the concept expressed in the title of this chapter, making the mystery of reality conspicuous by showing how people, places, and things appear as well as to supply visions of how they do not. Does not the struggle to define the book's genre offer a prominent example of such tension? To Harcourt, the book appeared to be a novel, but to Welty it seemed a grouping of interrelated stories. And this sense of indeterminacy carries over into a great many surreal textual iterations in *The Golden Apples*, some stylistic, some substantive, and some both. For instance, the surreal mode of presentation allows for the kind of writing that softens or elides physical and emotional boundaries, so that to Ran MacLain, Maideen Sumrall appears transformed into Snowdie, while the Sunset Oaks motel seems to be his boardinghouse. However, Ran is not alone in facing such dilemmas. His brother, Eugene— as well as Loch and Cassie Morrison, Nina Carmichael, Jinny Love, and Mattie Will—all see things "as they were not" (*Stories* 491), an experience that Welty extends to her audience through various cultural allusions embedded in the text. The presence of Hitchcock, Dalí, Buñuel, Schiaparelli, Simpson, and New York's World's Fair flaunts not only the crossing of the boundary between life from art (as well as high art from low), but also the more daring proposition that literature has the capacity to assimilate the media of film, painting, photography, fashion, and sculpture.

6

THE WILDNESS OF THE WORLD BEHIND THE LADIES' VIEW IN *THE BRIDE OF THE INNISFALLEN AND OTHER STORIES*

Long before her return from Europe to the United States in 1950, Welty had built a career out of confronting the wildness that roiled beyond what most women of her generation saw in the world. In fact, for the best part of her adult life—which then numbered forty-one years—her steady stream of fiction had made the dark recesses of human psychology its subject and its home. The 1955 publication of *The Bride of the Innisfallen* represented a continuation of this pattern. A student of the perverse, the cruel, and the brutal, and a champion of the heroic, the beautiful, and the elegiac, Welty challenged the ruse perpetrated on women whose parents, perhaps like those of the rueful protagonist in "A Memory," had shown them "nothing in the world which was not strictly coaxed into place like a vine on our garden trellis to be presented to my eyes" (*Stories* 92). Against this systematic cultivation of women's ignorance about the world, desire, men, and themselves, she had mounted an assault that fully participated in the revolution of consciousness that André Breton envisaged when he first leveled the institutions of bourgeois life in the "Manifesto of Surrealism," a broadside underwritten by psychoanalysis and pledging the "resolution of these two states, dream and reality" into a "kind of absolute reality, a *surreality*, if one may so speak" (14). Like the fantasist in "A Memory," Welty used her fiction to enter a "dual life, as observer and dreamer," and her conviction insisting on the permeability of consciousness produced a body of work that shows a profoundly surrealist sensibility at work (*Stories* 93).

"No Place for You, My Love" opens *The Bride of the Innisfallen*, presenting an intoxicating tour de force. This subtle yet electrifying story follows two anonymous strangers, a midwestern woman and a northeastern businessman, as they travel "south of South" (*Stories* 578). In a shabby rented car they drive beyond New Orleans to a landing called Venice, at the "End of the Road" where at last bayou yields to the deep waters of the Gulf (570). Clues to this story's composition under the influence of surrealism come from Welty's critical essay, "Writing and Analyzing a Story," which together with "Place in Fiction" establishes her criteria assessing fiction. In the former article, Welty selected "No Place for You, My Love" for extended examination, claiming that it "was a circumstantial, realistic story in which the reality *was* mystery" (779). This comment closely echoes similar assertions in the latter essay about the artist's responsibility to make "reality real" (791) by developing a "cultivated sensitivity for observing life, a capacity for receiving its impressions, a lonely, unremitting, unaided, unaidable vision, and transferring this vision without distortion to it onto the pages of a novel, where, if the reader is so persuaded, it will turn into the reader's illusion" (791–92). These statements reflect a general principle of surrealism, dictating that the artist has a duty to show reality's mystery, ideally through the presentation of a powerful vision. When she contends that the narrative "was a circumstantial, realistic story" ("Writing" 779), she discloses only her starting point. The narrative reproduces circumstantial detail using more or less referential language, but it filters its contents through a surreal consciousness.

"No Place for You, My Love" supplies an excellent vehicle for the expression of this approach, because it powerfully and persistently imbues whatever the strangers observe with the mood and tenor of their psychological preoccupations and idiosyncrasies. So forcefully does the narrative reflect the psychologies of both figures, in "Writing and Analyzing a Story" Welty argues "there had come to be a sort of third character along on the ride," adding that this presence represents the relationship "between the two," as well as the "domain" through which they pass. It also represents the role of "hypnosis" (777), forming the "straining, hallucinatory eyes and ears, the roused-up sentient being of that place." "No Place for You, My Love" is one of the more prominent examples of a surrealist narrative in all of Welty's fiction, because almost every line reveals what she calls the story's "vain courting of imperviousness in the face of exposure." At the narrative's deepest level, she reverses the convention through which fiction traditionally reveals character. Action usually bespeaks psychology, but here Welty externalizes the strangers' psychologies so that their actions, past or present, remain ancillary to a palpable sense of paranoia. "I was writing of exposure," Welty observes, "and the shock of the world; in the end I tried to make the story's inside outside and then leave the shell behind" (778). Driving "south of South" (*Stories* 578), the strangers' brittle imperviousness to exposure dissolves under the glare of the pervading light, which creates a surreal texture and illuminates the jaundiced state of these archetypal modern wanderers. They are the kind of characters Noel Polk declares populate modern literature, moving "through wastelands bemoaning the fact that they are on the outside, and . . . live out their frustrated and tragic lives beating on the doors, trying to get inside, trying to connect" ("Water" 102). Neither of these wanderers connects with anything or anyone, and by the close of the story Welty leaves her readers aghast at the danger her characters have faced.

A typically Weltian gambit opens the story, instantly effecting a suspension of time and space. In the oppressive heat of a summer afternoon, the two strangers, "seated side by side" at Galatoire's restaurant, sense "Time Out in New Orleans." It is as if time has stopped or at least begun to operate according to a counter logic (*Stories* 561), the regime of dreamtime that prevails over the entire story and a mood Diarmuid Russell quickly identifies in the story's "curious dreamlike affair" (qtd. in Kreyling *Author* 160). The highly self-conscious woman, who fears that her emotional fragility "must stick out all over me" (*Stories* 561), attracts the attention of a predatory businessman, who guesses her age at thirty-two, while he "himself was further along" (562). Welty's depiction of the New Orleans restaurant creates an atmosphere of uncertainty, a setting where the irrational forces of the unconscious permeate the fabric of an adroitly constructed scene. The strangers' thoughts of love, lust, hurt, and betrayal mix with the strange light and shade they experience when time halts, runs backward, stretches forward, or otherwise moves illogically as in dreams. A "recognizable shadow" cuts across the restaurant's space, in which they sit while "mirrors and fans were busy agitating the light" (561). The Northeasterner observes a curiously shadow between the woman's fingers before a "bold and full light, shot up under the brim of that hat, as close to them all as the flowers in the center of the table." Seen from this perspective, the woman assumes the provocative pose of a femme fatale, recalling the ghost in "The Purple Hat," yet the Midwesterner finds the "heat down here depressing" (562) and "*degrading*" (563). It seems that love has lead her into stormy waters before, because she shows a "bruise at her temple," (575) which comes "out like an evil star" (575–76), and now she feels the danger that the man opposite her poses. "The blades of fan shadows came down over their two heads," Welty writes, "as he saw inadvertently in the mirror, with himself smiling at her now like a villain." Such a deft evocation of Perseus, poised to decapitate Medusa, does not auger well for these out-of-towners. Neither has an appetite for food in this claustrophobic setting, more a reverie than a restaurant, where women put on the "Southern mask—of-life-is-a-dream irony," and where their friends want "to get back to their houses and sleep" (562). Instead, the strangers take off in a convertible, the man conceding that the rental company accused him of having lost his "mind" to wish to travel south in summertime with the top open (563). But these travelers appear to have nothing left to lose.

From the dream of the restaurant, they pass without rousing into the dream of the "strange land" that stretches south of the city to the Gulf (*Stories* 577). Suzanne Marrs provides a thorough account of the process by which Welty fictionalized an actual trip she took to this country in the company of a "young Harvard professor named Carvel Collins" (*One Writer's* 156). Marrs shows that the locations of "No Place for You, My Love" come "directly from this experience," and that the "setting is very realistically described" (157). In a sense, of course, the scene down south does show a high degree of verisimilitude. Welty uses the observations from her actual trip to imagine the fictional journey her characters take, and detail for detail and fact for fact, documentary observation and fictional result bear a striking resemblance. However, while the matrix of circumstantial detail does evoke actual bayou country, it also attains a surreality—or an intensified reality beyond the realism Marrs claims for the portrayal. Welty seems to have this enhanced envisioning of exterior life in mind when, in "Place in Fiction," she asserts that "art's responsibility" lies in "making reality real" (791). And in "No Place for You, My Love," she does not waver from this commitment, exploiting a variety of surreal literary effects to generate the travelers' sense of paranoia. Clearly, Cajun country had its charms for Welty, and she unreservedly lauded its beauty when she claimed that the places she visited on her trip "smote me." This world, she wrote, "started the story and made it for me—and *was* the story, really" (Kuehl 87). So heavily did the landscape impress itself upon her writer's eye that she could, with some heavy modification, render the inside of her characters outside. She achieved this outcome so effectively that readers scarcely know whether the characters travel down through a physical wasteland or through what Albert Devlin designates a "hypnotic country" ("Sharp Edge" 166) simulating a paranoiac state of mind.

The psychological malaise of these modern wanderers shows at every turn in this narrative, which takes as its organizing principle the relentless drive to expose the fraudulency of imperviousness, the kind of imperme-ability that all surrealists reveal as false. The promise of sex and the de-lirium this promise produces colors the hallucinogenic presentation of life down there. "A raging of insects" (*Stories* 563) comes from either side of the highway south, so the repellent the businessman suggests his companion wear seems like a futile gesture in this land where an exploding universe of "thousands, millions of mosquitoes and gnats" swarm. The threat of malarial infection hovers over them, recalling Loch Morrison's sweaty bed and the throbbing of desire newly awakened in his ravaged body. In bayou country, almost everything seen from the car evokes erotic associations. Evidence of or the prospect of copulation crowds in on the characters from all sides. "Families bigger than housefuls" throng the yards. A "family of eight or nine people on foot strung along the road." Young girls "disposing themselves over the porches," and naked "children running forth," litter the landscape. The frisson charging the language also emanates from repeated mention of animals. The crayfish "constantly crossed in front of the wheels" (564). Shrimp and the "other shell creatures" bestrew "their path, scuttling or dragging," as if Dalí's snapping lobsters, his signature emblem of sexual arousal and anxiety, have migrated to Arcadia. The landscape has narco-tized the businessman so heavily that he veers off the road, only to have the woman to nudge him and yell, "Wake up." That shout extends to readers whom Welty has caught in this daydream, which keeps unfolding down toward the "primeval mud" (565), where men exchange and boil shrimp and where a chained alligator—which boys toy with on board a ferry carrying them all over the river—provokes the woman to cry desperately, "What was there so hilarious about jaws that could bite?" (567). The conglomeration of biting mosquitoes, crayfish claws, men's mouths, and alligator jaws pro-vides a rich assortment of threats posed by desire's entanglements faced at Venice, the "jumping-off place" (571) where there "was water under every-thing" (568).

The road ends at a lounge called Baba's, where the businessman finds that his appetite has returned—not unlike Ran's when he flees from Morgana to Vicksburg in "The Whole World Knows." The woman only thirsts for water. Nonetheless, Baba forces her to eat and drink beer. Bayou country, transformed through the power of the author's pen, shows the midwestern woman the wildness beyond the view, a scene now familiar to Welty and a commonplace of her fiction.[1] Confronted by the overwhelming fecundity of the landscape, the sight of crawling, scabrous, and tough-hided animals, and the building tension of the moment, the woman "felt a panic rise, as sudden as nausea" and plaintively wonders, "How dear—how costly—could this ride be?" (*Stories* 569). Her distress and sense of seasickness, experienced as she and her partner move over water toward the evening's "threshold," parallels Maideen Sumrall's sensations in "The Whole World Knows" (575), where another unprepared woman is swept away by car, driven hard and fast, given alcohol, and taken to a place of seduction. However, unlike Maideen, and unlike Jenny from "At the Landing," the woman in "No Place for You, My Love" does not suffer sexual violation in the "camp" of "houses and shacks" that abut the water (570). She merely dances with the businessman "like people in love." Strangers to love and to each other, they glide like "Spanish dancers wearing masks" and represent "imperviousness in motion," revealing "separate hearts" (576). Of course, the enduring irony of this dance floor scene lies in the couple's perfect, completely hollow public display of affection, accompanied by "music you heard out of the distance at night—out of the roadside taverns you fled past, around the late corners in cities half-asleep, drifting up from the carnival over the hill, with one odd little strain always managing to repeat itself" (577). Like the nighttime music that the car screams past, that the pedestrian hears just around the bend, and that issues temptingly from over the rise, victims such as these endlessly wander after the riches of golden apples.

Like the journey south, the journey north "was wordless, quiet except for the motor and the insects driving themselves against the car." Still, the dream persists, cradling its sleepers, who abjure conversation yet feel their throbbing motors turning over below. Despite their need for connection, Welty undermines all the metaphors suggestive of building sexual tension and impending climax, continually reasserting the sense of loss, desperation, and frustration that these strangers feel. In the tapering beams of light from the headlights, "cones of flying things" threaten to "ignite at the last minute," as if passions may fire at any moment. But above a ghostly "ash-white moon" presides, while choking "dust lay thick and cratered on the roadside scrub." Stretches of water appear, but they no longer threaten to capsize the travelers as they did farther south. Open and unending vistas "like steppes, moors, like deserts" (*Stories* 577), ambiguously presented in their surreal multiplicity, present themselves to the Northeasterner, who stops as if to make last attempt at seduction. He kisses the woman without "knowing ever whether gently or harshly," but the meaningless embrace brings with it a disgusting aftermath, when the "heat came inside the car and wrapped them still, and the mosquitoes had begun to coat their arms and even their eyelids" (578). The armies of smothering insects seem to feast on their decomposing cadavers, a nightmare image of emotional and psychological decay capturing Welty's accentuation of love's homelessness and alienation in the story's title.

Love's tenuous placement, here between two people who cannot maintain connections and who wander existentially through dream landscapes, evokes the separateness that Robert Penn Warren famously claimed to be an abiding theme in Welty's work. He too argued that love, positioned at the other pole, maintained the tension ordering the action in her stories. In "No Place for You, My Love," strangers, driven by desire on a wild and desperate journey, arrive in a land of unyielding light and experience the heat of Welty's spotlight, switched full upon them, turning their insides outside and revealing fragility, rancor, and desperation. Desire for sexual gratification, desire for release from the cages that house them, and desire for finding a place for love in life bind the couple like the heat that wraps around them in the car. This time, however, the strangers escaped and "were getting safely back—by a slight margin, perhaps, but margin enough" (*Stories* 579). Insects have not suffocated them. Neither have fires burnt them too fiercely, leaving the businessman with the

> feeling that they had been riding for a long time across a face—great, wide, and upturned. In its eyes and open mouth were those fires they had had glimpses of, where the cattle had drawn together: a face, a head, far down here in the South—south of South, below it. A whole giant body sprawled downward then, on and on, always, constant as a constellation or an angel. Flaming and perhaps falling, he thought. (578)

If the surreal language Welty has used all along suggested the interiority of this drive into the swamp, the metaphor of the upturned face and spread out body, marked by roads and overlaid so conspicuously onto the landscape, confirms the story's dual reality. Readers travel with the strangers through an anthropomorphic landscape, a Newtonian universe bent and twisted by the distorting effects of nearly paralyzing neuroses.

The wildness witnessed through the aperture opened upon life in "No Place for You, My Love" receives amplification in the story that follows it in the collection. The first story written on her return from traveling "for almost a year" across Europe (Marrs *One Writer's* 143), "The Burning" presents Welty's only Civil War story. Delilah, a plantation slave, witnesses a brutal and probably sexual attack upon one of her owners, Miss Myra. Myra and her sister, Miss Theo, fail to flee their home even when warned that Union forces are advancing to burn and pillage. Following the razing of the plantation house, in which a mysterious child dies, the two white women die, leaving Delilah, the sole survivor, to contemplate her own trauma (possibly another rape) at the hands of the soldiers, the death of a child, Phinny, in the conflagration, and the meaning of what Vande Kieft deems the story's "major symbol" (130), a Venetian mirror that not only reflects but forms a screen upon which Welty projects Delilah's nightmares and resuscitation.[2] Although Welty roundly criticized "The Burning" as a fiction misadventure, her use of a Civil War setting to examine the imbricated themes of desire, hatred, miscegenation, racial purity, and xenophobic nationalism makes sense, allowing for the larger European context of war and genocide that inscribe the story.[3] "The Burning" directly announces this context in its title, which alludes to the millions of bodies that fascist ideologues incinerated in the death camps.

Western civilization in crisis and transformation forms the backdrop to "The Burning," and when the ex-slave, Delilah, turns for answers about her place in a world at the story's climactic end, she goes to a mirror and enters a dreamland where reason yields to the delirium of the reverie. Consumed by flames, the house has largely collapsed, but the mirror that once hung on the wall and reflected molestation by the soldiers, now lies in the fire's grate. Partly cloudy and partly clear, its surface presents a scene that Delilah (whose name may suggest a surreal play on Dalí) identifies as "Jackson before Sherman came" (*Stories* 594). In it, she sees a complex, poetic, and disquieting dream vision that conveys the structure of the social hierarchy and the distribution of power and wealth in planter society. "Black men" form the upright posts that support the "mirror's roof." Gazing into the frame returns their precious humanity to them, an experience expressed by repeated references to the honey that flows and the gold that they wear— and their exploitation by the elite planter class. Black labor transforms the land into "gold fields," which Welty reinforces by describing the fields as "hardening gold," as riches flow and twist "up into houses, trembling" on the mirror's watery screen (593). While "ladies with masks" peer icily from the "pointed windows" (594) of their cages, white men freely participate in a strange carnival, with "hives of houses on their heads, men in dresses, some with red birds; and monkeys in velvet" (593). The bizarre scene suddenly disappears, however, and Delilah watches her reflected and floating face, "pure as a water lily shadow," brought forward to the moment of the Civil War. The curious light behaves unpredictably, leaping, darting, and swimming like "minnows," and softening the unbending edge of material reality to illuminate "what men had done to Miss Theo and Miss Myra and the peacocks and to slaves, and sometimes what a slave had done and what anybody now could do to anybody" (594).

The scene of human carnage the mirror reveals to Delilah shows a conglomeration of internecine battles—white against black, master against slave, Union against Confederate, and man against woman—in which the winner inflicts terrible defeat upon the loser. Welty reveals all these aspects of the Civil War with the raping suggested by animals moving in the carnival parade evoked earlier, and the "horses," "butterflies," "bats," and "birds together, all with their weapons bared," as well as the vengeful "dragonflies" coming down upon her with "blades unconcealed and at point" (594). Delilah's vision seems to re-enact the violations brought by war and soldiers who discarded her "face-down in a ditch with her eyes scorched open," but contemplating the horror of a lifetime of burning through the dream depicted on the mirror delivers renewal and a sense of optimism (586). Unlike her masters, who feel the Civil War has left them obsolete and meaningless, Delilah prevails as she lifts herself from the frame, rising like a Phoenix from the ashes of this house of nightmares and catching herself heroically transformed in the mirror that had once reflected her subjugation. Now, she "cocked her head, looked sharp into the mirror, and caught the motherly image—head wagging in the flayed forehead of a horse with ears and crest up stiff, the shield and the drum of big swamp birdskins, the horns of deer sharpened to cut and kill with. She showed her teeth" (594–95). Confronting the potentially devastating pain and humiliation of this nightmare, Delilah emerges fortified and surreally metamorphosed into a woman warrior.

Women warriors also preoccupy Welty in "Circe," a twentieth-century renovation of Homer's account of the legendary witch. Written just before her departure for Europe, "Circe" reevaluates this narrative of female conquest, handed down from antiquity, by telling the "mythological tale of Circe and Odysseus from a woman's perspective" (Marrs *One Writer's* 145). Although Michael Kreyling forcefully argues that Welty's Circe "is as rich a presence as any character in *The Golden Apples*" (*Understanding* 168), she lacks the psychological depth that Welty plumbs elsewhere in her fiction through the deployment of surreal poetic effects. Her prose reassessment of Circe may evoke a world of dreams because of its fantastic setting, or because of the bravado Welty shows by directly rebutting the father of western literature, but at no point can the story escape the limitations of the epic genre, a poetic tradition reserved for the exploits of the high and the haughty. The epic form to which this story replies remains the backdrop to Welty's revisions. The constraints that she imposes upon herself by selecting a plot inherited from Homer and by choosing to mimic his august style, however satirically, preclude her from depicting Circe quite as humanly she does her other heroes. She exalts Virgie Rainey or Easter, for example, by manipulating the traditional style of realistic fiction. Surreal poetic effects appear so only because they reorient the reader in relation to received and quantifiable notions of time and space that realism tends to reinforce. In a narrative tracing events on a magical island, where no expectation of depiction of ordinary and mundane lives exists, no enlarged reality or sur-reality obtains. At no point does Circe dream as Virgie dreams, appear to hallucinate as Ran hallucinates, or indulge herself in a reverie like Robbie Reid. Of course, she has more dimensions than Homer's dupe, but because of her obvious extraction from a mythological epic, she hasn't the humanity of a Jenny Lockhart or a Joel Mays.

The world of most of Welty's characters seems very familiar. The fact that many commentators have viewed Welty's stories realistically, as actual transcriptions of Mississippi places and actual renderings of Mississippi people, attests to this assertion. However, as she says in "Place in Fiction," the "world of appearance in the novel has got to *seem* actuality" (785) in order that the writer's illusion "will turn into the reader's illusion" (792). Because of its source, "Circe" can offer no pretense of realism. By contrast, in a more conventional narrative, such as "At the Landing," apparent realism allows for the subversion of the world of appearances. In other words, surreal effects depend upon simulating a world of Newtonian stability, only to subvert those conventions by submitting them to the new physics of surrealism. When Welty observes that "there are only four words, of all the millions we've hatched, that a novel rules out: 'Once upon a time.' They make a story a fairy tale by the simple sweep of the remove—by abolishing the present and the place where we are instead of conveying them to us" ("Place" 782), she has stories like *The Robber Bridegroom* and "Circe" in mind. Because the genre of these narratives creates a context that forcefully abolishes the here and now, readers cannot imagine themselves entering these tales with quite the same ease as they imagine walking into the universe of a story like "At the Landing."

Unlike Circe's world—cut off from readers, utterly fantastic, and magical—the world of "Ladies in Spring" offers a universe that for twentieth and twenty-first century audiences, at least, appears familiar and known. Readers might know individuals like Blackie Coker and his son, Dewey, and if they don't, they would certainly recognize school buses and the "month of March." Nonetheless, Welty subtly challenges that sense of familiarity in the story's first line: "The pair moved through that gray landscape as though no one would see them—dressed alike in overalls and faded coats, one big, one little, one black-headed, one tow-headed, father and son." On the one hand, the two walk openly together without concealment, as if they do not care whether others see them. On the other hand, the sentence suggests that others, including readers, cannot observe the pair—either because Welty has recycled the "gray landscape" of San Francisco from "Music from Spain," or because the next paragraph reports that this scene has not yet taken place. It happens following the "quarter of an hour before." At once concrete and concretely insubstantial, this opening scene shows Welty's surreal sensibility emerging most subtly in moments like these, when situations familiar, known, and apparently rational reveal the irrational world of the dream. "Ladies in Spring" relates the most common of events: a father escorting his son on a fishing trip to the local river. However, rather than going to school that day and learning the fable of "*Excalibur*" from Miss Pruitt (*Stories* 625), Dewey plays truant with his father, who has another story to teach his son—a tale of ladies, lakes, and swords.

The whole narrative has the mood of a remembered dream, perhaps Dewey's own recollection of his initiation into the codes prescribing adult masculine behavior and the role his father plays in transmitting these conventions.[4] Indeed, Blackie Coker has organized this excursion to stage the events that follow and introduce Dewey to knowledge about relations between men and women. Why else would he walk "right down the road" with "two poles" in full view of the school bus, if not to tempt his son? Why would he carry two poles if fishing alone? And why go fishing at all if, as he admits, "we ain't going to catch us no fish, because there ain't no water left to catch 'em in"? Absent from school and warned by his father to "keep still about it at home," Dewey embarks on an illicit journey beyond the reach of his mother's authority (*Stories* 625).

Dewey abjures Miss Pruitt's story in favor of his father's, as father and son move into the dream of the forest and the surrealism of the swamp, where "vines, leafless and yet abundant and soft, covered the trees and thickets as if rainclouds had been dropped down from the sky over them" (*Stories* 625). Soon, they approach their fishing hole, an "old, unrailed, concrete bridge," which partially crosses the river and stands "like a table in the water." They precariously edge over the plank, which gives like a "hammock laid across to the bridge floor." On this island, a mesa of sleep that the fishermen have crossed onto, passing a sign reading "Cross at Own Risk," they bate their hooks and await bites. Of course, they catch no fish, as Blackie predicted. At about midday, a woman appears, haling from the riverbank as if the father has brought his son out to this liminal, dreamlike spot in order to sanction infidelity. "Another lady had dared to invade this place," Dewey remarks of the woman: "Over the water and through the trees, on the same side of the river they'd come from, her face shone clear as a lantern in nighttime. She'd found them." Like a ghost at dark, her voice sounding "like the dove-call of April or May" (627), the woman looks out from the forest and calls Blackie three times, while Dewey's thoughts turn immediately to her death and to sex, a subject that Welty introduces through the turtles that "now lay on logs." The boy counts the fourteen "baby turtles," observing that on a "giant log was a giant turtle, gray-tailed, the size of a dishpan, set at a laughable angle there, safe from everybody and everything" (628). This episode recalls Dabney's encounter with an obscenely depicted turtle on the banks of the whirlpool in *Delta Wedding*. The repeated calls of the woman to whom Blackie does not reply furnish a context for Dewey's initiation into sex—a springtime awakening announced as if by William Wallace—when the boy lands a dancing fish, "six inches long and jumping on the hook" (628–29). His father leads him to a remote and isolated spot in order to pass on to Dewey the dream of an equally distant and implacable masculine sexuality that admits no response or exchange, and associates women with ghouls and death.

The preoccupation with misogyny and dreams that reproduce and disseminate this fear within families also provides the thematic center for two other stories set outside the South, "The Bride of the Innisfallen" and "Going to Naples." Both narratives focus upon marriages imagined, endured, and suffered—and those on the point of collapse. Both deploy the metaphor of travel by rail and sea to enact the surreal blending of dreaming and waking realities. "The Bride of the Innisfallen," for example, includes a thinly veiled self-portrait of Welty, a quiet and innocuous American who assumes the position of discreet observer of events on a rail and sea journey from London, England, to Cork in Ireland. Marrs reports that Welty's "imagination was sparked in the early 1950s by the experience of travel—travel by train, ship, and car to states and countries not her own—and stories based very closely upon her various journeys dominate *The Bride of the Innisfallen*" (*One Writer's* 141). Both stories find Welty appropriating these modes of travel, transforming them into sites for social critiques. Furthermore, ships, trains, and cars often provide settings for Welty's undermining of purely rational strategies for comprehending the meaningfulness of place and for the evolution of personal identities.

The "American girl" (*Stories* 596) in "The Bride of the Innisfallen" has left her husband in London and travels to Cork. Welty does not disclose the cause of this marital estrangement, but the telegram the girl nearly sends her husband upon arrival in Ireland suggests he has suffered a loss of passion, an impotency, and a failure of imagination she remembers in his diagnosis of her problem as hoping "for too much" (624). The American girl, however, has her dreaming facility intact, and her journey through the darkness that mostly envelops the travellers inside the hull of the railway carriage creates a sense of claustrophobia, paranoia, and dreaming delirium. From the confines of the carriage waiting at the station, she spots her first traveling companion, a "middle-aged lady" (596) whose raincoat, rather than her legs, appears to transfer her around the platform. The girl's view, perhaps like Loch Morrison's, through the frame of a window, reveals the "strange, diminished light of the station," where people seem to "stand and move on some dark stage" (597). The woman's coat has "something of the pavilion" about it, catching the American's eye, which moves over the crowd on the platform.[5] The raincoat comes "parading through now," and its color and pattern in the shadowy station first appears "salmony-pink and yellow stripes," but then seems "rainbow-bright" inside the train. These apparently incidental details about the woman's billowy and "expanding" raincoat set the tone for what readers encounter on this dreaming voyage west. Everything Welty presents has dimensions, shapes, patterns, and colors that shift, harden, mollify, and metamorphose in time and place. She asserts this view through the world observed by the American, who daydreams the raincoat into a pavilion, a tent, and a vehicle for transporting its occupant over the platform in its bright billows and folds.

Subject to the laws of dreams, those in the carriage begin their journey. Among those who occupy the busy compartment, the boisterous, aggressive, and intimidating middle-aged woman assumes the role of a libidinous virago, with "flirtatious" hair that "went into two auburn-and-gray pomegranates along her cheeks" (*Stories* 596). As soon as the train has pulled out of the station and her officious husband disappears from view, she turns and puts "out her tongue, at everything just left behind" (599). She soon undoes her raincoat and requests a liberating rendition of "Wild Colonial Boy" (600). The winding and grinding train recalls other Weltian journeys into the heart of unconscious desires, such as the speeding flight of cars driven hard by Ran in "The Whole World Knows," Shelley in *Delta Wedding*, and the businessman going south in "No Place for You, My Love." Here, the woman in the raincoat draws attention to the train's subversive and dangerous ride when she observes, "railway trains are great systems for goings on of all kinds. You'll never take me by surprise" (601). The sounds of chatter about birds, wild looking dogs padding past, and mothers carrying babies supply the backdrop to this dream, an introverted narrative folding the passengers together in the dark of the "black windows—for the sun was down now, never having been out of the fogs and rains all day—coated warmly over between them and what flew by out there" (605). The middle-aged woman moves comfortably in this transitory world. She has come prepared with food and an appetite that exceeds everyone else's. She may well, as Polk intriguingly avers, lead "two lives between London and Cork, like an old Mr. Marblehall, perhaps, or in view of the children in Cork, more like a Remarkable Mrs. Pennypacker" ("Water" 115). She shares her provisions with the other passengers, yet still goes off to the dining car, leaving the American woman astonished at her appetite, "Did she really mean to eat still, and after all that largess?" Perhaps she seeks to satisfy her cravings through an encounter with a "delicious" stranger like the one she passes in the corridor, the "Tunnel of Love" (*Stories* 606), outside the compartment. Nobody else in the party "was, actually, booked for a berth on the *Innisfallen* except for the lady in the raincoat" (*Stories* 619), whose clothing presents an eye-catching sartorial advertisement for the present that it may conceal.

Boring through tunnels of rock, tunnels under water, and tunnels of blackness forged in the dark Welsh night, the train speeds toward its rendezvous with the *Innisfallen*, the boat ferrying the passengers to Ireland. The change of transport does not signal a change in mood, however. Now, they travel over water on a ship, but the dreamlike atmosphere persists. Welty condenses the train and the boat into one surreal image, the "boat train" (*Stories* 615), bobbing its way to Cork, caught on the world's surface over which rail tracks and shipping lanes direct passengers and cargo onwards through life. Beneath everything, motors turn over and throb, providing direction and propulsion down routes already assigned and ordered by convention and timetables. For example, the *Innisfallen* brings to harbor the bride referenced in the story's title. The American woman, fleeing *her* marriage, sees the bride emerge suddenly like an apparition as they approach the dock. A "girl who had not yet showed herself in public now appeared by the rail in a white spring hat and, over her hands, a little old-fashioned white bunny muff" (621). The dream vision, which Kreyling identifies as "sexual, religious, social, archetypal" (*Understanding* 176), presents readers with a delicate counterpoint to the domineering presence of the woman in the raincoat. Passive, huddled, virginal, sheltered, and restrained by the rail (in contrast to the unrailed bridge occupied by the Cokers in "Ladies in Spring"), the bride coyly smiles and navel gazes "down at her dazzling little fur muff," while those on shore delightedly celebrate her arrival by singing, ringing bells, and displaying flags that match the "color beating in their eyes." News of the bride creates excitement, stirring the townspeople, who glow at the prospect of a wedding. But the threat of danger subtly permeates this scene. Does she recognize the precariousness of her position high up above the dockside? Could she slip and fall like Easter in "Moon Lake"? Could the water take her like it does the newspaper that "slowly went down with its drowned news" (*Stories* 621)? Could she fall today into the whirlpool, a double of *Delta Wedding*'s maelstrom, and tomorrow seem yesterday's news? These grim alternatives suggest themselves to the sober American, whom marriage has dissatisfied and whose dreaming journey has brought a renewed sense of individuality.

In the fogginess of London and the dark of night as they cross to Ireland, ghosts both literal and dreamt haunt the girl's mind, introducing themes of confinement, paralysis, love, intoxication, and regret. She hears men talking coldly about caged birds that have starved to death. An unaccompanied pregnant woman and her troublesome ward, Victor, return from a wedding that has left a woman bedridden, while young, naïve lovers sit huddled against the threatening presence of the middle-aged woman and two hostile and overbearing men—the former coming along slowly because his mad wife has the "dagger stuck in him" (*Stories* 608)—who tell ghost stories about Lord and Lady Beagle. On board, all settle in for the night crossing: "In the deeps of night that bright room reached some vortex of quiet, like a room where all brains are at work and great decisions are on the brink. Occasionally there was a tapping, as of drumming fingernails—that meant to closed or hypnotized eyes that dogs were being sped through." At this strange and uncertain hour, both dark and light and sleeping and waking, confused "old men" (619) shuffle through the ship in search of stiff drinks. The pregnant woman abandons Victor as if he were a stranger. And the "man from Connemara sat up out of his sleep and stared at the American girl pinned to her chair across the room, as if he saw somebody desperate who had left her husband once, endangered herself among strangers, been turned back, and was here for the second go-around, asking again for a place to stay in Cork" (620). Defenseless and in the throes of a dream, the American traveller experiences a creeping sense of paranoia. She dreams of the stare of the man, who had earlier appeared a "starfish of exhaustion" (619), and whose fixed gaze dissects and insinuates moral laxity. Fortunately, the "streaming light" (620) of Cork dispels the gray figures and demons that populate her nightmares, and she experiences what Polk views as a "paradigmatic moment in Welty," when a "lone woman comes to herself in a dark wood but responds to it not as a moment of fear and perplexity, but rather savors it as a moment of epiphany, in which she discovers that she can be happy alone and stops to luxuriate in her freedom" ("Welty and Faulkner" 146). Beauty replaces horror, light shines into darkness, vitality substitutes for torpor, and elation displaces anxiety. Having discarded her husband's telegram and about to enter a lively pub, the American woman sees a wandering vision of herself in the barmaid, who "glimmered through the passage in her frill" (*Stories* 624), an allusion to glimmering wanderers like King MacLain and Virgie Rainey.

"Going to Naples" rounds out the collection, once again circulating Welty's always conjoined themes of desire, dreams, and the conventions that police behavior. Here, she reprises her surreal rhetoric, a poetic language that succeeds in artfully integrating dreaming realities into everyday experiences, so that readers scarcely sense the prose's delicate simulation of hallucinatory states. Mrs. Serto and her eighteen-year-old daughter, Gabriella, sail for Naples onboard the *Pomona*, a liner leaving from New York bound for Italy and echoing with Gabriella's wailing voice. Welty observes that she "was happy in Buffalo," but now appears "screaming and waving good-by to the Statue of Liberty" (*Stories* 682). Like the boat train that relentlessly forges onward over land and sea, the *Pomona* drives through ocean swells, another cork bobbing on the sea of desires building in Gabriella—young, distressed, and still unmarried, much to the chagrin of her mother. Constantly supervised by her mother and surrounded by a witch's coven of chaperones she cannot seem to shake, Gabriella goes on-board literarily kicking and screaming against the "black shawls, the same old caps, backed up against the blue—faces coming out of them that grew to be the only faces in the world, more solid a group than a family's, more persistent one by one than faces held fast in the memory or floating to nearness in dreams" (684). These oppressive figures from Gabriella's night-mare watch her every move and act like a collective superego, regulating desires and policing libido. These surreal descriptions show her crossing the Atlantic as if on a daydreamed journey, and Welty's prose creates a mood of suspended time, what Polk designates as "Time Out" for Gabriella and her suitor, Aldo Scampo ("Going" 160).

Dangers, threats, pitfalls, and barriers thwart easy movement on this boat and confront Gabriella on all sides. Should she manage to evade her mother's eye, other mothers take over surveillance. Should she fly too reck-lessly and far out to sea, like the birds that the crew shoot from the ship, she may get killed and "drop into the water" (*Stories* 684). Should she chose an unmarried life, she may suffer ostracism and end up spurned and ridiculed like La Zìngara, the gypsy, and a "popular passenger said to be an actress" (685). Yet, should she marry and capitulate to her mother's constant harp-ing, she may get saddled with an intolerable chauvinist like "Poldy some-body" (682), a dim bridegroom on his way to Italy to marry a woman he has never met. Presented with this dire set of options, Gabriella chooses to accept the favors of Aldo, another Italian-American about whom the "complete story was not yet known" (685). For the duration of the cruise, the engines pulse close beneath those, like the Sertos, traveling "*turistica*" (682), while the ship steadily plows toward Europe in a "strange, almost sad tranquility under the stars, as in a trance that might never be broken again" (688). And, although forces ranged against improper displays of feminine purity and convention attempt to keep Gabriella spellbound, she resists by responding to the rhythm of the ship's throbbing engine.

Throughout the narrative, Welty associates the "*Pomona* engines" and the "ship's crew—who looked wild in their half-undress, even their faces covered with black" with the eroticism investing the matchmaking taking place just above them (*Stories* 683). The ship's name itself suggests an orgasmic moan. It has a "humming and pounding bottom," and it may leak. Mrs. Serto and her daughter navigate a deep passage that "was wet" (682). Moreover, Gabriella and Aldo wrestle and frolic on the boat's "softly vibrating floor," while on deck warmth lulls "heads that were nodding of dreaming of home" (689). The heat, sea air, and throb from below even seem to overcome Mrs. Serto, who allows her daughter an unaccompanied stroll on board with Aldo. Unsupervised, the pair quickly duck below, making their way "through the depths of the ship" and along a passage "too narrow for Mrs. Serto and Gabriella," which nevertheless "seemed made for Gabriella and Aldo." Going down and along, they smell the "sour wine the crew drank," and at the "deepest part, the engines pounding just within that open door made a human being seem to go in momentary danger of being shaken asunder." Elated and dreaming of "Niagara Falls," Gabriella "felt as if she and Aldo were walking side by side in some still, lonely, even high place never seen before now, with mountains above, valleys below, and sky." While these travelers voyage across the sea, they also plumb its depths, going vertically and perhaps dangerously below the waterline, into spaces both literal and psychological. Near the engine room, Gabriella spots an old man, "who slept all day on top of that box asleep where he always was, but now as if he floated, with no box underneath him at all, in some spell" (693). Her awakening desire for Aldo and her escape from her mother create the delirious features of this reverie, a hallucinatory daydream that, in the old man, presents a slumbering superego asleep on the job.[6]

Eventually, this initiatory and forbidden trek through the bowels of the ship brings the couple up "steep stairs" and into the brightly-lit open shell of Venus, a waitress who dries her hair, which when let "loose from the towel . . . blew behind her straight as an arm" (*Stories* 693). This barely-disguised incarnation of the goddess crosses the "Mediterranean sea" (695) on an "altogether new deck" where "mysterious shapes" appear and where "no passenger was in sight." Here, in Gabriella's daydream, Welty redeploys the myth in order to enact a young girl's passage from screaming girlhood to adult femininity, an evolution toward clarity signified by the air's freshness, "bright and stiff as an open eye" (693). Like Virgie Rainey, another of Welty's Venuses, the waitress has long, luxurious hair and a sailor for a lover. Her deck, reached via the ship's darkest and deepest recesses, offers the lovers a space "where no eye oversaw them." Here they discover another passenger, Miss Crosby, whom Marrs suggests represents a veiled portrait of the author, who not only traveled Europe by boat in tourist class, but "spent a good bit of her voyage reading *Moby-Dick*" (*One Writer's* 162).

Beyond the writer herself is another Venusian candidate, Caresse Crosby, the wealthy socialite, patron, poet, and publisher, who embodied an ideal of modern femininity probably admired by Welty. Scandalously named Caresse married avant-garde poet Harry Crosby, and together in Paris they founded Black Sun Press in 1924 (Hamalian xi). Black Sun Press would ultimately publish Julien Levy's *Surrealism* in 1936 (104), as well as Faulkner's *Sanctuary* (91) and works by D. H. Lawrence, James Joyce, Ernest Hemingway, and Hart Crane (xi). The Crosbys travelled in Europe, lived a bohemian existence, and mixed with many modernist intellectuals. When Harry died in 1929, Caresse continued running the firm "for the next thirty years" (xi), promoted figures such as Dalí, Henry Miller, and Anaïs Nin (113), and developed a long friendship with Kay Boyle, one of Black Sun's writers and a friend of Eudora. In fact, Marrs reports that Welty worked on the story later titled "Going to Naples" in 1949, while staying in Paris, where, at a lunch, Mary Mian introduced her to Boyle, then serving as European correspondent for the *New Yorker* (*Eudora* 179–80). Adding Caresse Crosby and Kay Boyle to names such as Berenice Abbott, Elsa Schiaparelli, Katherine Anne Porter, and Mary Lou Aswell begins to build a limited but suggestive picture of women Welty could respect. And to these names perhaps add women who had, like the gypsy, La Zìngara, or the waitress, found their way up and out onto a hard-to-reach deck, a place difficult to find but not mythical, where a young woman like Gabriella can begin to acquire new insights about her identity. When La Zìngara appears, she trails a "horn-rimmed" priest, whom she treats to a dance, one that Gabriella later reprises on Gala Night. While Aldo sleeps, having thrown her baby picture into the ocean, Gabriella listens to the "dividing sea" as if through a "seashell," and happily drifts, feeling "caught in an element as languorous as it was strange, like a mermaid who has been netted into a fisherman's boat, only to find that the fisherman is dreaming" (695). She does not wake Aldo, though. The waitress has since left the hidden deck, but Gabriella has assumed her mantle as the Venus presiding at the ship's prow like the "figurehead on a Viking ship" (265) that Josie, the young girl in "The Winds," dreams is an emblem of resilience.

At one level or another and with varying degrees of conspicuousness, every Welty story so far considered creates and critiques realistic fiction's representational assumptions. Stories such as "A Memory," for instance, make the squared fingers of an artist's capturing frame a prominent symbol for the essentially narcissistic position that writers attempt to overcome. And, in stories such as "A Still Moment," Welty critiques purely rational approaches to presentation by mounting an attack on representational strategies that aim crudely at reproducing life in purely representational detail. Audubon's art fails to capture the life of his subject because his neoclassical philosophical values create a painting that enshrines and celebrates the bird's death. To these two accounts written in the thirties and forties, one can add "Kin," written in the fifties with the intent to dissect and render spurious representational approaches to life that claim a monopoly on truth. The narrative follows Dicey Hastings and her cousin, Kate, as they journey out to Mingo, the home of their sick Uncle, Felix, whom Sister Anne, a very distant relative, supposedly nurses. Set back in the Mississippi wilderness, "in a part the highway had deserted long ago" (*Stories* 656), the old house sits beyond an "iron bridge" and down a turning "off on a still narrower, bumpier road." Upon reaching their almost-hidden destination, the women sense they have wandered into a dream. Every light burns, despite their daytime arrival, and the large house, filled with strangers, appears "vaguely powdered over with the golden dust of their thick arrival here in mid-afternoon" (657). Sister Anne, a once-jilted bride who had attempted suicide in Mingo's well, has transformed the parlor into a photographer's studio for an itinerant conman, the shady Mr. Puryear, always on the make, to take portraits. In order to create room for the customers and for the photographer, Anne has cruelly relegated the sick patient to a ramshackle room at Mingo's rear while locals sit, stand, smoke, and otherwise wait in comfort for their turn in front of the camera. Sister Anne benefits from the arrangement, getting her own picture taken for free after everyone else.

Like *The Golden Apples*'s MacLain house or *Delta Wedding*'s Marmion, which act as focal points for the concentration of dream life, Mingo functions in "Kin" to create a kaleidoscopic stage for surreal events. It supplies a surreal context for reappraising all the values to which the visiting women subscribe. Dicey's remembrances of happy family occasions spent at Mingo sit uneasily alongside the present spectacle of the house, filled with taciturn outsiders. Her memories contradict what she now sees, as if she daydreams the scene. Astonished at the number of customers, she exclaims the "way she did last night in her sleep." She cannot keep from thinking, as she passes through Mingo's gate, "I'd either forgotten or never known how *primitive* the old place was" (*Stories* 658). More a state of mind than an actual place, Mingo sounds bizarre and seems like a "house of death" where, like the faulty clocks running behind in *Delta Wedding*'s Shellmound, the "clock was wrong," even though Dicey "was deeply aware that all clocks worked in this house" (660).[7] In Dicey's long absence from Mississippi, the house has changed irrevocably. A rational processing of events does not explain the depth of the alteration. What was a happy and beautiful place in her dreams and memories now appears grotesque and distorted, like a house of horrors at a carnival—complete with flashing lights, exploding gunpowder, ghostly strangers, a corpse seemingly from the Civil War, a bear, a charlatan, and a vampire.

In fact, Mingo presents a hive of illusions and surreal frauds. At the center of the action, a conman acts as a photographer, a creator of pictorial illusions, and successfully accomplishes the most obvious illusion of all: pulling the wool over his customers' eyes by leading them to believe he honestly plans to return with the pictures for which they have paid. Readers last see him running from the house and tearing away in his Ford. To Dicey, Mingo seems that most indecipherable of places, because as a child she saw the house radiating with family life and familiarity and love. But when she returns, she sees the house marked by death and populated by miscreants. On closer inspection, the mistress of the house and "nurse" to Uncle Felix has turned mad torturer, her very name, Sister Anne, perpetrating a lie. Nobody claims her as a sister.

Furthermore, when Welty introduces the stereopticon, she extends a long-running discussion on the duality of perception and the role of dreams in molding opinions. As a child, Dicey dearly treasured this device, which she could operate "in lieu of any nap" (670). It has affected her so deeply that she seems to have entered the world that the stereopticon depicted: "It's strange to think that since then I've gone to live in one of those picture cities" (671). Danièle Pitavy-Souques also claims the instrument as a representative of imagination when she argues that it provides a metaphor for describing the way "Kin" creates layered points of view—none of which readers should trust—in order to deliver social satire. Welty uses this satire to juxtapose variant images of the South, as if viewed through the instrument's blending lenses ("Blazing" 134–36). Truly, the stereopticon operates like a surreal prism through which viewers' dreams come into focus. It acts as a kaleidoscopic dream portal opened to Dicey as a child, displaying fantastic "sandpink cities and passionate fountains," "islands in the sea," "volcanoes," and "the Lakes, like starry fields," as well as things that she "couldn't see, which could make Uncle Felix pucker his lips for a kiss." Felix peers through the viewing device rather like Loch gazes at the MacLain house through his telescope, Delilah stares into her mirror, or the girl in "A Memory" composes the world inside her framed fingers. What appears to all these daydreamers so powerfully affects their consciousnesses that rational control slips under the weight of hallucination, and they appear spellbound, like Uncle Felix, who acts as "though, while he held the stereopticon to his eye, *we* did not see *him*" (*Stories* 671). Lost in the spectacle of dreams, these somnambulists yield to the illusion that enthralls them.

If the stereopticon supplies pictures that productively engage imagination and foster liberty, Sister Anne's wedding photograph symbolizes imprisonment through an image that looks backwards and fabricates a history that never existed. Her wedding ended in a debacle, but she wants a wedding photograph nonetheless. In preparation for her free picture, she stages the shot by arranging foliage over the fireplace "as for a country wedding" (*Stories* 673). Despite her energetic primping and coordinating of the scene, Welty portrays Anne's efforts as futile, because the picture would reveal "none of Mingo at all, but the itinerant backdrop—the same old thing, a scene that never was, a black and white and gray blur of unrolled, yanked-down moonlight, weighted at the bottom with the cast-iron parlor rabbit doorstep, just behind Sister Anne's restless heel." Indeed, witnessing her melodramatic posing moves Dicey to dream of "what was behind the photographer's backdrop," a portrait of her great grandmother, Evelina Mackaill, seated romantically on a "fallen tree under brooding skies" (674). In what Polk describes as an "epiphany of sisterhood" ("Going" 163), Dicey acknowledges the illusions that these representations of women perpetuate. Sister Anne appears moonlit in daytime, peaceful despite her illness. Evelina's picture appears equally staged, her form having "been fitted to the ready-made portrait by the painter who had called at the door." This idealized image presents her demurely seated, posed according to the conventions of feminine gentility, yet Dicey knows that Evelina had lived a life poles apart from the picture. She had faced the "Mississippi wilderness," consumed "bear meat," encountered "Indians," lived with "slaves," known "unknown feelings," and died of "yellow fever." Rather like a feminized version of Joseph Conrad's Mr. Kurtz, a man who tested the limits of civility in *Heart of Darkness*, Evelina experienced the "wildness of the world behind the ladies' view" (*Stories* 675), a perspective now shared by Dicey.

For reasons not altogether clear, the publication of *The Bride of the Innisfallen* marked the moment at which the influence of surrealism began to diminish significantly in Welty's work. When *Losing Battles* appeared fifteen years later, vestiges of this once-prominent characteristic remained, but surreal stylistic effects commonplace in her work from the thirties through the fifties had ceded ground to other formal preoccupations, probably as a consequence of Welty's intention to redefine her writing in the sixties and seventies. If *The Bride of the Innisfallen* aimed to reveal what the deceptions of tradition wanted to hide from women, the book appears to have made good on its promise. Welty remarked that "No Place for You, My Love" signaled her purpose to write about "exposure" and "shock" ("Writing" 778), but nearly all of its companion stories enact this desire in one way or another—and do so by exploiting surrealism's ever-malleable point of view, a perspective bearing a force both revelatory and concussive.

7

AMONG ARTISTIC LEADERS

This study began by situating itself in the context of oversight, particularly by American and British academics who studied modernism and modernist figures through interpretive structures, which minimized and/or excluded the achievements of many writers. Even so, Welty fared better than many women, not least because she came from a country with a respectable literary past that produced cosmopolitans par excellence, among them Ezra Pound, T. S. Eliot, and Gertrude Stein, and wrote in a way amenable to critics with formalist priorities. Then came "theory" that by the 1990s, according to Susan Stanford Friedman, left the study of modernism

> split into camps: an old guard holding to restrictive canons of a Eurocentric experimentalism and avant-garde and/or primarily formalist definitions of modernism; and a raucous crowd at the gate assaulting such restrictions and insisting on the inclusion of those the field had marginalized (e.g. women) or excluded (e.g. the Harlem Renaissance; non-western; popular culture). The uprising of the interdisciplines—women's studies, race studies, popular culture studies, gay/lesbian/queer studies—into the heart of modernist studies in the 1980s and 1990s divided the field. . . . (260)

Before theory's revolt against New Criticism, scholars had already established Welty the modernist, bestowing on her a modestly high reputation, assessed using myth criticism and undergirded by "local color" status. After theory—and particularly after Rebecca Mark's 1994 *The Dragon's Blood: Feminist Intertextuality in Eudora Welty's* The Golden Apples—Welty's star shone even brighter, as critics began revealing her fiction's engagement with the world at large, a project still underway. A book like this one, then, seems heir to both the older and the newer currents propelling Welty studies forward. On the one hand, it reads Welty's work formally, perhaps completing a long-running discussion investigating Welty's modernist influences by tracing the lineaments of her prose style back to surrealism as it represented the avant-garde. On the other, it carries out the analysis using an interdisciplinary method, probably the only strategy available for such a study. Derived from the recent uprising Friedman outlines, it is an approach to interpreting Welty that makes few apologies for freely merging close readings of texts with close readings of images; for mixing art history with cultural history and the history of fashion; for blending photography with cinema; for mingling theories of writing with theories of visual representation; for conflating the insider with the outsider; for collapsing the lofty world of high art into the realm of popular culture; or for finding the apparently postmodern asserting itself in the late modern period. This approach concedes little in its justification of these boundary-breaking approaches, because its method grew out of attempts to assess Welty by imitating the interdisciplinary life she herself led, which forged the worldview that shaped her art.

For many observers, Welty's literary and probably her lifestyle choices exile her from modernism's central precincts, perhaps because she gave up trying to establish herself in a large city, chose mostly to write about southern life, and challenged the novel as the supreme test of a writer's talent. When she elected to make Jackson her permanent home, she must have recognized the possibly skewed reception her work might receive at the hands of urbanites. For noteworthy reasons, many critics now and then view the metropolis and modernism as almost synonymous, so Welty presented a tricky taxonomic problem. She was someone who lived and wrote about somewhere other than New York, London, or Paris, but who clearly had a style of writing developed and transmitted from these urban centers.[1] Perhaps the expression "regional modernist" represents her contribution to American letters well. Defining Welty as part of "Southern cosmopolitanism" (178), to adopt Leigh Ann Duck's recent coinage, may supply a just definition. But in Welty's case both phrases still carry a whiff of snobbery about them, as if these compromise terms, reflecting the schism in modernist studies that Friedman outlines, require a measure of nose holding. Whatever the choice, such phrases still make Welty and many other writers outsiders on the fringes of the modernist enterprise, a perhaps not unreasonable or necessarily demeaning view.[2] Nonetheless, how peripheral a perspective can she occupy, allowing not only for her well-established modernist mythmaking, but her equally well-established engagement with James Joyce, T. S. Eliot, W. B. Yeats, William Faulkner, Katherine Anne Porter, Virginia Woolf, and Elizabeth Bowen? Had she successfully transferred to New York, moved in "legitimate" artistic circles, and used her surrealist aesthetic to convey urban alienation, would her reputation have gained a brighter luster? Moreover, when Eliot poetically appropriates rural English or American scenes, when Yeats and Synge evoke "West Ireland" (McWhirter "Eudora Welty Goes" 69), when Faulkner remakes Mississippi, Frost transforms New England, or D. H. Lawrence depicts rural Nottingham, do critics deem them "regional modernists"? Hardly.[3] Critical expressions like "modernist" or "regional modernist" have historically depended for their meaning on sustaining of geographical boundaries that the modernist began to destroy. Either the writer in question lived in the city or the provinces, and this distinction formed part of the calculation determining the validity of a writer's claim to modernism. However, assessments of this kind, typical of "old guard" commentators (Friedman 260), overlook the way that material conditions of early twentieth-century life quickly began erasing boundaries. By the twenties and thirties, railways, ocean liners, newspapers, magazines and, later, cars, planes, telephones, radios, cinemas, and skyscrapers began to destabilize spatial and intellectual frontiers. These technical innovations also played havoc with language, especially the sort of referential language that draws apparently impermeable lines. The material conditions of life that modernity revolutionized could make insiders of outsiders and outsiders of insiders, regionalists into modernists and modernists into regionalists, and even southerners into cosmopolitans and cosmopolitans into southerners. Take Welty's agent, Diarmuid Russell, as a prime example of the final shift listed above. Or consider Ruth and Charles Henri Ford, Herschel Brickell, and Lehman Engel as examples of individuals shifting in the opposite direction. Technological conveniences of modern life could rapidly transport a somewhat-sheltered young woman from a rural province to somewhere like Julien Levy's or Pierre Matisse's, temples of surrealist art in New York. Could Welty not, given her keen sensitivity to art and culture, modernize representation of the life she knew at home? Such a theory does not require as great a suspension of prejudice as imagining the idea that, among the productions of all the surrealists, Dalí's art resonated most strongly with Welty.

The readings offered in this study give Dalí an obvious priority when they offer surrealism generally as a cultural influence, not least because his great fame in the United States during the thirties and forties makes him a logical choice. When this conclusion reasserts his name, it does so only to expose the nature of the rhetorical problem at the heart of this study. Assuming that surrealism as a general movement influenced Welty offers a plausible claim, but how does one compellingly demonstrate the exact result of the influence—especially when the writer in question indicates no obvious direction to explore? Welty simply never mentions surrealism as a potential influence. Aside from Joseph Cornell and Charles Henri Ford, she completely—and surely in some contexts coyly—declines any mention of the surrealist artists with whom she must have had great familiarity. This movement dominated the visual arts during the thirties, when her gallery and museum going probably reached its peak. In order to pursue a meaningful analysis of unacknowledged influence, one has to make some reasonable assumptions. For example, this study assumes that Welty read some surrealist theory, in newspapers, in magazines, or in exhibition catalogs with informative essays like Alfred H. Barr's in *Fantastic Art, Dada, Surrealism*, a volume Welty owned. In the absence of determinative evidence, one has to assume also that she saw many examples of art composed in the surrealist style in any number of exhibited paintings, photographs, and films shown in the cities she frequented, such as New York and Chicago.

However faulty, these assumptions provide enough leverage to start opening an otherwise closed discussion of the widespread dispersal of surreal figurative language. The discussion should include Welty's apparent acknowledgement, in numerous textual parallels, parodies, allusions, and inferences, of the movement at large in the United States. The idea that many of her books would adopt surrealism as a primary theme in their production gains further momentum when considered in light of letters that she and Frank Lyell exchanged. This correspondence colorfully and comically reflects the zeitgeist of the thirties. Economic devastation had brought the nation to its knees, but the arrival of modern art—epitomized by, but clearly not exclusive to a figure like Dalí—on American shores began the gradual process that eventually substituted New York for Paris as the center of the art world. Like Welty, a keen follower of cultural trends, Lyell attended and reported on Dalí's first solo exhibition in the United States in 1933. But the Spaniard only formed one member of a large cast of characters the friends knew about and followed. Combining the personalities referenced in their letters with some of the celebrity names published in *Vanity Fair: A Cavalcade of the 1920s and 1930s*, a book Welty owned, gives a broad sense of the large and varied assortment of writers, artists, intellectuals, actors, models, publishers, editors, directors, designers, dancers, and filmmakers who formed the dominant cultural milieu during Welty's formative artistic years. These figures include: Jean Cocteau, Tallulah Bankhead, D. H. Lawrence, Josephine Baker, the Sitwells, Virginia Woolf, Gabrielle Chanel, Caresse Crosby, Marlene Dietrich, Mae West, Cecil Beaton, Shirley Temple, Miriam Hopkins, Jean Harlow (Amory 66–304), Elsa Schiaparelli, Tilly Losch, Daisy Fellowes, Salvador Dalí, George Hoyningen-Heuné, Djuna Barnes, George Balanchine, William Dollar, Peter Neagoe, James Pendleton, Augustus John, Nicolas Nabokov and Paul Bowles. Of course, the mere positing of such a world does not necessarily show Dalí's influence to be more significant than that of other, less famous surrealists, such as Max Ernst or Yves Tanguy. But placing Dalí among his celebrated ilk does provide a tantalizing starting point from which to reconceptualize Welty. The artist provides an indispensable and illuminating focal point, because of which the influence of surrealism gains clarity for the first time in studies of Welty's work.

Finally, let this chapter turn briefly to make some basic remarks about books not examined here—*The Robber Bridegroom* (1942), *The Ponder Heart* (1954), *Losing Battles* (1970), and *The Optimist's Daughter* (1972)— and about the later phases of Welty's career. The fantasy of *The Robber Bridegroom* is the basis for excluding this book's investigation as a surrealist novella. Although much about the text recommends an absurdist interpretation, the fairytale form that it assumes undermines expectations that novels or short stories exploit. Welty herself asserts as much when she observes that the "novel from the start has been bound up in the local, the 'real,' the present, the ordinary day-to-day of human experience. Where imagination comes in is in directing the use of all this. That use is endless, and there are only four words, of all the millions we've hatched, that a novel rules out: 'Once upon a time.' They make a story a fairytale . . ." ("Place" 782). Thus, writing a work as a fairytale removes the action and characters so far from the mundane experiences of life, the surreal point of view does not obtain. The enlargement of reality that surrealism promises only emerges where the typical and the realistic unexpectedly mix with the world of dreams. Surrealism does not offer an escape from the ordinary world; rather, it promises the ordinary world's elevation. At the other extreme, *The Ponder Heart* has its foot too much in the world. As an apparent experiment in the power of the spoken word to shape a character's opinions and values, it succeeds because, in Edna Earle, Welty contrives a character who exists as an ebullient but, from a surrealist perspective, largely superficial, comic figure. Deploying the interior language of surrealism, the kind of language always associated with characters like Shelley in *Delta Wedding* or Virgie in *The Golden Apples*, would undermine her purpose in this text, which seems to be an investigation of the consequences of language for a public, rather than a private audience. This interest in the power of verbalized thoughts continues in *Losing Battles*, Welty's longest book and, together with *The Ponder Heart*, one that decisively breaks with the inclination toward the extended lyricism of dreams characteristic of a majority of her fiction from the thirties until the fifties. Finding some scattered and gemlike examples of surreal figurative language does not pose great difficulties in *Losing Battles*, but they appear as vestigial remains of an artistic strategy which, for whatever reasons, had reached the end of the road. Perhaps the influence of surrealism emerges to a greater extent in *The Optimist's Daughter*, but still, the moment when the movement exerted its greatest influence on her had passed.

In the forties and fifties, surrealism gradually ceded artistic ground to the products of abstract expressionism, a phrase coined by Robert Coates of *The Outlaw Years* fame (Roza 143). Yet surrealism did not die, continuing to have influence.[4] Around the time of its gradual diminishment, Welty began her experiments prioritizing spoken language in fiction—not necessarily as a reaction to surrealism's eclipse, but probably as a response to what had prompted the emergence of abstract expressionism. The triggers were various: the terror of the nuclear age; the ascendancy of American power; the horror of fascism; the ruthlessness of communism; and, at the national level, the failure of liberal democracy to protect the civil rights of black Americans, as well as to promote the interests of women. If the visual arts turned to the abstractions of Pollock, Rothko, and de Kooning for a resolution of and/or an encounter with the dilemmas facing the West, Welty seems to have steered her fiction in the opposite direction, eschewing abstraction and concentrating increasingly on writing stories that examined the language that people used publicly and politically, perhaps through characters who frequently speechify. In this decisive step away from what Katherine Anne Porter defined as the kind of writing that mixed "dreaming and waking" realities (969), perhaps Welty began acknowledging that quiet imaginative acts of self-reflection and discovery needed pairing with vocalizations in language designed for the public sphere. And she may have done so especially to counter public accusations like the complicity with white supremacy maintained by Diana Trilling in her 1946 review of *Delta Wedding*.[5]

A deep reserve of daring supplied courage for the personal and professional struggles that marked the final phases of Welty's career. Daring had always served her well. It informed her reading, her education, her travel, her friendships, her gallery and museum going, her photography, and her serious fiction when she came to write it. When this bravery happened to coincide with surrealism's arrival in the United States, something fantastic happened: The products of France's avant-garde merged with a quietly developing literary talent from Mississippi to form a new artistic alloy of enormous originality. On the one hand, Welty turned her pen to shattering all kinds of myths about women, and by extension other historically marginalized groups. And on the other hand, she invited a surrealistic aesthetic home to help her carry out the critique. Writing a thoroughgoing and decades-long satire on moral complacency and unquestioned traditionalism took guts, but to write it from inside a region known for its reactionary politics amplified the stakes. The way that Welty's fiction lampooned and lamented southern power by rather proudly borrowing from an imported aesthetic meant potentially facing the strongest sort of social ostracism. Notwithstanding the dangers, Welty won the day through canniness and charm, and somehow, perhaps as a consequence of numerous national and international accolades, her fiction made her a local treasure and not a traitor.

Can a writer permanently alter the course of American literature without fair critical acknowledgement? Can one of the twentieth century's "artistic leaders" (to borrow a phrase from Danièle Pitavy-Souques ["Eudora Welty as Twentieth-Century" 72]) repeatedly escape full notice and endure all manner of subtle and not-so-subtle slights and misunderstandings before getting just credit? This book implicitly proposes these questions and explicitly gives an affirmative reply, but it does not necessarily predict a rise in Welty's artistic stock as a result. Of course, one hopes for such an outcome, but beyond academic interpretation stands the body of work itself, clear-eyed, courageous, profound, and ultimately durable. It is durable because of its integrity, a word Welty used to defend Faulkner's literature against the myopia of philistines dismissing him owing to matters outside his control, his ethnicity and birthplace. "Integrity," she averred, "can be neither lost nor concealed nor faked nor quenched nor artificially come by nor outlived, nor, I believe, in the long run denied. Integrity is no greater and no less today than it was yesterday and will be tomorrow. It stands outside time" ("Must the Novelist Crusade" 803). In the long run, the only kind of time that matters in literature, the integrity of great writing cannot but emerge from its unmistakable outlines to manifest a beauty that seems to multiply as the years age Welty's canon.

NOTES

Chapter 1

1. The phrase, "early years in New York," comes from a letter Welty sent to Emily and William Maxwell, her editor at the *New Yorker*, in February 1978 (qtd. in Marrs *What There* 336). In it, she thanks the couple for a book, probably Diane Waldman's 1977 *Joseph Cornell* (469), they have sent her. The gift triggers a brief reminiscence about her correspondence with this American surrealist, whom she observes formed a "part of my early years in New York, as I suspect he was of yours too," and of whom she says, if "we were all cooks, we would be often using the same ingredients" (336). The letter goes on to introduce Cornell's friend and collaborator, Mississippian Charles Henri Ford, as well as to mention Ford's important literary and artistic periodicals, *Blues* and *View*. I return to this significant set of interrelationships at greater length later in the book.

2. Michael Kreyling's analysis of this and other passages in "A Memory" parallels Welty's technical virtuosity with the formalized bathers that "have probably migrated from Seurat, Cezanne, or Picasso" (*Understanding* 26). In a similar vein, Jan Nordby Gretlund comments on the stylistic as well as the thematic overlap between Picasso's *La Femme des Saltimbanques* and Welty's early story, "Acrobats in the Park" (*Eudora* 24–28). However, neither commentator views Welty's perspective as surreal in orientation, despite the migration of the bather archetype from Cezanne to Seurat to Picasso and also to a surrealist like Dalí, who also produced a number of early paintings dwelling on this theme, including his 1923 *Bathers of Es Llaner* and his 1925 *Venus and Cupids*.

3. For a sampling of these widespread claims, see Porter (966), Vande Kieft (88–89), Appel (205–37), Eisinger (3–25) Bloom (10), Kreyling (*Eudora Welty's* xi–xx), Devlin (*Eudora Welty's* xi), Pitavy-Souques ("Blazing Butterfly" 113–38), Westling (24 *Eudora Welty*), Schmidt (xix), Mark (*Dragon's Blood* 4), and Harrison.

4. For full expressions of this interpretation see Gretlund (*Eudora Welty's Aesthetics* 39–75), as well as Brooks ("Eudora Welty" 3–24), Randisi (vii–xxviii), Westling (*Sacred Groves* 36–37), and Manning (ix–xi).

5. Studies of modernism that stress its interdisciplinary and international dimensions do much to redress a historical bias in the Anglo-American academy, which has tended

to canonize a small number of English-speaking poets and writers and to minimize the enormous contributions of the avant-garde. For example, Astradur Eysteinsson observes that in contrast to the study of modernism in Britain and the United States, "critical discourse around modernism in, say, the German-speaking countries and France is heavily influenced by the presence of avant-garde movements like surrealism, Dada, and expressionism, and is therefore less likely to be shaped by the shadows of iconic individuals" (85). Conscious of such criticism, the 1999 edition of *The Cambridge Companion to Modernism* presents a broader and more diverse picture of modernism, offering conventional analyses of Pound, Eliot, and Lewis, alongside chapters devoted to drama, gender, the visual arts, and film. Critics may have overlooked Welty's relationship to surrealism because of these institutional prejudices against the avant-garde and against scholarship that sought to violate disciplinary margins. Eysteinsson rightly notes that students of modernism must commit to viewing it as a "literary or aesthetic concept" (5) that "belongs within a broader cultural framework in which modernism is to be seen as a semiotic and historical project."

6. This book did not grow out of reading and responding to recent scholarship that seeks a redefinition of the "US South" as a meaningful critical expression. Studies of this sort include but are not limited to *American Literature*'s special issue, "Violence, the Body and 'The South,'" edited by Houston A. Baker and Dana D. Nelson; Michael Kreyling's *Inventing Southern Literature*; Jon Smith and Deborah Cohn's *Look Away! The U.S. South in New World Studies*; James L. Peacock, Harry L. Watson, and Carrie R. Matthews's *The American South in Global World*; and Leigh Anne Duck's *The Nation's Region*. Instead, this study began with both the European and American strands of my education, as they encountered Eudora Welty's work, entwining and resulting in scholarship such as my article, "South of South Again." Happily, this book contributes to revising parochial interpretations of the South and, specifically, to revealing a southern writer in a broader context than traditional appraisals allow.

7. My brief summary synthesizes a number of sources. For studies that primarily treat the European phases of surrealism's evolution see Nadeau, Jean (*History of Surrealist*), Jean (*Documents*), Rubin, Alquié, and Short. For more general and wide-ranging analyses of surrealism's larger cultural contexts, see Seigel and Shattuck. For works that spotlight Breton's leadership, see biographies of Breton by Balakian and Polizzotti, and Breton's surrealist manifestoes. For women's contribution to surrealism, see Caws et al. and Rosemont. For works that relate surrealism's development in the United States, see Tashjian, Schaffner & Jacobs, and Sawin.

8. Breton's biographer, Mark Polizzotti, notes that "Every one of the twenty-four antecedents [Breton] named in the *Manifesto* was a writer, and only in a footnote did he credit some visual artists—Seurat, Moreau, Derain, Picasso, and a few of his contemporaries— with having occasionally demonstrated the same spirit" (208).

9. The debacle at the 1935 Congress of Writers in Paris "served as the final break between Surrealism and organized Communism" (Polizzotti 424).

10. Balakian's pivotal contribution to scholarship on surrealism began in 1947 with her classic *Literary Origins of Surrealism*, and concluded with a full-length biography of André Breton, *Magus of Surrealism*, in 1971. Balakian knew many of the figures who moved in

Breton's circle, as well as the man himself, to whom she gained access as a graduate student through Julien Levy (Schaffner "Alchemy" 46). That Welty became a very close friend of Anna's sister, Nona, an editor at the *New York Times Book Review*, is perhaps a mere coincidence, but certainly one worth noting. When Nona died, Anna wrote Welty touching notes and cards acknowledging their mutual loss.

11. Steven Watson's "Julien Levy: Exhibitionist and Harvard Modernist" locates Levy in the elevated company of such innovators as "Lincoln Kirstein, Arthur Everett ("Chick") Austin, Jr., Alfred Barr, Jr., Kirk Askew, Philip Johnson, Henry-Russell Hitchcock, John McAndrew, Agnes Rindge, and secondarily, John Becker, Jere Abbott, Arthur McComb, and Edward Warburg" (80). Watson goes on to list the mighty achievements of some of these individuals: "They created institutions: the Museum of Modern Art, the School of American Ballet, the Wadsworth Atheneum. They embraced new disciplines in the museum: film, architecture, industrial design. They introduced to the United States Surrealism, International Style architecture, and Neo-Romanticism. Taken together, they functioned as a monopoly on modernist culture in New York" (84–85).

12. This assortment of venues where patrons and buyers could view avant-garde European and American art derives from the citing of these museums and galleries in the following publications: Julien Levy's *Surrealism* (31), Nicholas Fox Weber's *Patron Saints* (166, 231, 234), and Isabelle Dervaux's *Surrealism USA* (172–85).

13. For a complete listing of Dalí's individual and group exhibitions in the United States in the thirties, forties, and beyond, see Julien Kreinick's "Biographical Chronology" (Lubar 161–75). For biographies of Dalí, see Seacrest and especially Gibson.

14. Indeed, book publication of Welty photographs did not occur until 1971, when the University Press of Mississippi issued *One Time, One Place.*

15. In interviews, Welty repeatedly emphasizes her visual facility as a writer. For further examples see *Comment* (22), Mitchell (70) Kuehl (85), and Ferris (157–58, 162–63).

16. Welty's second New York show opened at the Camera House and ran March 6–31, 1937 (Marrs *Welty Collection* 78).

17. That Welty probably had great familiarity with many of these photographic innovators made her qualified in 1974 to write "Africa and Paris and Russia," an essay for the *New York Times Book Review* evaluating three new books of photography, by Leni Riefenstahl, André Kertész, and Henri Cartier-Bresson. All the books receive Welty's approval, but her treatment of Kertész and his pictures of Paris seems especially affectionate, perhaps because these images returned the reviewer to images of the city in its bohemian heyday, the cultural context that so strongly influenced Welty's art.

18. For biographical information, photographs, and commentary on Abbott's work, see O'Neal, Sullivan, and Yochelson.

19. In jocular letters and postcards that passed between Welty and Lyell, Mae West's name frequently appears as part of the comedy. Contemplating a 1944 visit with Lyell to see *Catherine Was Great*, she writes, "It's probably awful but it would be fun to go to see Mae." Other examples include Lyell's regular allusions to West, as if she forms the center of jokes shared between friends. See correspondence dated June 4, 1932, March 10, 1933, and March 25, 1933.

As for West's literary abilities, her biographer, Leider, observes that

> her name appears as the author of plays, screenplays, novels, magazine and newspaper articles, an autobiography, and a book of advice on sex, health, and ESP. For her, being a writer meant taking control of her professional vehicles. By creating or participating in the creation of her own material, sometimes co-producing her own plays, and consistently minimizing or denying credit to writing collaborators, she could literally run the show, which mattered more to her than anything else. (4)

20. For discussions of the Prince of Wales's noted promiscuity, personal affability, and disinclination to assume the throne, see Ziegler (196–239). Furthermore, Welty may have had a more informed perspective on the next king than those in Britain. Her favorite paper, the *New York Times*, reported closely on the "prince's movements" between 1931 and 1934, when the "London *Times* gave a more censored calendar of events" (Higham 491).

21. Elsa Schiaparelli (1890–1973), Italian-born French fashion designer, left Rome for Paris and New York, where Man Ray, then in his New York Dada phase, photographed her before she returned to France to witness the advent of surrealism in 1924. As her reputation for cutting-edge fashion grew, she established a company in Paris, and distributors for her clothing in the United States, such as Wm. H. Davidow Sons Co., Saks Fifth Avenue, and M. C. Shrank, appeared regularly in leading fashion magazines. In 1932, Schiaparelli began acting as a buyer for Hattie Carnegie's New York store. In 1934, *Time* cemented her stature when it featured her on its cover. From then on, her fame grew immense, not least because of her whimsical collaborations with Dalí. By the time of her firm's eventually closure in 1954, she had emerged as one of the interwar period's most influential couturiers (Blum 292–301).

22. Sir Cecil Walter Hardy Beaton (1904–80), English photographer, painter, writer, and scene and costume designer. At the beginning of his career, he designed scenery for stage shows before developing into one of the leading fashion and celebrity photographers of the twentieth century ("Sir Cecil").

23. Like Mae West and Cecil Beaton, Schiaparelli enters into several comic and not-so-comic exchanges between Welty and Lyell in letters and postcards. See Welty's references to Schiaparelli and her circle in a postcard dated June 12, 1933, in which she puns on "Daisy Fellowes," "Lady Muñoz," "Elsa," and "Cec' Beaton," as well as her letter dated October 1, 1934, where she comments on, "Schiaparelli's last models" in *Vogue*. In addition, see Lyell's November 30, 1934, postcard to Welty, which reinvents several lines of Cole Porter's *You're the Top*, including the gag, "You're Schiaparelli, You're guava jelly."

24. Along with three other stores in Mississippi, located in Greenville, Meridian, and Vicksburg, and with many other outlets across the nation, The Emporium of Jackson advertised its New York fashions in the pages of *Vogue*. One such advertisement for Russeks Fifth Avenue appears in an issue dated September 1, 1936 (30–31).

25. For extended treatments of the interrelation between surrealism and fashion see Dickran Tashjian (66–90) and Richard Martin's *Fashion and Surrealism*.

26. The Levy Gallery acted as a distributor for avant-garde journals such as *La Révolution Surréaliste* and sold imported poetry and prose by Louis Aragon, René Crevel, and Paul Eluard (Schaffner "Alchemy" 33). In his memoir, Levy highlights the availability of publications that would have carried news of surrealism when he recalls a Madison Avenue stationary shop where one "would pick up a copy of *Art News*, or *Dial*, or *Creative Arts* and sooner or later most of the better foreign art publications." Over time, the owners "built up a considerable knowledge of books and revues of special interest to us"—and perhaps to bright young intellectuals like Welty (16).

27. For additional examples of the mainstream media's coverage of Dalí's work, see *Life*'s advertising of his 1939 Levy exhibition in "Salvador Dalí," as well as *Life*'s and *Vogue*'s publicizing of his surrealist installation at the New York World's Fair in "Dali's Surrealist Dream House." Moreover, both *Life* and Welty's favorite newspaper, the *New York Times*, covered his extravagant set designs for the 1939 ballet, *Bacchanale*, based on Wagner's *Tannhäuser*, in, respectively, "Life Goes to Dali's New Ballet" and Morgan's "The Dance: Surrealism and Americana." Welty may well have seen the giant surrealist sets, lavishly reproduced in *Life*, showing Venus emerging in "full-length white tights from a huge swan." The ballet's cooption of the Leda and the swan myth, a narrative more famously appropriated by W. B. Yeats, may have influenced Welty's decision to integrate the legend into *The Golden Apples*. Furthermore, *Life* reports that *Bacchanale* "is based on the Venusburg scene" (91) in the opera, so when Welty writes in "June Recital" that Fate Rainey tears the "Venusberg pictures" from Miss Eckhart's German-language books "about the lives of the masters" (*Stories* 371), she perhaps echoes this 1939 surrealist ballet.

28. In addition to the dissemination of the newest artistic ideas through magazines based in New York, avant-gardism came to Welty in the form of Henry Miller when he came south to visit her in 1941. In interviews, Welty tends to disparage Miller, who had ventured to Jackson in order to suggest that Welty exploit his connections in the pornography market (Ferguson 276). Miller had spent the best part of the thirties in Paris and elsewhere in Europe and had only returned to the United States when ordered to do so because of the war (Dearborn 208). Working on the book published in 1945 as *The Air-Conditioned Nightmare*, he visited Welty sometime in 1941, having spent the previous summer with the Dalís at the estate of Caresse Crosby in Virginia. Despite the Dalís' snubbing him and the "group of visiting writers" (214), over the summer Miller wrote what one of his biographers describes as a "surreal paean" to America's great black jazz musicians (Ferguson 273). He could not have failed to admire Dalí, if only because of the painter's early surrealist films, which the American had watched in the early thirties and which had a "profoundly liberating effect on Miller's approach to the art of writing" (176). Miller's arrival in Jackson at the beginning of a new decade reveals just how porous the nation had become to advanced cultural ideas—if one knew where to look and knew the right people.

29. Little could Welty have known that in the late forties *she* would appear as the celebrity when Beaton, Louise Dahl-Wolfe, and Irving Penn all photographed her in a shoot organized by *Harper's Bazaar*. Welty recalls that Penn's attitude and technique were "venturesome," while Dahl-Wolfe and Beaton "were majestic figures, whose work everybody knew" (Cole & Srinivason 200). Employed as a fashion photographer for *Harper's Bazaar*,

Dahl-Wolfe interested Welty, who enjoyed the shoot, perhaps because of the writer's early interest in fashion photography and her background in advertising.

30. Lyell may have begun the Beaton jokes in a tongue-in-cheek letter that he wrote to Welty in the September of 1932: "Just a line from the Côte D'Azur—Met Cecil Beaton, Noel Coward, & Mrs Tiffany Supporters on the 'plage' (beach to you) 'ce matin'—all were eating [illegible]." A few months later, in March 1933, Welty continued the running joke in a full-page mock letter to Beaton applying for the position of his "amanuensis," claiming, "i [*sic*] can maintain a deftly remote attitude and then suddenly at a nod fly to and decorate a Sitwell with decorum, although I realise that won't be required." In June of that year, Welty used Beaton again for comic effect in a postcard, and in October of the next year remarked that somebody, probably a mutual friend, named a male puppy after the photographer. In a final example from April 1935, Lyell sent Welty a mock memo punning on "Mr Beaton," "Mrs A Knops" and Jean Cocteau. Lyell and Welty certainly made comic capital out of Beaton's name and what he represented, but Beaton also had knowledge of Welty. In his book, *Portrait of New York*, written with the assistance of "Mr. Charles Henri Ford" (vii), Beaton admires Welty's and Carson McCullers's literary contributions to *Harper's Bazaar* as examples of "now famous 'unusual' talent" (50).

31. George Hoyningen-Huené (1900–1968) was a Russian born American photographer who ultimately moved to the United States and made it his permanent home. Huené moved to London and then Paris after the Russian Revolution. and worked with Man Ray before joining *Vogue* as chief photographer in 1925. After moving to the America in 1929, he continued working for *Vogue*, then moved to *Harper's Bazaar* in 1935 (Conkelton).

32. Djuna Barnes (1892–1982), an American novelist, short story writer, playwright, and poet, began her career as journalist in New York City and soon decamped for Paris, living in the expatriate community there for the next twenty years. In Europe, she wrote among other works *Nightwood* (1936), the novel on which her reputation as a key American modernist rest. At the outbreak of war, she returned to the United States, living in Greenwich Village (Fuchs).

33. George Balanchine (1904–83), a Russian-born American dancer and choreographer, successfully toured Europe in his youth before moving to the United States in 1933. There, he founded the American School of Ballet with Lincoln Kirstein in 1934, and, in the next decade, created the organization that developed into the New York City Ballet. He had an inestimable influence on twentieth-century ballet ("George Balanchine").

34. William Dollar (1907–86), an American dancer and choreographer, worked closely with George Balanchine in the thirties and forties and later directed many ballets himself ("William Dollar").

35. Peter Neagoe (1881–1960), a Romanian-born American artist, writer, and editor who lived in Paris during the twenties and New York in the thirties, made the United States his home. In his bibliography of key works in *Surrealism*, Julien Levy cites Neagoe's 1932 "What is Surrealism?" which appeared in the *New Review*, a journal with which Neagoe would assume an editorial position. He also published surrealist fiction in *transition* and edited *Americans Abroad*, an anthology of expatriate writers, including such figures as Kay Boyle and Gertrude Stein (Ernst).

36. Little biographical information exists on James Pendleton; however, Billy Baldwin, the American interior designer, remembers Pendleton as a decorator in his autobiography. On one occasion Pendleton worked for Hattie Carnegie, and he was the owner of the "most attractive shop in New York," where Baldwin and Ruby Wood shopped for furnishings (208).

37. Augustus Edwin John (1878–1961), a British landscape and portrait artist, began his career living the life of a gypsy in England and Wales. After World War I, he focused on portraiture, a talent ensuring that he "painted many of the best-known figures of the day" (Lloyd-Morgan), including two paintings of the cosmetics magnate Elizabeth Arden (Woodhead 190). Her rival, Helena Rubinstein, chose Dalí for her likeness and for contributing painted panels to her Manhattan apartment's "Dream Room" (275).

38. Nicolas Nabokov (1903–78), Belorussian composer, professor, and political organizer, fled the Red Army in 1919 and continued his musical studies, first in Germany and then at the Sorbonne in France, where he befriended Prokofiev, Stravinsky, and Diaghilev. Traveling to the United States in the thirties, he taught at Wells College from 1936 to 1941 and took up American citizenship. At the war's close, he worked for the American government in Germany, where he promoted the "re-establishment of Berlin's cultural life" (Wellens 1), and later assumed the secretary-generalship of the Congress for Cultural Freedom (CCF). In the sixties and seventies, he taught at the City University of New York and the Aspen Institute for Humanistic Studies (Wellens 1–2).

39. Paul Bowles (1910–99), an American writer, composer, and photographer, traveled widely, making homes in Paris, New York, and Algiers. Moving in Parisian artistic circles in the early thirties, he met, among others, Gertrude Stein, Ezra Pound, and Jean Cocteau, and wrote poetry and music. In 1933, he returned to New York and pursued a large variety of musical and literary projects, including collaborations with Lincoln Kirstein, Tennessee Williams, Salvador Dalí, and Charles Henri Ford, notably contributing reviews and translations to Ford's *View* magazine (Carr 339–51).

40. Tallulah Bankhead (1903–68), an American actor born in Huntsville, Alabama, left the South and the United States for the London stage, where she gained considerable fame. Her role as a journalist in the 1944 film, *Lifeboat*, showcased the "wit, sophisticated aplomb, and uninhibited behavior that made her a legend" ("Tallulah Bankhead").

41. Daisy Fellowes (1890–1962), French born socialite, heiress, aristocrat, and editor, led a life of luxury and glamour. Heir to the Singer sewing machine fortune and to the wealth of a "noble French family" (Tapert & Edkins 75), she prized men, money, and fashion, formed part of Frances's "Les Dames de Vogue," the clique of women who "dictated fashion" (79), and wore Chanel in the twenties and Schiaparelli in the thirties. "Other women also bought Schiap's famous lobster dress and hat shaped like a shoe with a shocking pink velvet heel inspired by Salvador Dalí," observe Annette Tapert and Diana Edkins, "but when Daisy wore it, it made news. On her, this surrealistic design seemed as practical as a mackintosh" (79). Much photographed by Cecil Beaton and a regular in the pages of *Vogue* and *Harper's Bazaar*, Daisy even did a stint as the latter magazine's Paris editor, a position offered by Carmel Snow (82), *Bazaar*'s imperious editor, now "almost vanishing" from the public view (Rowlands xiv).

On at least one occasion (and probably on others too), Welty penetrated to the heart of this elite milieu through Mary Lou Aswell, fiction editor for *Bazaar*, Welty champion, and coauthor of Snow's 1962 autobiography, *The World of Carmel Snow*. In the "Epilogue," Aswell records the following fascinating reminiscence, indicative of the high esteem Welty commanded and worth quoting in full:

> Many glamorous people she'd known weren't mentioned by Carmel in telling me her story because they were all in the day's work to her, however thoroughly she enjoyed her encounters with them—and she did enjoy them. During my years as fiction editor of *Harper's Bazaar* I knew it was worth my job not to let her know when an interesting writer was in town. I'd pop my head in her office to say, "Eudora Welty's coming in from Jackson," and she'd call for her calendar. Dorothy Monger might say, "I'm sorry, Mrs. Snow, you're booked solid."
>
> Carmel would look over the closely scribbled pages. "Oh—that advertising lunch. Tell them I've been called out of town." On the day of Eudora's arrival I'd help Dorothy extricate Bossy from a meeting, we would often skip out the back way via the freight elevator to avoid someone waiting in the front hall to pounce, and then, in those days, we generally walked around the corner to the Savoy-Plaza, where she entertained the people who didn't care about being seen by the fashion world. (206)

42. Ottilie Ethel Losch (1907–75), Austrian dancer, choreographer, and actor, traveled Europe as a ballerina before coming to the United States with the theater director Max Reinhardt. In the thirties, she worked in New York with George Balanchine and Fred and Adele Astaire, danced for the Columbus Circle Theatre, married the surrealist patron Edward James, as well as the Earl of Carnarvon, and acted in Hollywood (Poetzl). "Her close friends at one time were the Sitwells, Cecil Beaton and Pavel Tchelitchew," reports Herbert Poetzl, the author of the "Biographical Note" that prefaces the *Tilly Losche Collection*, housed as part of the *Max Reinhardt Archives* at the State University of New York at Binghamton.

43. The combined contribution of the Sitwells, Edith (1887–1964), Osbert (1892–1969), and Sacheverell (1897–1988), to literary culture has few peers. Edith wrote poetry, criticism, and biographies, Osbert wrote poetry and fiction, and Sacheverell wrote art criticism, poetry, and biographies. They produced their work prolifically and have justifiably high reputations ("Sitwell").

44. For a further consideration of Cornell, Ford, and Welty, see Pearl McHaney's unpublished essay, "Eudora Welty's 'The Winds' and 'A Sketching Trip': Wonderful and Explicit and Authentically 'sur-real.'"

45. Episodes like the one shortly before their return to Europe in 1935 illustrate Salvador and Gala's ability to create a stir and draw press coverage. They attended a costume ball, the "Bal Onirique," to which guests would come "as a dream." Salvador sported a shirt with a glass window in its chest panel, showcasing a pink bra, while Gala turned out in a red cellophane gown and ornamented her head with doll and lobster images (Tashjian 54). *Vanity*

Fair participated in garnering and solidifying Dalí's considerable public appeal. In 1934, the magazine ranked him among "The New Reputations of the Year" and in 1935 illustrated "two Dalis" in their magazine (56).

46. For comprehensive analyses of Dalí's "Dream of Venus" pavilion, see Lewis Kachur's *Displaying the Marvelous* and Ingrid Schaffner's *Salvador's Dalí's Dream of Venus.*

47. Brenda Putnam (1890–1975), American sculptor and author, studied art in Boston before opening a studio in New York and later traveling to Florence. She "was a successful academic sculptor who made the transition to an art deco style and hovered on the border of modernism" (Rubinstein 248), an evolution evident in the figure she produced for the world's fair.

Why Welty mixed Chalmers Alexander, a Jackson lawyer and city council member, and Allie Blanche Ruff, a public school teacher (Marrs "Re: Welty and Surrealism"), with the unknown Reba Tull and Miss Fletcher remains mysterious. For whatever reason, these figures from Welty's life seem to have come into focus at the very moment of her visiting the fair.

48. Should Welty have visited the attraction in August 1940, she would have witnessed the pavilion as a "shell of its former self" just prior to closing in October (Schaffner *Salvador* 142). Rank commercialization had destroyed the initial allure, to which she may have responded when *Life* and *Vogue* advertised its opening in "Life Goes to the World's Fair" and "Dalí's Surrealist Dream House at the World's Fair," respectively.

49. One measure of Welty's uncertainty about the direction of her artistic strengths comes in an amusing 1936 letter she sent to "Miss Monroe," the editor of *Poetry: A Magazine of Verse*, based in Chicago: "I enclose three poems which I hope you will read for your magazine. They are the first I have written since submitting to you in college days, when Miss Jessica North used to write me nice rejection slips. Thanks for your consideration." (Special Collections Research Center at The University of Chicago). In the year that her first serious stories would find publication, Welty still appears wholly uncommitted to prose as the only available path to success.

50. For recent translations of Dalí's key texts, see Finkelstein (*Salvador Dalí's Art & Collected Writings*), and for biographical and theoretical examinations of Dalí's corpus, see Ades, Schiebler, and Tashjian.

51. For some representative examples of surrealism as a mainstream magazine promulgated it, see *Vogue's* "Surrealism or the Purple Cow" by M. F. Agha, "Vogue's 3 Man Show," featuring Dalí, De Chirico, and Tchelitchew, as well as "Surrealism in Paris" and "Surrealism in New York Shops."

52. The verbal/visual analysis that follows takes Levy's assertion that "surrealism is a point of view" (4) at face value, and with this premise, aligns naturalism in visual representation with realism in literary representation. Creating such a coincidence allows for certain parallels among theories that have either a visual or verbal emphasis. At the same time, Welty's acknowledgement of painting and writing as the "closest two of the sister arts" should not obfuscate her later qualification of the word "being ultimately as different from the pigment as the note of the scale is from the chisel" ("Place" 783).

53. Haim Finkelstein, the editor of *The Conquest of the Irrational*, admits he can find no painting to which this commentary applies, but offers that the "description, however, points to the multiple images of 1938, and, in particular, to *The Endless Enigma*, with its six different images" (*Collected Writings* 421).

54. Intriguingly, Noel Polk points out that when William Faulkner first read Welty's *The Robber Bridegroom*, he "told her that he thought of Djuna Barnes" ("Welty and Faulkner" 134), the author of *Nightwood* (1936) and a novelist widely acknowledged to have been influenced by Parisian surrealism.

55. Haftmann classifies Max Ernst, Yves Tanguy, and Salvador Dalí as Veristic Surrealists. Joan Miró and André Masson are classified as Absolute Surrealists because, in contrast to the former grouping, the latter pairing's art tends toward the abstract and "is neither reproductive nor illusionistic" (268).

Chapter 2

1. See Nadeau's chapter, "The Aragon Affair" (175–82), for a representative example of the contentiousness that characterized membership in the Parisian group.

2. For a further consideration of "Flowers for Marjorie," as well as other Welty stories, in the context of surrealism and modernism more generally, see Daniéle Pitavy-Souques's "'The Inspired Child of [Her] Times': Eudora Welty as a Twentieth-Century Artist."

3. Using Julia Kristeva's theory of abjection, Don James McLaughlin reads Clytie's obsession with faces as part of her failure to establish "any coherent sense of self or agency" (54).

4. For a reading of the way "Old Mr Marblehall" remakes the world from a dizzying array of points of view, which switch around seamlessly between inside and outside and the dreamt and the observed, see Noel Polk's "Welty, Hawthorne, and Poe: Men of the Crowd and the Landscape of Alienation."

5. In Diana Almeida's essay, "'Keela, the Outcast Indian Maiden': (Story)Telling the Southern Ideology," she too foregrounds the narrative's resistance to the idea of perception as universally consistent when she writes, "In fact, Welty's texts deconstruct the Southern hegemonic ideologies, favoring indeterminacy of meaning over totalitarian narrative" (37).

6. See Rebecca Mark's "Carnival Geeks and Voudoun Healing" for a recent reconsideration of this story, interpreting Keela/Lee Roy's performance as returning "white liberal readers," embodied in the character Steve, "an image of their own narcissistic racism" (14)

Chapter 3

1. This long line of critical descent reaches its apogee in Michael Kreyling's *Eudora Welty's Achievement of Order*. However, critics have not ceased exploring or expanding Anglo-American lines of modernist influence. Prominent examples include Suzan Harrison's and Rebecca Mark's studies, which identify Welty as either the recipient of

English-speaking modernism's insights, or as replying to and revising modernism's masterworks.

2. In *Author and Agent*, Michael Kreyling reproduces a 1940 letter Welty sent to her agent, Diarmuid Russell, in which she contemplated the relevance of the Trace to the stories that she would collect as *The Wide Net*: "I believe that the Natchez Trace, like many another beautiful and timeworn place, casts a spell, because I have felt it, and many other people must have; and if I can show this spell, in a few of its dramatic or modest aspects, that is what I hope to do. An old trail like that passes through so many times and enters so many lives, and stands for so many things, functioning heavily or lightly in the course it follows, that it could be a thing to hold a group of stories together as well as any other, and better than any other that I have heard of yet for me" (52–53).

3. Welty seems to pun, here, on this term drawn from photography. Audubon represents the nineteenth-century equivalent of a documentary photographer who records his or her subject for posterity.

4. See Vande Kieft (57–58), Appel (63–69), Kreyling (*Eudora* 19–21; *Understanding* 65–68), and Schmidt (135–44).

5. In one of the few critical appraisals of this story's remarkable setting, Louise Westling observes that "Welty's descriptions bestow dimensions of the marvellous upon natural settings and actions that would seem otherwise less remarkable" (75). Although brief, this comment does point up, here and widely throughout her work, Welty's preoccupation with manifestations of the irrational and the wondrous in places that she evokes.

6. The notion of William Wallace's masculinity in despair also finds support in David McWhirter's recent essay, in which he argues that Welty's narrative "is less a rewriting of a specific male intertext than a general response to the anxious, beleaguered masculinity that pervades *The Waste Land, The Sound and the Fury, Light in August,* "The Bear," *In Our Time, The Sun Also Rises,* and *A Farewell to Arms*" ("Fish Stories" 37).

7. Gibson notes, "Once he got a good pictorial idea, Dalí tended to go for over-kill. Having devised his head of the Great Masturbator, he produced hundreds of them" (338). In addition to the head's first appearance in his 1929 *The Great Masturbator*, other versions feature prominently in his 1929–30 *Profanation of the Host*, and more subtly in his 1931 *Memory of the Child-Woman* and his 1932 *Fantasies Diurnes* (Lubar 57–76).

8. Both Gibson (256-57) and Radford (128) attribute the head's petrified appearance to Dalí's preoccupation with the Spanish coastline at Cape Creus; the head's shape "was inspired by a rock in the inlet of Cullaró at Cape Creus" (Gibson 257).

9. Ruth D. Weston's *Gothic Traditions and Narrative Techniques in the Fiction of Eudora Welty* comprehensively assesses Welty's appropriation and development of gothic conventions. Weston argues that in addition to borrowing from European gothic traditions, Welty also draws on the American variety. Revealing the influence of such writers as Poe, Cooper, Hawthorne, Melville, and James, "Welty's subtle and sophisticated depictions of the mysteries of nature and human nature owe much to this tradition of the American romance" (27).

10. In a 1972 interview, Welty criticizes "The Purple Hat," stating, "I wish I hadn't written that story. I saw it dramatized last year, an off-Broadway thing, which only brought home to me its failings" (Bunting 63).

11. Welty's "A Memory" provides a parallel example of stories nested within stories. See Stephen M. Fuller's "Memory's Narrative Gossamer."

12. See Patti Carr Black's *Early Escapades* for a thorough analysis of Welty's love of cartooning.

13. Westling cleverly glosses this allusion by commenting, "Any reader familiar with classical mythology would begin to grow uneasy at the mention of pomegranates, remembering that this fruit was sacred to Dionysus and that Persephone's eating even a few seeds created a bond between herself and her gloomy ravisher Pluto which even her powerful mother Demeter could not break" (*Eudora* 77).

14. Possible surreal analogues for Welty's heady mixture of wavering columns, dreaming women, sexual anxiety, egregious nakedness, and threatening lions include several Dalí paintings that pictorially merge a congruent set of subjects. For example, see *The Great Masturbator* and *The Enigma of Desire*.

15. Critical divergences mostly stem from differing interpretations of the consequences of Jenny's sex with men. Those who view sex as initiatory (Appel l88–92; Kreyling *Eudora* 28–31 and *Understanding* 75–80) tend to see the story more optimistically and follow Vande Kieft's early assessment (27–29). In contrast, others tend to consider the sex rape and view the outcome of violations much more problematically (Brookhart & Marrs 82–95; Westling *Eudora* 80–84; Schmidt 27–30; Weston 40–42; Marrs *One Writer's* 57–58) and read the story bleakly.

16. See Welty's brief remarks in interviews decades after the story's publication (Freeman 190; Wheatley 126).

17. Matica Swain's *Surrealism in Exile* traces the formative effect on the American arts scene of surrealism's displacement between January 1938, the year of the movement's largest exhibition in Paris, to the summer of 1947, when a major exhibition signaled the "return of the exiles to a less-than-welcoming France" (x). Her analysis explores the shifting of the avant-garde art world from Paris to New York in the forties with the arrival of a sizable contingent of surrealist insiders: Salvador Dalí, Max Ernst, Leonora Carrington, Stanley William Hayter, André Masson, Roberto Matta, Gordon Onslow Ford, Wolfgang Paalen, Kurt Seligman, Yves Tanguy, and André Breton. This European presence, she argues, spurred the development of a "new mode of painting" (vi), then sometimes called "abstract surrealism" (ix) and latterly termed abstract expressionism.

18. Kreyling notes that the story draws on the lives of the "Expeditions of settlers" who "had been flowing into the Mississippi territory after the Louisiana Purchase" (*Understanding* 52), as well as the "frigid winter associated with the New Madrid quake" in 1811 (53).

19. Kreyling argues that Welty triangulates Josie, Cornella, and the cornetist in desire, so that they "become superimposed personae" (*Understanding* 74). This interpretation certainly accords with my own, in that the dream identifies these figures so strongly with each other that they merge into a Dalínian multiple image, signifying the right of women to have meaningful artistic lives.

20. Joseph Cornell's 1945 letter/collage of admiration to Welty reprises the figurehead imagery in the form of a "Moorish pirate," who "once proudly scanned the waves from an

East Indiaman" and then shoots bizarrely, like a firework, from a house's crumbling chimney.

Chapter 4

1. For commentary on this transformation, see Kreyling (*Eudora* 52–76).

2. Fry invented the term postimpressionism for his inaugural exhibition of imported European art at the Grafton Galleries in 1910, and, with the aid of Clive Bell, he staged a second exhibition two years later (Kolocotroni 189).

3. In her forward to Harcourt Brace's 1981 edition of *To the Lighthouse*, Welty remarks that it seems incredible to her that she had the fortune to come across the novel in Mississippi in 1930, and that she "fell upon the novel that once and forever opened the door of imaginative fiction for me, and read it cold, in all its wonder and magnitude" (vii).

4. Brannon Costello's *Plantation Airs* focuses closely on the historical context of the novel when he quite rightly claims:

> [W]ritten in the wake of New Deal reforms that set in motion forces that would irrevocably alter Delta life, and with the influence of World War II on the African American population already becoming apparent, *Delta Wedding* reflects anxieties about the naturalness, coherence, and perpetuation of aristocratic identity and traditional ways of life that many elite Deltans felt in the 1940s. (39)

This study concurs and augments Costello's analysis by concentrating on the surreal style of the prose that in a variety of episodes destabilizes what Shellmound's masters would claim to be natural, coherent, and perpetual.

5. Perhaps Laura supplies the best metaphor for the Shellmound lives of the Fairchilds, bound by history and immured in tradition. Early in the novel, she sits at the family dining table pondering their seeming immutability: "Laughter at something went over the table; Laura found herself with a picture in her mind of a great bowerlike cage full of tropical birds her father had shown her in a zoo in a city—the sparkle of motion was like a rainbow, while it was the very thing that broke your heart, for the birds that flew were caged all the time and could not fly out" (103). Welty's image of the caged birds forms a central emblem in *Delta Wedding*, where the mounting dissatisfaction of the younger women over limitations proscribed by the genteel plantation life provides material for many of their frustrated reflections.

6. Troy's name alludes to the destruction visited upon that mythical city by Greek invaders. *Delta Wedding*, too, presents a city in flames in the china nightlight that the Fairchild aunts give Dabney as a wedding gift. Troy's marriage to a Fairchild, then, adds to the conflagration that ultimately consumes the civilization of the southern planters, beset by outside forces of modernization.

7. Welty repeatedly draws attention to Troy's conspicuous virility, such as when she identifies him with George's big knife, which Dabney imagines "was as big as the one Troy could pull out" (123). Kreyling observes that Welty also describes "[Troy's] full head of red

hair and the hairs sprouting from the backs of his hands" that makes him a "satyr," and that when "on horseback, he is doubly sexualized as a centaur" (Kreyling *Understanding* 97).

8. Dorothy G. Griffen, too, argues for Marmion as Shellmound's double when she describes the abandoned mansion as the "preamble to Shellmound" (105).

9. Tenley Gwen Bank's insightful analysis of Pinchy and the role that she plays in the novel's treatment of race and sex contends that when Robbie discovers her, the "girl has begun to have contractions and needs to find a safe place to give birth; reduced to animalistic behavior, as the white Fairchilds expect her to be, she seeks a private, protected space in which to welcome her baby" (64).

Chapter 5

1. Welty's fame grew significantly throughout the forties. Between 1940 and 1949, her stories began appearing in national magazines with high literary reputations, including *Atlantic Monthly*, the *New Yorker*, and *Harper's Bazaar*. She published three collections of short stories, a novella, and a novel. She won a Guggenheim fellowship in 1942, later renewed in 1949. She worked at the *New York Times Book Review* during the summer of 1944. She won or came close to winning writing prizes (Welty *Stories* 954–56). And in 1947, E. M. Forster wrote her a short letter generously expressing his admiration for her work, especially *The Wide Net, and Other Stories*, "with the wild and lovely things it brings up" (qtd. in Kreyling *Author* 129).

2. For other examples of Welty's linking the town of Morgana to the mythical mirage of the fata morgana, see Gretlund ("An Interview" 214) and Jones (332).

3. Welty displayed an uncharacteristic degree of inflexibility on this matter. Writing to her agent, she flatly refused Harcourt's proposal to market *The Golden Apples* as a novel, despite their generous $5000 advance: "I'll turn it down if that's the catch and maybe they'll turn back the book but nothing changes the book into a novel or play or poem, if it's a book of related stories, then it is" (qtd. in Kreyling *Author* 146). Kreyling observes that ultimately Harcourt conceded to Welty's wishes and billed the book as a "'chronicle' of the Mississippi town of Morgana" (Kreyling *Author* 146).

4. For a complex and insightful account of how "The Whole World Knows" subtly revises Faulkner's unforgivingly bleak assessment of human relations in *The Sound and the Fury*, see Mark (*Dragon's Blood* 145–74).

5. See Dina Smith's "Cinematic Modernism and Eudora Welty's *The Golden Apples*" for an enlightening analysis contending that "Welty renders her fictional Morgana in cinematic terms, where image meets word," serving as a "reminder of the historically complicated and intertwined relationship of literary and filmic modernisms" (81).

6. Peter Schmidt persuasively shows that both Ran's and Eugene's characterizations reveal the deleterious effects of their father's prolonged absence and of King's insistence upon enacting "stereotypes of 'male' behavior that destroys any possibility for fluid and nonsexist role-playing for both the parents and their child." As a result, the boys harbor a "mixture of repressed emotions" toward their father, including guilt for falling short of

King's "standards of masculinity" and "deep anger toward him for abandoning them and making their relations with women so troubled" (66).

7. That Ran doesn't actually confront Woody about the affair, but has to imagine a fight in which he emerges victorious and heroic, indicates the sense of feebleness and inferiority he feels inside. Moreover, the stiff and unbending shaft of the "croquet" mallet, which he only wields in his daydream, echoes Miss Lizzie Starks's "crochet" hook, which she raps threateningly on the window when Ran arrives at her house. Ran's actual inability to raise his mallet and confront Woody about the affair suggests his fear of castration, which Welty also associates with the crochet hook, with its drooping and folded spike at once a symbol of castration anxiety and impotence.

8. In *The Dragon's Blood*, Rebecca Mark shows Welty's intertextual appropriation and redeployment of textual elements from Faulkner's *The Sound and the Fury* (144–74), claiming that Mississippi "is the place of Welty's literary imagination, and it is populated with Ran and Maideen, with frogs and nightbirds, and with the literary ghosts of Faulkner's world" (150). Another of Faulkner's and T. S. Eliot's ghosts haunts Ran, here, when Welty recycles the prominent water imagery, originally drawn from Eliot's "The Waste Land," in Quentin's section in *The Sound and the Fury*, where the imagery prefigures his drowning in Boston.

9. The conclusion to Hitchcock's *Spellbound* may have influenced Welty's decision to conclude "The Whole World Knows" with a parallel suicide attempt. At the movie's close, a pistol trains a threatening woman in its sights before turning frighteningly upon the camera and firing in a red flash, the only moment of color in an otherwise colorless film. Although Ran's gun sticks, his turning the barrel upon the reader mimics Hitchcock's action. In both examples, the seeing eye confronts death, a metaphor recycled in the dream sequences of the film and originally conceived in Dalí and Buñel's 1929 surrealist classic, *Un Chien Andalou*, which opens with a "famous act of aggression" against the feminine, as a razor slits open a woman's eye (Krohn 78).

10. Later in the narrative and in "The Wanderers," Welty closely identifies Virgie with Venus, the mythological goddess of desire, whose form also "recurs in the work of Dalí" (Romero 240). In Dalí's 1925 *Venus and a Sailor (Homage to Salvat-Papasseit)* and *Venus and Sailor* of the same year, he twice produced paintings depicting Venus with sailors acting as lovers. Apparently, both painter and writer saw in the figure of the wandering sailor an archetype that they could deploy to emphasize the idea of Venusian liberty.

11. Rebecca Mark observes that Loch's viewing through the telescope's lens reveals "everything in the minutest detail but leaves out any personal comment, feeling, or experience" (*Dragon's Blood* 53). But much evidence from "June Recital" demonstrates the reverse, because Welty excludes nothing in the way of feeling or experience from Loch's sighting of the MacLain house, which develops into the stage upon which his nascent desire and misogyny play out.

12. In addition to the allusion to Botticelli's masterpiece in the recital night scene, Welty also identifies Virgie with Venus when she goes swimming naked in "The Wanderers." Noel Polk makes this parallel when he argues that this swimming scene shows Virgie's merging with the universe: "[S]he melds with it, absorbs it, assumes her position in the larger,

the truly 'universal,' scheme of things as unselfconsciously and magisterially as Botticelli's Venus" ("Welty and Faulkner" 145).

13. Ian Gibson reports that the archive of Dalí's English patron, Edward James, contains "three boxes of press cuttings" focusing upon the two-year attraction (723).

14. The funhouse also contains a hall of mirrors in which Cassie sees herself changed into a man, Mr. Voight, in a kind of Dalínian multiple image. In her room, she assumes Voight's frenzied expression, with bared teeth and a "frantic look." But his overpowering sexual energy disturbs Cassie, who "could not now, any more than then, really describe Mr. Voight, but without thinking she could *be* Mr. Voight, which was more frightening still" (*Stories* 358).

15. The symbolism of the metronome resists easy interpretation, but reading the item in the context of Man Ray's surrealism does supply various possibilities. In 1932, he had famously memorialized the death of his relationship with Lee Miller by sketching a metronome, to whose pendulum he attached a cutout image of Miller's eye. He titled the drawing *Object of Destruction* and later that year made it into an object. He then instructed abandoned lovers to imitate his actions by attaching to their own metronomes eyes of partners no longer seen. Then he urged using a hammer to destroy the whole creation. One can only speculate about whether Welty may have seen the drawing when in 1932 it appeared in the magazine *This Quarter*, edited by Edward Titus in Paris (Baldwin 168), but evidence does show that she read other little magazines, such as Ford's *Blues* and *View*, as well as frequenting areas of New York City where customers could buy "foreign art publications" (Levy *Memoir* 16). Man Ray's fetish obtained celebrity in artistic circles and perhaps provides an overdetermined locus for the clustering of themes raised in *The Golden Apples*, highlighting the intersection between the concept of the woman artist and the threat of violence. When Miller left Man Ray, he retaliated by using his art to publicly obliterate her memory. One wonders if "June Recital" reproduces a version of this cause and effect in the forlorn figure of Miss Eckhart, as Mr. Fatty Bowles attempts to destroy her metronome by launching it through a window.

16. Through her description of the well-handled "mint-white bust of Beethoven" (*Stories* 349) that sits on Miss Eckert's piano's corner, Welty may allude to Josef Danhauser's 1840 "best known portrait of Liszt" (Leppert 256), which shows the pianist seated at the instrument, staring "intently at the looming, oversized bust of Beethoven on the piano, looking up at the sculpture as if playing for a god" (257). Four listening men, Alexandre Dumas, Victor Hugo, Niccolò Paganini, and Gioacchino Rossini, appear overwhelmed by the power of the music, but less so than the women who "are represented as emotionally undone by their response" (256). Danhauser presents George Sand's face as "that of a woman in thrall" and Liszt's lover, Marie d'Agoult, collapsed at his feet with her back to the audience showing her "hair in long loose curls: cascading hair was a then-standard visual metaphor for women's sexuality. In other words, Marie, as well as Sand, serve as overdetermined metaphors for awakened desire." With Liszt's eyes transfixed upon the commanding bust of Beethoven, Danhauser identifies the two pianists with each other and with "Lord Byron, Romanticism's ideal of the heroic (read masculine) artist, via the portrait-within-the-portrait on the wall at the rear center" (257). Welty, however, has renovated the set of gender

expectations inscribed in this image. She replaces Danhauser's Romantic heroes with two women of her own devising, Miss Eckhart and Virgie, and raises them from the helpless swoons of Sand and Marie to the position of the Romantic hero, the musician ecstatic at the keys.

17. One could easily cycle through *The Golden Apples* by starting at any given point. Welty presents the narratives kaleidoscopically, variously intersected by time and place and gathering strength through the accretion of meaning invested in repeated themes, symbols, and metaphors. *The Golden Apples* has splintered the emphasis on storyline so completely that mood and atmosphere dominate plot, allowing readers to enter or exit the narrative where they wish. This loose assortment of stories may help to explain why Welty forbade it to be designated a novel.

18. See James Shimkus's "The Habit of Sir Rabbit: Harris, Hurston, and Welty" for other parallels linking King to rabbits and for a general analysis demonstrating the commonalities between "Sir Rabbit" and the "Brer Rabbit tales, particularly as presented by Hurston" (107).

19. Welty's image of the piano transformed into a cow represents one of hundreds of surreal juxtapositions dispersed throughout her work, collectively suggesting an allusion to the surrealist icon, the Comte de Lautréamont, and his utterance defining beauty "as the chance meeting on a dissecting-table of a sewing machine and an umbrella" (177). According to Robert Radford, this much-quoted line "was revered as a kind of talisman by the Surrealists, representing their ideal of a memorable, poetic image which had the potential to suggest a complex of symbolic associations, largely by the surprising and irrational juxtaposition of objects" (88). Welty's surreal imagery evokes a parallel logic demanding widespread reassessment of putatively comprehensive categories of thought.

20. Fate Rainey's attendance on recital night isolates him from the other men in town, who have no appreciation for music— except for Mr. Sissum, the cello player Miss Eckhart adores, but whose name and tragic demise suggest his homosexuality. Another ridiculed outsider like his friend, Miss Eckhart, he commits suicide by drowning. Perhaps Welty hints at Fate Rainey's homosexuality through his appearance at the recital, especially when considering his wife's emasculating assessment of him in comparison to King MacLain, "Fate Rainey ain't got a surprise in him, and proud of it" (*Stories* 322).

21. For an extended analysis that parallels Eliot's poem and Welty's story, see Kreyling (*Eudora* 94–100).

22. A few years later, Welty seems to allude again, much more directly, to Dalí's Cadaqués coastline when she describes the voyagers crossing the Mediterranean onboard the *Pomona* in "Going to Naples": "All afternoon, with the sun going down on their backs, they had been drawing nearer and nearer the tinted Coast of Spain. It grew long, pink, and caverned as the side of a melon. Chances were it would never come close enough for them to see much: they would see no face" (688). In this presentation of the Spanish coastline—geologic, vegetative, and anatomic— Welty evokes a Mediterranean seashore like Cadaqués, whose bizarrely formed boulders, rocky caves, and stony outcroppings fascinated Dalí so greatly he painted them compulsively, making them foci for the genesis of trompe l'oeil effects.

Chapter 6

1. The notion of a reserved midwesterner feeling the dangerous heat of a southern summer may reenact, in reverse, Welty's experience of wintery Wisconsin, where she obtained her degree. In her biography, Marrs quotes from a letter that Welty sent Diarmuid Russell, reflecting on that time when "those people up there seemed to me like sticks of flint, that lived in the icy world. I am afraid of flintiness—I had to penetrate that, but not through *their* hearts" (22–23). "No Place for You, My Love" reverses the actual, however, by having the apparently cold midwesterner travel south, rather than having the Southerner go north.

2. Apertures, screens, mirrors, and other reflecting surfaces of various kinds frequently mark thresholds leading into the Weltian unconscious. Parallel openings into surreal worlds include the eyepiece to Loch Morrison's telescope and his screen window in *The Golden Apples*, the open door through which Robbie Reid gazes on the road to Shellmound and the churning whirlpool that Dabney feasts her eyes on in *Delta Wedding*, and the frame made by the young girl bathing at the lakeside in "A Memory."

3. For example, in a 1976 interview with Jan Nordby Gretlund, Welty denigrates "The Burning" when she avers that it "is a bad story," adding that "it is the worst story I ever wrote" ("An Interview" 221). Later, in 1986, she condemned the setting she had chosen, insisting, "You know, I don't like reading anything about the Civil War, that's the truth. I hate the Civil War. I hate it. I never have read *Gone with the Wind*. I'm totally ignorant about the Civil War" (Devlin & Prenshaw 113).

4. This assertion gains strength in light of the interjection Dewey makes from a point "fifteen years later," when he speculates that the girl in the woods "had very likely been Opal" (636). Furthermore, the narrative skips at the end to a moment after "Days passed" (637).

5. The surreal depiction of the raincoat probably finds its provenance in George IV's Royal Pavilion at Brighton, a building described by its onetime director as an "opium dream beside the English channel" (Morley 22)—not least because of "its utter lack of restraint; its wild mingling of various exoticism, a soufflé of Chinese, Indian, French and English motifs; its daring and extreme colour harmonies, which give the frisson of approaching discordance; its lavish use of gold in every form and in every material; its sybaritic luxury; its brilliant and witty use of *faux* surfaces" (29). While spending time in Brighton in 1951, Welty grew enamored of the town and its "Prince Regent's Palace" and "managed to do some work in the seaside city; she wrote Robinson that she had finished the Irish story based on her boat-train journey from London to Cork" (Marrs *Eudora* 197).

6. The old man whom Gabriella sees levitating while asleep in the engine room, despite the "deafening" (*Stories* 693) pounding of the pistons, parallels the slumbering night watchman, Mr. Holifield, in "June Recital." Both men symbolize unguarded superegos rendered defenseless by sleep.

7. From the outset, Welty introduces an element of confusion into the question of Mingo's identity. Dicey opens, "'Mingo?' I repeated, and for the first moment I didn't know what my aunt meant. The name sounded like *something* instead of *somewhere*" (647).

Chapter 7

1. In his introduction to a special issue on "Regional Modernisms" in *Modern Fiction Studies*, Scott Herring remarks:

> Across the United States, the United Kingdom, and continental Europe, modernism's reliance on the metropolitan appears unshakable. Its major movements crystallized in global metropoles such as London, New York, Paris, and Berlin. Publishing houses and small presses in these same cities vetted many of its major productions. Its affective repertoire often hinges on two acute responses to the supposed anonymity of the urban environment, shock and blasé. And the gregariousness of a large city seems to nurture ideals of cosmopolitanism and worldliness that continue well into the present. (2)

Nonetheless, he goes on to remark, "[W]e should be wary of collapsing metropolitanism with modernism and regionalism with ruralism" because of the critical oversights enabled by such parallels (3).

2. In his recent study, *American Literary Regionalism in a Global Age*, Philip Joseph retains "regionalism" as a periodizing concept, but then offers analyses of writers, such as Hamlin Garland, Abraham Cahan, Willa Cather, and Zora Neale Hurston, who redefined their regionalist labels, "writers who attempted to revitalize the discussion of local community by situating a given community and its subjects squarely in an interconnected nation and world" (11). Surely this description, which throws the definition of "local color" writer into question, fits Welty's context handily.

3. Welty's "Place in Fiction" stringently takes up this point in the context of Austen, Brontë, Hardy, Cervantes, Turgenev, and the writers of the Old Testament, all of whom, she argues, necessarily depicted regions in their writing. Railing against critical usage of the word *regional*, she argues that it fails to "differentiate between the localized raw material of life and its outcome as art. 'Regional' is an outsider's term; it has no meaning for the insider who is doing the writing, because as far as he knows he is simply writing about life" (796). Has the argument for the limitations of descriptive literary terms found more powerful expression?

4. Isabelle Dervaux argues that with the return of émigré artists to Europe after the war, and with the 1947 closure of Peggy Guggenheim's Art of This Century and the Julien Levy Gallery in 1949 came surrealism's decline: "Criticized as academic and literary by Clement Greenberg, the champion of Abstract Expressionism, Surrealism had grown out of fashion in New York by the end of the decade" (17).

5. This new focus on literary language as it enters political contexts finds expression in the following additional works from the fifties and sixties: "Writing and Analyzing a Story" (1955), "Place in Fiction" (1955), "Where is the Voice Coming From" (1963), "Must the Novelist Crusade" (1965), and "The Demonstrators" (1968).

WORKS CITED

Ades, Dawn. *Dalí*. London: Thames & Hudson, 1995. Print.

Agha, M. F. "Surrealism or the Purple Cow." *Vogue* 1 Nov. 1936: 60+. Print.

Almeida, Diana. "'Keela, the Outcast Indian Maiden': (Story) Telling the Southern Ideology." *Eudora Welty Review* 2 (2010): 35–52. Print.

Alquié, Ferdinand. *The Philosophy of Surrealism*. Trans. Bernard Waldrop. Ann Arbor, MI: U of Michigan P, 1965. Print.

Amory, Cleveland, and Frederic Bradlee, eds. *Vanity Fair, Selections from America's Most Memorable Magazine: A Cavalcade of the 1920s and 1930s*. New York: Viking P, 1960. Print.

Appel, Alfred. *A Season of Dreams: The Fiction of Eudora Welty*. Baton Rouge, LA: Louisiana State UP, 1965. Print.

Audubon, John James. "Account of the Method of Drawing Birds Employed by J. J. Audubon, Esq. F.R.S.E." *Writings and Drawings*. New York: Library of America, 1999. 753–58. Print.

Bach, Friedrich, Margit Rowell, and Ann Temkin. *Constantin Brancusi*. Cambridge, MA: MIT P, 1995. Print.

Baker, Houston A. and Dana D. Nelson, eds. "Violence, the Body, and 'The South.'" Special Issue. *American Literature* 73.2 (2001). Print.

Balakian, Anna. *André Breton: Magus of Surrealism*. New York: Oxford UP, 1971. Print.

———. *Surrealism: The Road to the Absolute*. Chicago: U of Chicago P, 1986. Print.

Baldwin, Billy. *Billy Baldwin: An Autobiography with Michael Gardine*. Boston: Little, Brown, and Company, 1985. Print.

Baldwin, Neil. *Man Ray: American Artist*. New York: Da Capo P, 1988. Print.

Bank, Gwen Tenley. "Dark-Purple Faces and Pitiful Whiteness: Maternity and Coming Through in *Delta Wedding*." *Mississippi Quarterly* Supplement (2009): 59–79. Print.

Barilleaux, René Paul, ed. *Passionate Observer: Eudora Welty Among Artists of the Thirties*. Jackson, MS: Mississippi Museum of Art, 2002. Print.

Barr, Alfred H., ed. *Cubism and Abstract Art*. New York: Museum of Modern Art, 1936. Print.

———, ed. *Fantastic Art, Dada, Surrealism*. New York: Museum of Modern Art, 1937. Print.

———, ed. *Modern Works of Art: Fifth Anniversary Exhibition*. New York: Museum of Modern Art, 1936. Print.

Baudot, François. *Elsa Schiaparelli*. New York: Universe Publishing, 1997. Print.

Beaton, Cecil. *Portrait of New York*. London: B. T. Batsford, 1948. Print.

Benjamin, Walter. "Surrealism: The Last Snapshot of European Intelligentsia." *Walter Benjamin: Selected Writings*. Trans. Rodney Livingstone et al. Eds. Michael W. Jennings, Howard Eiland, and Gary Smith. Cambridge, MA: The Belknap P of Harvard UP, 1999. 207–21. Print.

Black, Patti Carr. "Back Home in Jackson." *Passionate*. Barilleaux 33–55.

Bloom, Harold, ed. Introduction. *Eudora Welty*. New York: Chelsea House Publishers, 1986. 1–10. Print.

Blum, Dilys E. *Shocking! The Art and Fashion of Elsa Schiaparelli*. New Haven: Yale UP, 2003. Print.

Bradbury, Malcolm. *The Modern American Novel*. Oxford: Oxford UP, 1992. Print.

Breton, André. "Manifesto of Surrealism." *Manifestos* Breton 1–47.

———. *Manifestos of Surrealism*. Trans. Richard Seaver and Helen R. Lane. Ann Arbor, MI: U of Michigan P, 1969. Print.

———. "Second Manifesto of Surrealism." *Manifestos* Breton 117–87.

Brickell, Herschel. "Some Books About America." *North American Review* 230.4 (1930): 505–6. Print.

Brookhart, Mary Hughes, and Suzanne Marrs. "More Notes on River Country." *Welty: A Life*. Devlin 82–95.

Bunting, Charles T. "An Interior World: An Interview with Eudora Welty." *Conversations*. Prenshaw 40–63.

Burns, Martha Dennis. "A Gallery of Teachers and Students: The Female Piano Teacher in Antebellum America." *Piano*. Parakilas 165–79.

Carr, Virginia Spencer. *Paul Bowles: A Life*. New York: Scribner, 2004. Print.

Catalogue of a Century of Progress Exhibition of Paintings and Sculpture. Chicago: The Art Institute of Chicago, 1933. Print.

Caws, Mary Ann, Rudolf Keunzli, and Gwen Raaberg, eds. *Surrealism and Women*. Cambridge, MA: MIT P, 1991. Print.

Champion, Laurie, ed. *The Critical Response to Eudora Welty's Fiction*. Westport, CT: Greenwood Press, 1994. Print.

Childs, Peter. *Modernism*. London: Routledge, 2000. Print.

Cochran, Sara. "Spellbound." *Dalí and Film*. Ed. Matthew Gale. London: Tate Publishing, 2007. 174–85. Print.

Cole, Hunter, and Seetha Srinivasan. "Eudora Welty and Photography: An Interview." *More Conversations*. Prenshaw 188–213.

Comment Magazine. "An Interview with Eudora Welty." *Conversations*. Prenshaw 18–25.

Conkelton, Sheryl. "Hoyningen-Huene, George." *Oxford Art Online*. Oxford UP. n. pag. Web. 31 March 2011.

Cornell, Joseph. Letter to Eudora Welty. 5 February 1945. TS. Private Collection.

Costello, Brannon. *Plantation Airs: Racial Paternalism and the Transformations of Class in Southern Fiction, 1945–1971*. Baton Rouge: Louisiana State UP, 2007. Print.

Crews, Elizabeth. "Cixous' New Woman: Laura and Shelley in Eudora Welty's *Delta Wedding*." *Eudora Welty's Delta Wedding*. Ed. Reine Dugas Bouton. New York: Rodopi, 2008. 65–78. Print.

Dalí, Salvador. *Atmospheric Skull Sodomizing a Grand Piano*. 1934. Oil on wood panel. The Salvador Dalí Museum, Florida.

——. *Bathers of Es Llaner*. 1923. Oil on plywood and cardboard panel. Fundació Gala-Salvador Dalí, Figueres.

——. *The Conquest of the Irrational. Collected*. 1935. Finkelstein 262–72.

——. *Dream Caused by the Flight of a Bee Around a Pomegranate, a Second Before Waking Up*. 1944. Oil on wood panel. Thyssen-Bornemisza Collection, Madrid.

——. *Enigma of Desire*. 1929. Oil on canvas. Pinakothek der Moderne, Munich.

——. *The Great Masturbator*. 1929. Oil on canvas. Museo Nacional Centro de Arte Reina Sofia, Madrid.

——. *The Hand, Remorse*. 1930. Oil and collage on canvas. The Salvador Dalí Museum, Florida.

——. *Mae West's Face Which May be Used as a Surrealist Apartment*. 1934–35. Gouache, with graphite, on commercially prited magazine paper. The Art Insitute of Chicago.

——. *The Old Age of William Tell*. 1931. Oil on canvas. Private collection.

——. *The Persistence of Memory*. 1931. Oil on canvas. Museum of Modern Art, New York.

——. "The Rotting Donkey." *Collected*. Finkelstein 223–26.

——. *Skull with its Lyric Appendage Leaning on a Night Table Which Should Have the Exact Temperature of a Cardinal Bird's Nest*. 1934. Oil on wood panel. The Salvador Dalí Museum, Florida.

——. *Venus and Cupids*. 1925. Oil on wood panel. Private collection.

——. *Venus and Sailor*. 1925. Oil on canvas on wood. Fundació Gala-Salvador Dalí, Figueres.

——. *Venus and a Sailor (Homage to Salvat-Papasseit)*. 1925. Oil on canvas. Ikeda Museum of Twentieth-Century Art, Sizuoka-Ken.

——. *Venus de Milo with Drawers*. 1936. Painted plaster with metal pulls and mink pompons. The Art Institute of Chicago.

——. *William Tell*. 1930. Oil and collage on canvas. Musée National d'Art Moderne, Centre Pompidou, Paris.

"Dali's Surrealist Dream House at the World's Fair." *Vogue* 1 June 1939: 56–57. Print.

Dearborn, Mary V. *The Happiest Man Alive: A Biography of Henry Miller*. New York: Simon & Schuster, 1992. Print.

Dervaux, Isabelle, ed. *Surrealism USA*. New York: Hatje Cantz, 2004. Print.

Descharnes, Robert, and Gilles Néret. *Salvadore Dalí 1904–1989*. Trans. Michael Hulse. Köln: Taschen, 1998. Print.

Devlin, Albert J. *Eudora Welty's Chronicle: A Story of Mississippi Life*. Jackson: UP of Mississippi, 1983. Print.

——. "The Sharp Edge of Experiment: The Poetics of *No Place for You, My Love*." Champion 163–70.

———, ed. *Welty: A Life in Literature*. Jackson: UP of Mississippi, 1987. Print.

Devlin, Albert J., and Peggy Whitman Prenshaw. "A Conversation with Eudora Welty." *More Conversations*. Prenshaw 100–19.

Doherty, Thomas. *Pre-Code Hollywood: Sex, Immorality, and Insurrection in American Cinema, 1930–1934*. New York: Columbia UP, 1999. Print.

Dollarhide, Louis, and Ann J. Abadie. *Eudora Welty: A Form of Thanks*. Jackson: UP of Mississippi, 1979. Print.

Duck, Leigh Anne. *The Nation's Region: Southern Modernism, Segregation, and U.S. Nationalism*. Athens, GA: U of Georgia P, 2009. Print.

Eichelberger, Julia. "'The Way for Girls in the World': Laura's Escape from Drowning in *Delta Wedding*." *Eudora Welty's Delta Wedding*. Ed. Reine Dugas Bouton. New York: Rodopi, 2008. 47–63. Print.

Eisinger, Chester E. "Traditionalism and Modernism in Eudora Welty." *Critical*. Prenshaw 3–25.

Ernst, Stephanie A. "Peter Neagoe." *Guide to Literary Masters & Their Works*. Salem P. n. pag. *Literary Reference Center*. Web. 29 June 2011.

"Exhibition History List." *The Museum of Modern Art*. The Museum of Modern Art. N.d. Web. 30 July 2011.

Eysteinsson, Astradur. *The Concept of Modernism*. Ithaca, NY: Cornell UP, 1990. Print.

Ferguson, Robert. *Henry Miller: A Life*. New York: W. W. Norton & Company, 1991. Print.

Ferris, Bill. "A Visit with Eudora Welty." *Conversations*. Prenshaw 154–71.

Finkelstein, Haim, ed. and trans. *The Collected Writings of Salvador Dalí*. Cambridge: Cambridge UP, 1998. Print.

———. *Salvador Dalí's Art and Writing 1927–1942: The Metamorphoses of Narcissus*. Cambridge: Cambridge UP, 1996. Print.

Ford, Charles Henri, ed. *Blues: A Magazine of New Rhythms*. Vol. 1. New York: Johnson Reprint Corporation, 1967. Print.

Freeman, Jean Todd. "An Interview with Eudora Welty." *Conversations*. Prenshaw 172–99.

Friedman, Susan Stanford. "Afterword." *Disciplining Modernism*. Ed. Pamela L. Caughie. London: Palgrave Macmillan, 2009. 259–63. Print.

Fuchs, Miriam. "Djuna Barnes." *Critical Survey of Long Fiction*. Salem P. n. pag. *Literary Reference Center*. Web. 14 July 2011.

Fuller, Stephen M. "Memory's Narrative Gossamer: Configurations of Desire in Eudora Welty's "A Memory." *Studies in Short Fiction*. 35 (1998): 331–37. Print.

———. "South of South Again: Eudora Welty's Late Surreal Lament, 'No Place for You, My Love.'" *Southern Quarterly* 47.2 (2010): 39–55. Print.

Gale, Matthew. "Un Chien Andalou." *Dalí and Film*. Ed. Matthew Gale. London: Tate Publishing, 2007. 82–93. Print.

"George Balanchine." *Columbia Electronic Encyclopedia*. Columbia UP. n. pag. *Literary Reference Center*. Web. 29 June 2011.

Gibson, Ian. *The Shameful Life of Salvador Dalí*. New York: W. W. Norton & Company, 1998. Print.

Gretlund, Jan Nordby. *Eudora Welty's Aesthetics of Place*. Newark: U of Delaware P, 1994. Print.

———. "An Interview with Eudora Welty." *Conversations*. Prenshaw 211–29.

———. "Seeing Real Things: An Interview with Eudora Welty." *More Conversations*. Prenshaw 248–61.

Griffin, Dorothy G. "The House as Container: Architecture and Myth in Delta Wedding." *A Life*. Devlin 96–112.

Haftmann, Werner. *Painting in the Twentieth Century*. New York: Frederick A. Praeger, 1960. Print.

Hamalian, Linda. *The Cramoisy Queen: A Life of Caresse Crosby*. Carbondale, IL: Southern Illinois UP, 2005. Print.

Harrison, Suzan. *Eudora Welty and Virginia Woolf: Gender, Genre, and Influence*. Baton Rouge, LA: Louisiana State UP, 1997. Print.

Hartshorn, Willis. Introduction. *Man Ray: Bazaar Years*. By John Esten. New York: Rizzoli International Publications, 1988. Print.

Hartshorn, Willis, and Merry Foresta. Introduction. *Man Ray in Fashion*. New York: International Center of Photography, 1990. Print.

Henningfeld, Diane. "Charles Henri Ford." *Guide to Literary Masters & Their Works*. Salem P. n. pag. *Literary Reference Center*. Web. 29 June 2011.

Herring, Scott. "Regional Modernism: A Reintroduction." *Modern Fiction Studies* 55.1 (2009): 1–10. Print.

Higham, Charles. *The Duchess of Windsor: The Secret Life*. Hoboken, NJ: John Wiley, 2005. Print.

Jacobs, Lisa. "Chronology of Exhibitions." *Julien Levy*. Schaffner & Jacobs 173–89.

Jean, Marcel. Ed. *The Autobiography of Surrealism*. New York: Viking P, 1980. Print.

———. *The History of Surrealist Painting*. Trans. Simon Watson Taylor. New York: Grove P, 1960. Print.

Jones, John Griffin. "Eudora Welty." *Conversations*. Prenshaw 316–41.

Joseph, Philip. *American Literary Regionalism in a Global Age*. Baton Rouge: Louisiana State UP, 2007. Print.

Kachur, Lewis. *Displaying the Marvelous: Marcel Duchamp, Salvador Dalí, and Surrealist Exhibition Installations*. Cambridge, MA: MIT P, 2001. Print.

Keith, Don Lee. "Eudora Welty: 'I Worry Over My Stories.'" *Conversations*. Prenshaw 141–53.

Kolocotroni, Vassiliki, Jane Goldman, and Olga Taxidou. *Modernism: An Anthology of Sources and Documents*. Chicago: U of Chicago P, 1998. Print.

Kreyling, Michael. *Author and Agent: Eudora Welty and Diarmuid Russell*. New York: Farrar Straus & Giroux, 1991. Print.

———. *Eudora Welty's Achievement of Order*. Baton Rouge, LA: Louisiana State UP, 1980. Print.

———. "History and Imagination: Writing 'The Winds.'" *Mississippi Quarterly* 50.4 (1997): 585–99. Print.

———. *Inventing Southern Literature*. Jackson, MS: UP of Mississippi, 1998. Print.

——. *Understanding Eudora Welty*. Columbia, SC: U of South Carolina P, 1999. Print.

Krohn, Bill. *Hitchcock at Work*. London: Phaidon P, 2000. Print.

Kuehl, Linda. "The Art of Fiction XLVII: Eudora Welty." *Conversations*. Prenshaw 74–91.

Lacan, Jacques. "The Mirror Stage as Formative of the Function of the I as Revealed in Psychoanalytic Experience." *Écrits: A Selection*. Trans. Alan Sheridan. New York: W. W. Norton & Company, 1977. Print.

L'Age D'Or. Dir. Luis Buñuel. Screenplay by Luis Buñuel and Salvador Dalí. Perf. Gaston Modot and Lya Lys. 1930. Kino Video, 2004. DVD.

Lautréamont. *Maldoror*. Trans. Alexis Lykiard. New York: Thomas Y. Crowell Company, 1972. Print.

Leider, Emily Wortis. *Becoming Mae West*. New York: Farrar, Straus & Giroux, 1997. Print.

Leppert, Richard. "Cultural Contradiction, Idolatry, and the Piano Virtuoso: Franz Liszt." *Piano*. Parakilas 252–81.

Levenson, Michael, ed. *The Cambridge Companion to Modernism*. Cambridge: Cambridge UP, 1999. Print.

Levy, Julien. *Memoir of an Art Gallery*. New York: G. P. Putnam's Sons, 1977. Print.

——. *Surrealism*. 1936. New York: Da Capo P, 1995. Print.

"Life Goes to Dali's New Ballet: A Surrealist 'Bacchanale' with a Mad Bavarian and a Venus in White Tights." *Life* 27 Nov. 1939: 90–93. Print.

"Life Goes to the World's Fair: It Turns Out to be a Wonderful Place." *Life* 3 July 1939: 54–70. Print.

Lloyd-Morgan, Ceridwen. "Augustus (Edwin) John." *Oxford Art Online*. Oxford UP. n. pag. Web. 3 March 2011.

Lubar, Robert S. *Dali: The Salvador Dali Museum Collection*. Boston, MA: Bulfinch P, 2000. Print.

Lyell, Frank. Letter to Eudora Welty. September 25 1932. MS. Eudora Welty Collection. Mississippi Department of Archives and History, Jackson, MS.

——. Letter to Eudora Welty. March 10 1933. MS. Eudora Welty Collection. Mississippi Department of Archives and History, Jackson, MS.

——. Letter to Eudora Welty. March 25 1933. MS. Eudora Welty Collection. Mississippi Department of Archives and History, Jackson, MS.

——. Letter to Eudora Welty. 24 July 1933. MS. Eudora Welty Collection. Mississippi Department of Archives and History, Jackson, MS.

——. Letter to Eudora Welty. December 1933. MS. Eudora Welty Collection. Mississippi Department of Archives and History, Jackson, MS.

——. Letter to Eudora Welty. 7 April 1935. MS. Eudora Welty Collection. Mississippi Department of Archives and History, Jackson, MS.

——. Mock memo to Eudora Welty. 7 April 1935. MS. Eudora Welty Collection. Mississippi Department of Archives and History, Jackson, MS.

——. Postcard to Eudora Welty. 4 June 1932. MS. Eudora Welty Collection. Mississippi Department of Archives and History, Jackson, MS.

——. Postcard to Eudora Welty. 30 November 1934. MS. Eudora Welty Collection. Mississippi Department of Archives and History, Jackson, MS.

Manning, Carol S. "Hurston and Welty, Janie and Livvie." *Southern Literary Journal* 34.2 (2002): 64–72. Print.

———. *With Ears Opening Like Morning Glories: Eudora Welty and the Love of Storytelling.* Westport, CT: Greenwood P, 1985. Print.

Mark, Rebecca. "Carnival Geeks and Voudoun Healing: The Performance of White Guilt and African American Empowerment in Eudora Welty's 'Keela, the Outcast Indian Maiden.'" *Mississippi Quarterly* Supplement (2009): 13–33. Print.

———. *The Dragon's Blood: Feminist Intertextuality in Eudora Welty's* The Golden Apples. Jackson: UP of Mississippi, 1994. Print.

Marrs, Suzanne. *Eudora Welty: A Biography.* Orlando, FL: Harcourt, 2005. Print.

———. "Eudora Welty's Enduring Images: Photography and Fiction." *Passionate.* Barilleaux 9–31.

———. *One Writer's Imagination: The Fiction of Eudora Welty.* Baton Rouge, LA: Louisiana State UP, 2002. Print.

———. "Re: Welty and Surrealism." Message to the author. 4 May 2011. E-Mail.

———. *The Welty Collection: A Guide to the Eudora Welty Manuscripts and Documents at the Mississippi Department of Archives and History.* Jackson: UP of Mississippi, 1988. Print.

Morgan, Barbara. "The Dance: Surrealism and Americana." *New York Times* 19 Nov. 1939: 8x. Print.

Martin, Richard. *Fashion and Surrealism.* New York: Rizzoli Publications, 1989. Print.

McHaney, Pearl Amelia. *Eudora Welty: The Contemporary Reviews.* Cambridge: Cambridge UP, 2005. Print.

———. "Eudora Welty's 'The Winds' and 'A Sketching Trip': Wonderful and Explicit and Authentically 'sur-real.'" 2011. Unpublished TS.

McLaughlin, Don James. "Finding (M)other's Face: A Psychoanalytic Approach to Eudora Welty's 'Clytie.'" *Eudora Welty Review* 1 (2009): 53–62. Print.

McWhirter, David. "Eudora Welty Goes to the Movies: Modernism, Regionalism, Global Media." *Modern Fiction Studies* 55.1 (2009): 68–91. Print.

———. "Fish Stories: Revising Masculine Ritual in Eudora Welty's 'The Wide Net.'" *Mississippi Quarterly* Supplement (2009): 35–57. Print.

Mitchell, Henry. "Eudora Welty: Rose-Garden Realist, Storyteller of the South." *Conversations.* Prenshaw 64–73.

Moorehouse, Paul. *Dali.* London: PRC Publishing, 2004. Print.

Morley, John. *The Making of the Royal Pavilion Brighton.* Boston: David R. Godine, 1984. Print.

Mortimer, Gail L. *Daughter of the Swan: Love and Knowledge in Eudora Welty's Fiction.* Athens, GA: U of Georgia P, 1994. Print.

Mundy, Jennifer. *Surrealism: Desire Unbound.* Princeton, NJ: Princeton UP, 2001. Print.

Nadeau, Maurice. *The History of Surrealism.* Trans. Richard Howard. New York: MacMillan, 1965. Print.

O'Connor, Francis V. "Framing Time in Expressive Places: Eudora Welty's Stories, Photographs, and the Art of Mississippi in the 1930s." *Passionate.* Barilleaux 56–83.

O'Neal, Hank. *Berenice Abbott: American Photographer*. New York: Artpress Books, 1982. Print.

Parakilas, James et al. *Piano Roles: Three Hundred Years of Life with the Piano*. New Haven, CT: Yale UP, 1999. Print.

Peacock, James L., Harry L. Watson, and Carrie R. Matthews, eds. *The American South in a Global World*. Chapel Hill: U of North Carolina P, 2005. Print.

Phillips, Sandra S. "Eudora Welty and Photography." *Eudora Welty as Photographer: Photographs by Eudora Welty*. Ed. Pearl Amelia McHaney. Jackson, MS: UP of Mississippi, 2009. Print.

Pitavy-Souques, Danièle. "A Blazing Butterfly: The Modernity of Eudora Welty." *Welty: A Life*. Devlin 113–38.

———. "'The Inspired Child of [Her] Times': Eudora Welty as a Twentieth-Century Artist." *Eudora Welty Review* 2 (2010): 69–92. Print.

———. "Watches and Watching: Point of View in Eudora Welty's 'June Recital.'" *Southern Review* 19 (1983): 483–509. Print.

Pitxot, Antoni, Montse Aguer, and Anna Otero. "Dream Caused by the Flight of a Bee around a Pomegranate One Second Before Awakening." *Fundació Gala-Salvador Dalí*. Fundació Gala-Salvador Dalí, 16 Feb. 2010. Web. Aug. 11 2011.

Poe, Edgar Allan. *The Complete Tales & Poems of Edgar Allan Poe*. Edison, NJ: Castle Books, 2002. Print.

Poetzl, Herbert. "Biographical Note: Biography and Career of Tilly Losch." *Tilly Losch Collection*. Special Collections, Preservation and University Archives at Binghamton University. 1 July 2011. Web. 14 July 2011.

Polizzotti, Mark. Introduction. *Surrealism*. By Julien Levy. v–viii.

———. *Revolution of the Mind: The Life of André Breton*. New York: Farrar, Straus & Giroux, 1995. Print.

Polk, Noel. "Going to Naples and Other Places in Eudora Welty's Fiction." *Eudora Welty: Eye of the Storyteller*. Ed. Dawn Trouard. Kent, OH: Kent State UP, 1989. 153–64. Print.

———. "Water, Wanderers, and Weddings: Love in Eudora Welty." Dollarhide & Abadie 95–122.

———. "Welty and Faulkner and the Southern Literary Tradition." *Value and Vision in American Literature: Literary Essays in Honor of Ray Lewis White*. Ed. Joseph Candido. Athens, OH: Ohio UP, 1999. 132–50. Print.

———. "Welty, Hawthorne, and Poe: Men of the Crowd and the Landscape of Alienation." *Mississippi Quarterly*. 50.4 (1997): 553–66. Print.

Porter, Katherine Anne. Introduction. *Stories*. Welty 965–70.

Prenshaw, Peggy Whitman, ed. *Conversations with Eudora Welty*. Jackson, MS: UP of Mississippi, 1984. Print.

———, ed. *Eudora Welty: Critical Essays*. Jackson, MS: UP of Mississippi, 1979. Print.

———, ed. *More Conversations with Eudora Welty*. Jackson, MS: UP of Mississippi, 1996.

———. "Persephone in Eudora Welty's *Livvie*." Champion 91–97.

———. "Woman's World, Man's Place: The Fiction of Eudora Welty." Dollarhide & Abadie 46–77.

Price, Marshall N. "Chronology of Surrealism in the United States, 1931–1950." *Surrealism USA*. Dervaux 172–85.

Price, Reynolds. Forward. *Eudora Welty: Photographs*. Welty vii–xii.

Radford, Robert. *Dalí*. London: Phaidon Press, 1998. Print.

Randisi, Jennifer Lynn. *A Tissue of Lies: Eudora Welty and the Southern Romance*. Washington: UP of America, 1982. Print.

Ransom, John Crowe. "Delta Fiction." Rev. of *Delta Wedding*, by Eudora Welty. *Kenyon Review* 8 (1946): 503–7. Print.

Reid, Panthea. *Art and Affection: A Life of Virginia Woolf*. Oxford: Oxford UP, 1996. Print.

Romero, Luis. *Salvador Dalí*. Barcelona: Ediciones Polígrafa, 2003. Print.

Rosemont, Penelope, ed. Introduction. *Surrealist Women: An International Anthology*. Austin, TX: U of Texas P, 1998. Print.

Roudinesco, Elisabeth. *Jaques Lacan: Outline of a Life, History of a System of Thought*. Trans. Barbara Bray. New York: Columbia UP, 1997. Print.

Rowlands, Penelope. *A Dash of Daring: Carmel Snow and her Life in Fashion, Art, and Letters*. New York: Atria Books, 2005.

Roza, Mathilde. *Following Strangers: the Life and Literary Works of Robert M. Coates*. Columbia: U of South Carolina P, 2011. Print.

Rubin, William S. *Surrealist Art*. New York: Harry N. Abrams, 1968. Print.

Rubinstein, Charlotte Streifer. *American Women Sculptors: A History of Women Working in Three Dimensions*. Boston: G. K. Hall, 1990.

Russeks Fifth Avenue. Advertisement. *Vogue* September 1 1936: 30–31. Print.

"Salvador Dalí Arrives. Surrealist Painter Brings 25 of His Pictures for Show Here." *New York Times* 15 Nov. 1934. n. pag. *NYTimes.com*. Web. 30 July 2011.

"Salvador Dalí: New Yorkers Stand in Line to See His Six-in-One Surrealist Painting." *Life* 17 Apr. 1939: 44–45.

Sawin, Martica. *Surrealism in Exile and the Beginning of the New York School*. Cambridge, MA: MIT P, 1995. Print.

Schaffner, Ingrid. "Alchemy of the Gallery." Schaffner & Jacobs 20–59.

———. *Salvador Dalí's Dream of Venus: The Surrealist Funhouse from the 1939 World's Fair*. New York: Princeton Architectural P, 2002. Print.

Schaffner, Ingrid, and Lisa Jacobs, eds. Introduction. *Julien Levy: Portrait of an Art Gallery*. Cambridge, MA: MIT P, 1988.

Schmidt, Peter. *The Heart of the Story: Eudora Welty's Short Fiction*. Jackson, MS: UP of Mississippi, 1991. Print.

Schiebler, Ralf. *Dalí: Genius, Obsession and Lust*. Trans. Fiona Elliott. Munich: Prestel-Verlag, 1996. Print.

Secrest, Meryle. *Salvador Dalí: A Biography*. New York: E. P. Dutton, 1987. Print.

Seigel, Jerrold. *Bohemian Paris: Culture, Politics, and the Boundaries of Bourgeois Life 1830–1930*. Baltimore, MD: Johns Hopkins UP, 1999. Print.

Shattuck, Roger. *The Banquet Years: The Arts in France 1885–1918*. New York: Harcourt, Brace & Company, 1958. Print.

Shimkus, James. "The Habit of Sir Rabbit: Harris, Hurston, and Welty." *Eudora Welty Review* 1 (2009): 107–113. Print.

Short, Robert. "Dada and Surrealism." *Modernism: A Guide to European Literature 1890–1930.* Eds. Malcolm Bradbury and James McFarlane. London: Penguin Books, 1991. 292–308. Print.

———. *Dada and Surrealism.* London: Lawrence King, 1994. Print.

"Sir Cecil Walter Hardy Beaton." *Columbia Electronic Encyclopedia.* Columbia UP. n. pag. *Literary Reference Center.* Web. 14 July 2011.

"Sitwell." *Columbia Electronic Encyclopedia.* Columbia UP. n. pag. *Literary Reference Center.* Web. 29 June 2011.

Smith, Dina. "Cinematic Modernism and Eudora Welty's *The Golden Apples.*" *Mississippi Quarterly* Supplement (2009): 81–100. Print.

Smith, Jon, and Deborah Cohn. *Look Away! The U.S. South in New World Studies.* Durham, NC: Duke UP, 2004. Print.

Smith, Meredith E. *The Persistence of Memory: A Biography of Dalí.* New York: Random House, 1993. Print.

Snow, Carmel, and Mary Lou Aswell. *The World of Carmel Snow.* New York: McGraw-Hill, 1962. Print.

Spellbound. Dir. Alfred Hitchcock. Perf. Ingrid Bergman and Gregory Peck. 1945. MGM, 2008. DVD.

Sullivan, George. *Berenice Abbott, Photographer: An Independent Vision.* New York: Clarion Books, 2006. Print.

"Surrealism in New York Shops." *Vogue* 1 Mar. 1938: 108–9. Print.

"Surrealism in Paris" *Vogue* 1 Mar. 1938: 106–7. Print.

Tapert, Annette, and Diana Edkins. *The Power of Style: The Women Who Defined the Art of Living Well.* New York: Crown, 1994. Print.

Tashjian, Dickran. *A Boatload of Madmen: Surrealism and the American Avant-Garde 1920–1950.* New York: Thames & Hudson, 1995. Print.

Trilling, Diana. "Fiction in Review." *Nation* 2 October 1943: 386–87. Print.

———. "Fiction in Review." *Nation* 11 May 1946: 578. *Eudora Welty: The Contemporary Reviews.* Ed. Pearl Amelia McHaney. Cambridge: Cambridge UP, 2005: 60–61. Print.

"Tullulah Bankhead." *Columbia Electronic Encyclopedia.* Columbia UP. n. pag. *Literary Reference Center.* Web. 14 July 2011.

Tyler, Parker. *The Divine Comedy of Pavel Tchelitchew.* New York: Fleet, 1967. Print.

Un Chien Andalou. Dir. Luis Buñuel. Screenplay by Luis Buñuel and Salvador Dalí. Perf. Simone Mareuil and Pierre Batcheff. 1929. Transflux Films, 2004. DVD.

Vande Kieft, Ruth M. *Eudora Welty.* Rev. Ed. Boston: Twayne, 1987. Print.

Vella, Christina. "Dorothy Dix: The World Brought Her Its Secrets." *Louisiana Women: Their Lives and Times.* Eds. Janet Allured and Judith F. Gentry. Athens, GA: U of Georgia P, 2009. 195–214. Print.

"Vogue's Three Man Show." *Vogue* 15 Mar. 1937: 82–85. Print.

Walker, Alice. "Eudora Welty: An Interview." *Conversations.* Prenshaw 131–40.

Warren, Robert Penn. "Love and Separateness in Eudora Welty." Bloom 19–28.

Watson, Steven. "Julien Levy: Exhibitionist and Harvard Modernist." *Julien Levy.* Schaffner & Jacobs 80–95.

Watt, Ian. *The Rise of the Novel: Studies in Defoe, Richardson and Fielding.* Berkeley: U of California P, 1957. Print.

Weber, Nicholas Fox. *Patron Saints: Five Rebels Who Opened America to a New Art, 1928–1943.* New Haven: Yale UP, 1992. Print.

Wellins, Ian. *Music on the Front Line: Nicola Nabokov's Struggle Against Communism and Middlebrow Culture.* Bodmin, Cornwall: Ashgate, 2002. Print.

Welty, Eudora. "Africa and Paris and Russia." *A Writer's Eye.* Welty 185–90.

——. "The Bride of the Innisfallen and Other Stories." *Stories.* Welty 557–722.

——. *Complete Novels.* Ed. Richard Ford and Michael Kreyling. New York: Library of America, 1998. Print.

——. "A Curtain of Green and Other Stories." *Stories.* Welty 1–179.

——. "Delta Wedding." *Complete Novels.* Welty 89–336.

——. "The Demonstrators." *Stories.* Welty 733–50.

——. *Early Escapades.* Ed. Patti Carr Black. Jackson, MS: UP of Mississippi, 2005. Print.

——. *Eudora Welty: Photographs.* Jackson, MS: UP of Mississippi, 1989. Print.

——. "The Golden Apples." *Stories.* Welty 313–556.

——. "Ida M'Toy." *Accent: A Quarterly of New Literature.* 2.4 (1942): 214–22. Print.

——. Introduction. *To the Lighthouse.* By Virginia Woolf. San Diego: Harcourt, 1981. vii–xii. Print.

——. "Is Phoenix Jackson's Grandson Really Dead?" *Stories.* Welty 815–18.

——. Letter to Charles Henri Ford. 16 January 1943. TS. Special Collections. J. D. Williams Library, University of Mississippi, Oxford, MS.

——. Letter to Emily and William Maxwell. 15 February 1978. *What There Is to Say We Have Said: The Correspondence of Eudora Welty and William Maxwell.* Ed. Suzanne Marrs. Boston: Houghton Mifflin Harcourt, 2011. 335–37. Print.

——. Letter to Frank Lyell. N.d. 1932? MS. Eudora Welty Collection. Mississippi Department of Archives and History, Jackson, MS.

——. Letter to Frank Lyell. 1933. Cartoon of "Mae West." The Eudora Welty House and Museum, Jackson, MS.

——. Letter to Frank Lyell. 1933. Cartoon of "Prince of Wales." The Eudora Welty House and Museum, Jackson, MS.

——. Letter to Frank Lyell. 27 March 1933. TS. Eudora Welty Collection. Mississippi Department of Archives and History, Jackson, MS.

——. Letter to Frank Lyell. 25 May 1933. MS. Eudora Welty Collection. Mississippi Department of Archives and History, Jackson, MS.

——. Letter to Frank Lyell. 1 October 1934. MS. Eudora Welty Collection. Mississippi Department of Archives and History, Jackson, MS.

——. Letter to Frank Lyell. 25 November 1942(?). TS. Eudora Welty Collection. Mississippi Department of Archives and History, Jackson, MS.

——. Letter to Frank Lyell. 4 August 1944. TS. Eudora Welty Collection. Mississippi Department of Archives and History, Jackson, MS.

———. Letter to Harriet Monroe. 2 May 1936. TS. Special Collections Research Center. The University of Chicago Library, Chicago, IL.

———. "Literature and the Lens." *Vogue* 1 Aug. 1944: 102–3. Print.

———. Losing Battles. *Complete Novels.* Welty 425–879.

———. "Mirrors for Reality." Rev. of *A Haunted House and Other Short Stories*, by Virginia Woolf. *A Writer's Eye.* McHaney 25–29.

———. "Must the Novelist Crusade." *Stories.* Welty 803–14.

———. "One Writer's Beginnings." *Stories.* Welty 831–948.

———. "Place in Fiction." *Stories.* Welty 781–96.

———. The Ponder Heart. *Complete Novels.* Welty 337–424.

———. Postcard to Frank Lyell. 12 June 1933. MS. Eudora Welty Collection. Mississippi Department of Archives and History, Jackson, MS.

———. Postcard to Frank Lyell. 6 August 1940. MS. Eudora Welty Collection. Mississippi Department of Archives and History, Jackson, MS.

———. "Retreat." *Occasions: Selected Writings.* Ed. Pearl Amelia McHaney. Jackson: UP of Mississippi, 2009: 34–40. Print.

———. The Robber Bridegroom. *Complete Novels.* Welty 1–88.

———. "Some Notes on River Country." *Stories.* Welty 760–72.

———. Stories, Essays & Memoir. Ed. Richard Ford and Michael Kreyling. New York: Library of America, 1998. Print.

———. "Where Is the Voice Coming From?" *Stories.* Welty 727–32.

———. "The Wide Net, and Other Stories." *Stories.* Welty 181–312.

———. A Writer's Eye: Collected Book Reviews. Ed. Pearl Amelia McHaney. Jackson, MS: UP of Mississippi, 1994. Print.

———. "Writing and Analyzing a Story." *Stories.* Welty 773–80.

Westling, Louise. *Eudora Welty.* Totowa, NJ: Barnes & Noble Books, 1989. Print.

———. Sacred Groves and Ravaged Gardens: The Fiction of Eudora Welty, Carson McCullers, and Flannery O'Connor. Athens, GA: U of Georgia P, 1985. Print.

Weston, Ruth D. *Gothic Traditions and Narrative Techniques in the Fiction of Eudora Welty.* Baton Rouge, LA: Louisiana State UP, 1994. Print.

Wheatley, Patricia. "Eudora Welty: A Writer's Beginnings." *More Conversations.* Prenshaw 120–45.

"William Dollar." *Encyclopedia Britannica Online.* n. pag. Web. 31 March 2011.

Woodhead, Lindy. *War Paint: Madame Helena Rubinstein and Miss Elizabeth Arden, Their Lives, Their Times, Their Rivalry.* Hoboken, NJ: John Wiley, 2003. Print.

Woolf, Virginia. "Pictures." *The Moment and Other Essays.* San Diego, CA: Harcourt Brace Jovanovich, 1975. 173–78. Print.

Yaeger, Patricia S. "Because a Fire was in My Head: Eudora Welty and the Dialogic Imagination." *A Life.* Devlin 139–67.

Yates, Gayle Graham. "My Visit with Eudora Welty." *More Conversations.* Prenshaw 87–99.

Yochelson, Bonnie. *Berenice Abbott: Changing New York.* New York: W. W. Norton & Company, 1997. Print.

Ziegler, Philip. *King Edward VIII.* Stroud, Gloucestershire: Sutton Publishing, 2001. Print.

INDEX